THE WORLD OF

Ripley's Believe It or Not!®

THE WORLD OF

Ripley's Believe It or Not!®

**by AEI's Julie Mooney
and the Editors of
Ripley's Believe It or Not!**

BLACK DOG
& LEVENTHAL
PUBLISHERS
NEW YORK

Black Dog & Leventhal Publishers

New York

Published by
Black Dog & Leventhal Publishers, Inc.
151 W 19th St.
New York, NY 10011

In Association with AEI's Writer's Lifeline

Distributed by
Workman Publishing Company
708 Broadway
New York, NY 10003

Manufactured in Hong Kong

ISBN: 1-57912-272-8

h g f e d c

CONTENTS

Acknowledgements

AEI/Writers Lifeline and Julie
Mooney wish to thank the
editors and staff of Ripley
Entertainment, especially Bob
Masterson (President, Ripley
Entertainment), Norm Deska
(Executive Vice President),
Edward Meyer (Vice President,
Publishing) and Christy Barnes
(Keeper of the Strange and
Unusual.) This book never
would have happened without
Jessica MacMurray (Editor,
Black Dog & Leventhal), JP
Leventhal (Publisher, Black
Dog & Leventhal), Dell Furano
of Signatures Network and Bob
Whiteman (Ripley's Director of
Licensing).

INTRODUCTION

"I make a living out of the fact that truth is stranger than fiction," Robert L. Ripley once said of his peculiar profession. Ripley invented the famous Ripley's Believe It or Not! cartoon feature filled with amazing-but-true facts in 1918. Since Ripley wrote the first Believe It or Not!, the world has been able to indulge its passion for the weird on a daily basis. A tireless world traveler, adventurer and collector of the strange and unusual, Ripley loved to be called a liar. He took it as a compliment, because it meant that somebody found the facts he reported too bizarre to believe.

Today we're living in an era when jaded cynicism is hip. It's not cool to have a sense of wonder. But without that wonder, without that sense of adventure, discovery, and awe, without that feeling of being slightly off balance when something doesn't fit our sense of reality, we end up missing out on a lot of joy in the world.

Just a couple of generations ago, our sense of wonder was still alive and well, in the comic books we snuck under the covers to read with a flashlight, in the National Geographics we ogled behind the bleachers and in a daily feature that arrived in the newspaper, called Ripley's Believe It or Not! Ripley was there to remind us every day that we shared our world with two-headed calves, chasms where stars could be seen in the daytime and people with horns growing out of their heads.

Ripley's is still around, ready to be rediscovered. Today more than ever before, we need a regular dose of Ripley's in our lives. There's something about the things Ripley's shows us about ourselves that renews our hope in humankind. How can you help but feel affection for human beings when you discover that they'll spend five years of their lives learning how to toe-skate? Or that they'll ski down the roof of a barn on chicken feathers? Or build a suit of armor for a cat, fight a duel for the love of a woman at age 94, eat an entire bag of Portland cement or bestow upon a baby daughter a name for every letter of the alphabet?

This is an exciting time for Ripley's. Ripley's is on a quest to reclaim the reputation it held during the first half of the twentieth century as the indisputable champion of the strange but true. As Ripley's reasserts itself in the new millennium, the emphasis is on believability. Everybody loves the bizarre, but the bizarre is only spine-tingling when it's true. Ripley's original phrase, "Believe It or Not!" left room for fans to choose the "not" option, even though Ripley himself took great pride in carefully documenting each of his statements. At heart Ripley's is, and always will be, about the undeniable fact that truth is stranger than fiction. That's a reputation that the passing of time can't take away.

We need our sense of wonder. We need that innocence and wide-eyed amazement if we're going to keep our lives fresh. Besides, the real truth is, we haven't been everywhere or done it all. If we truly do go forth in life as Robert Ripley did, on a quest for the things that don't fit our comfortable models of the way the universe works, we'll discover how little we truly know. We'll be able to revel in the fact that the world is full of strange things and that we human beings are the strangest things of all!

Now that Ripley's is moving into the new millennium, this is a good time to look back on what has come before. This book is a preview of things to come, by way of an affectionate glance back at what has gone before. We'll begin at the beginning, with the birth of Robert Ripley, trace the Believe It or Not! phenomenon from the first cobbled-together cartoon through the "Golden Era" of radio shows and Vitaphone movies, up to the TV shows, Odditoriums, aquariums, and motion theaters of the present and maybe a little bit beyond. We'll explore Ripley's most beloved categories of oddities, from amazing anatomy and eccentric epitaphs to nutty names and whimsical wonders.

When asked, "where do you get all your facts?" Ripley always replied, "Everywhere, all the time." When asked if he would ever run out of bizarre, unbelievable stories to tell, he answered, "It's impossible to run dry on astonishing facts about our world." Our universe is full of more amazing things than we can possibly imagine. Welcome to the truly incredible world of Robert Ripley. It'll be your strangest adventure yet. Believe It!

Around the World with
ROBERT RIPLEY

Robert Ripley in his trademark pith helmet, circa 1935. The helmet was a constant part of his wardrobe throughout the 1930s.

Ripley in his New York City office, packed and ready to travel

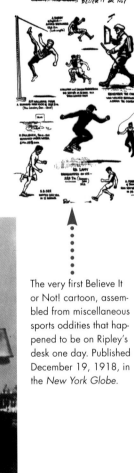

The very first Believe It or Not! cartoon, assembled from miscellaneous sports oddities that happened to be on Ripley's desk one day. Published December 19, 1918, in the *New York Globe*.

It started one day in 1918, when a young cartoonist named Robert Ripley was drawing his regular sports feature for the *New York Globe*. Ripley casually put together a spread of nine cartoons featuring unusual sports feats. He called it "Champs and Chumps", a title which would later be changed to "Believe It or Not!" Then, without thinking that he'd done anything particularly special, he went across the street for a cup of coffee. When it was published the next day, Ripley's cartoon caused a stir. Readers were clamoring for more unusual facts. And Ripley's "Believe it or Not!" was born.

Ripley spent the next three decades indulging in his love of the bizarre, searching the globe for the weirdest, most unbelievable facts, and sharing them with his avid fans. He shocked and amazed the world in his syndicated cartoon feature, weekly radio show, Vitaphone movies, and "Odditorium" museums. He created an institution that is recognized the world over in the familiar phrase and logo, "Believe It or Not!"

The Life of Robert Ripley

Robert Ripley came from adventurous stock. His mother, Lily Belle Yucca, was born in a covered wagon heading west. His father, David Isaac Ripley, ran away from home and swam the Mississippi river on his way west because he lacked boat fare. Robert LeRoy Ripley was born on December 25, 1893 in Santa Rosa California. Ripley's childhood was a difficult one. His father died in 1905, and Lily Belle had to struggle to care for her family alone. At a young age, Ripley started making money from his passion, drawing, by selling cartoon posters for local baseball games. When his mother took in as a boarder an Oakland, California newspaperwoman named Carol Ennis, Ripley got himself noticed. Ennis returned to San Francisco and promoted Ripley's work, quickly getting him a job at the *San Francisco Bulletin* as a sports cartoonist.

The young cartoonist loved to travel the streets of San Francisco. He was especially fond of Chinatown, where he often went to eat and to listen to amazing tales of that exotic, faraway land. In San Francisco, Ripley also met writer Jack London, who was perhaps his first model for what a successful life might look like. In any case, Ripley soon headed east for bigger and better opportunities. While working for the *New York Globe*, Ripley met fellow cartoonist "Bugs" Baer (so named because of his habit of adding tiny bugs to each of his drawings) who would be his life-long best friend. Ripley began to go by "Bob" or "Rip" instead of "Roy", and adopted his trademark spat shoes and bowtie attire.

On December 18, 1918, Ripley was stricken with a bad case of "cartoonist's block," and couldn't come up with a cartoon for the next day's newspaper. He hastily assembled a strip of sports oddities from his collection, and titled it "Champs and Chumps." The cartoon was an overnight sensation. Readers clamored for more strange sports facts. Robert Ripley's destiny was fixed.

Ripley's Ramble 'Round the World

In December 1922, Robert Ripley embarked on his first trip around the world, a journey he'd dreamed about ever since his boyhood. The experience would change his life forever. Ripley started from New York on December 2nd, traveled west to his old stomping grounds in San Francisco, then on to Hawaii, Japan, China, India, the Middle East, Europe, and finally arriving back in New York again, a changed man.

The "Ramble" transformed Ripley's life; it moved him out of his narrow focus on sports oddities and into a broader global and cultural realm. It also whetted his appetite for travel, an insatiable hunger he would feed whenever the opportunity arose, for the remainder of his life.

Over the next several years, Ripley's empire grew. "Believe It or Not!" quickly became a household phrase. Ripley curried a reputation as a dashing man-about-town, thwarted only by a brief, unhappy marriage

Ripley takes in the view on the banks of the Shameen, the busy water thorough-fare in Canton, China, 1923

in 1919 that lasted scarcely three months, although the divorce wouldn't be final until a week after Ripley returned from his famous "Ramble."

Ripley continued to scour the globe for oddities. During a 1927 trip to Paris, Ripley met "Oakie," a sophisticated Russian refugee, and one of the only women ever to sustain his interest. Oakie taught Ripley the finer points of etiquette, and traveled with him for a while. Ripley spoke of Oakie with a tenderness he never expressed toward any other woman. Indeed, she may have been the only woman he ever truly loved.

In 1929, Ripley signed on with newspaper mogul William Randolph Hearst, launching "Believe It or Not!" into the bigtime. Ripley quickly became the first millionaire cartoonist in history. The Golden Era of Ripley's had begun!

Ripley muses upon the wonders of the world while steaming home toward New York, April 6, 1923.

Excerpt from "Ripley's Ramble 'Round the World", published as Ripley traveled, mailing daily installments back to New York City for publication, from December 1922 to April 1923.

Ripley the Human Post Office

From the beginning, Ripley welcomed letters from his fans. He encouraged people across the nation, and later, around the globe, to write in with interesting material they thought would make a good Believe It or Not!—the stranger the better.

But not even Ripley anticipated how strange his fan mail would get. Letters arrived written on turkey bones, grains of rice, eggs, glass, rocks, and tin. When fans learned of Ripley's passion for having fun with languages, postcards and letters poured in that were written in signs, codes, obscure languages, and anagrams. A letter addressed, "What happens if your trousers are tight and you bend over to pick a flower?" was delivered promptly, as was one which bore as its address nothing more than, "?"

The Post Office Department once estimated that Ripley alone received as much mail as the entire town of Coral Gables, Florida. "All the world does my work," Ripley chortled "and I don't have to pay 'em a cent!" But after a while, the Post Office Department stopped finding all that bizarre mail amusing. It issued a statement that it would no longer deliver letters to Ripley that were addressed "incorrectly."

But fans were undeterred. Ripley claimed he gleaned about 90 per cent of his Believe It or Not!s from unsolicited ideas, and that each new day brought at least seven items that could be turned into great car-

Morocco, 1931: Ripley shops through a "camel parking lot" for suitable desert transportation.

His home at BION Island in Mamaroneck, New York was constantly being rearranged to make extra room for his ever-growing collection.

Believe It or Not! Hits the Airwaves

In the 1930s and 1940s, Ripley added another item to his astonishing resume: radio host. Despite his knock-kneed stage fright, Ripley's weekly radio program was a hit. Ripley featured unusual performers on his show such as Kuda Bux, the Hindu firewalker, and Zaro Agha, the oldest man in the world.

As enthusiasm for the broadcasts grew, so did the scope of Ripley's show. Ripley began broadcasting from remote locations.... very remote. One week he would broadcast from the bottom of the Grand Canyon, another week he would be deep underground in the Carlsbad Caverns. Another week would find him at the bottom of a shark tank, or pioneering the first ship-to-shore broadcast from the deck of the homeward-bound S.S. *Leviathan.* And of course, the radio show was a great excuse for more traveling. Ripley became a pioneer in the field of overseas broadcasting.

Of course, a "Believe It or Not!" radio show couldn't help but attract a certain "weird" element. One day a middle-aged man appeared at Ripley's studio and requested an interview, claiming that he had a stunt to sell, something which had never been done over the air. "You may have read, Mr. Ripley, that condemned prisoners frequently make arrangements to have their bodies sold after their execution. The money received for the cadaver goes to the family of the man." The gentleman then announced that he planned to

toons. Ripley's fans were all the more loyal because they were able to become a part of Ripley history just by submitting a good idea. Ripley's still honors this tradition today, and welcomes fans' submissions.

In the early 1930s, Ripley used his newfound wealth to indulge in more travel. In 1932 he returned to his beloved China, and made excursions to Korea, Australia and New Zealand. In 1933, Ripley visited Java, Thailand and Bali. He also made a grueling trek into the Sudan desert of Africa, traveling largely on donkey and camelback, seeking out the most remote locations.

Freaks and Fakirs, Collections and Curioddities: Ripley's Odditoriums

Later in 1933, Ripley's odd career gained a new facet when investor C. C. Pyle approached him with the idea of opening a live exhibition of human oddities at the Century of Progress Fair in Chicago. Fairgoers flocked to see Ripley's odd assortment of sword swallowers, fakirs, and contortionists, and Ripley had another hit on his hands. Ripley's so-called "Odditoriums" appeared at several world's fairs thereafter, and in 1939, Ripley opened the first permanent Odditorium in New York City. In years to come, several more Odditoriums would open in cities across the United States, and later, across the world.

In 1934, Ripley bought a 28-room mansion on an island in Mamaroneck, New York, and dubbed it BION (for "Believe It or Not!") Island. He spent the next several years filling it with exotic artifacts from around the world and entertaining a "harem" of beautiful women

in it. He treated his guests, famous "names" and ordinary folk alike, to lavish parties with bizarre themes in true Ripley style.

It was about this time that Oakie, Ripley's only true love, died. Grieving, Ripley threw himself into his travels more ferociously than before. He visited the British Isles and Europe, though scrupulously avoiding France and the places that would remind him of his lost Oakie.

Ripley The Collector

To Robert Ripley, anything weird, creepy, exotic, or unusual was "artistic." And anything "artistic" was worth having. Ripley collected everything from unconventional artwork to native watercraft. In 1943 he even tried to buy a small volcano that had recently emerged in a Mexican cornfield. Ripley was forever coming home from his travels with a customs officer's nightmare of medieval torture devices, gaudy furniture, shrunken heads, and whatever else piqued his curiosity.

Ripley broadcasts live from the bottom of a St. Augustine, Florida shark tank. (February 23, 1940)

commit suicide, live, on air, in exchange for a large sum to be donated to his family.

"I'd leave the modus operandi up to you, Mr. Ripley." The man insisted. Ripley hemmed and hawed, his mental wheels spinning as he tried to figure out what to say to the man. Finally, it came to him. "Sir, I'm not saying that your idea doesn't have commercial appeal, but it just wouldn't be practical. You see, once we finish broadcasting our show each evening, we wait four hours, then broadcast it again for the folks on the West coast. If you committed suicide during the first broadcast, it would leave us nothing for the second." And thus Ripley got himself off the hook.

In the early 1940s, World War II began to close the door on Ripley's ability to travel. Ripley used the time to reinvest in his cartoon feature, soliciting unusual war stories from his readers, and offering weekly prizes for the most unbelievable tales. But without the ability to indulge his gypsy spirit, Ripley became increasingly morose and withdrawn. Over the next decade, it could be seen that Believe It or Not! had truly come of age, and would soon take wing independently of its creator.

Ripley drew copious numbers of cartoons on his travels. This is one of only a small handful of drawings in which Ripley put himself into the picture. (July 17, 1938.)

The 204 "Countries" Visited by Robert Ripley in his Quest for the Strange

Aden	Czecho-Slovakia	Korea	Samoa
Afghanistan	Dalmatia	Kurdistan	San Blas
Ajmer-Merwara	Danzig	Kwangtung	San Marino
Alaska	Delhi	Lappland	Sardinia
Albania	Denmark	Latvia	Sark
Algeria	Diebel Druse	Lebanon	Scotland
Andorra	Djerba	Liechtenstein	Serbia
Antigua	Dominican Republic	Lithuania	Shetland Islands
Arabia	Dutch East Indies	Llivia	Siam
Argentina	East Prussia	Luxembourg	Sicily
Armenia	Ecuador	Macao	Sinai
Australia	Egypt	Madeira	Sindh
Austria	El Salvador	Madoera	Southern Rhodesia
Azerbaijan	England	Madras	Soviet Russia
Azores	Er Rif	Mallorca	Spain
Bahamas	Estonia	Malta	St. Croix
Bahawalpur	Fiji Islands	Manchukuo	St. Lucia
Bali	Finland	Martinique	St. Pierre-Miquelon
Baluchistan	Formosa	Mexico	St. Thomas
Barbados	France	Mombasa	Straits Settlements
Baroda	French Guiana	Monaco	Sudan
Basque	Frontier Provinces	Montenegro	Sumatra
Bechuanaland	Garden of Eden	Morocco	Surinam
Belgium	Georgia	Mozambique	Swaziland
Bengal	Germany	Natal	Sweden
Bermudas	Gibraltar	Newfoundland	Switzerland
Bihar & Orissa	Greece	New Zealand	Syria
Bolivia	Guadeloupe	Nicaragua	Tonga Islands
Bombay Presidency	Guatemala	Northern Rhodesia	Tanganyika
Bosnia	Haiti	North Caucasus	Tangier
Brazil	Hawaiian Islands	Northern Ireland	Tchad
British Guiana	Herzegovina	Norway	Transjordan
British Honduras	Holland	Orange Free States	Transvaal
Bulgaria	Honduras	Orkney Islands	Trinidad
Burma	Hong Kong	Palestine	Tripoli
Canada	Hungary	Panama	Tunisia
Canal Zone	Iceland	Papua	Turkey
Cape Colony	Inini Territory	Paraguay	Uganda
Celebes	Iraq	Persia	Ukrania
Central Provinces	Irish Free State	Peru	U.P. of India
Ceylon	Isle of Man	Philippine Islands	United States
Channel Islands	Italy	Poland	Uruguay
Chile	Jamaica	Portugal	Vatican State
China	Japan	Puerto Rico	Venezuela
Colombia	Java	Punjab	Virgin Islands
Corsica	Jehol	Quelimane	Wales
Costa Rica	Johore	Rajputana	Wurtemberg
Croatia	Karelia	Rhodes	Yucatan
Cuba	Kashmir-Jammu	Saar	Yugo-Slavia
Curacao	Kenya Colony	Sahara (French)	Zanzibar
Cyrenaica	Khairpur	Salvador	Zara

RIPLEY'S LOVE AFFAIR
WITH CHINA

Ripley explores the Ming Emperors' Tombs north of Beijing, 1932. Stone animals and warriors line the road to the tombs for miles. The presence of elephants at the tombs suggests that China had established trade routes with India at the time of the monument's creation.

History will probably never uncover the reason behind it, but it was an established fact that Robert Ripley was completely, utterly, and unabashedly in love with China. To Ripley, China stood for everything that was exotic, romantic, and mysterious. Ripley's writings portray a wistful longing, even an inexplicable belonging, to that faraway land. Ripley wrote of his first travel to the land he'd longed to see, "It was like coming home."

Ripley first visited China during his famous 1922-1923 "Ramble 'Round the World." He marveled at the fact that the Yellow Sea was truly yellow. He found Tsingtao filthy and dangerous, full of beggars, and Shanghai to be too much like a miniature New York, with the scurrying rickshaws seeming out of place. What Ripley really wanted to see was China's interior, away from seaports and tourist spots, the places he thought of as the "real" China.

In Hong Kong, on January 18, Ripley wrote, "The daily papers flare headlines about the war in Canton...the American consul at Canton refused permission to go there, but Bob Ellis (a traveling companion) and I are going anyway...they say it is very dangerous and we are strongly advised not to go, but I have always wanted to be a war correspondent like Herb Corey, so I cannot very well pass up a chance like this." All the railway bridges had been blown up, so the trains were no longer running. Ripley and Ellis had to go in stealthily, aboard a tiny private boat that sailed at midnight.

Ripley's experiences over the next several days were inarguably seminal moments in his life. He wrote passionately of the thousands of Cantonese sampan dwellers living out their lives aboard their rivercraft: "...a floating city. It even has its own government." Ripley was struck by Canton's sheer oldness; the city was several centuries older than the birth of Christ. He drank in the foul smells and clamoring sounds of Canton's dark streets, too narrow even for rickshaws. "This is China, real China," Ripley wrote on January 20, "I saw more of China in five minutes here than I would see in a year in Hong Kong or Shanghai." Ripley would return to China again and again, ever after naming Canton as one of the most remarkable cities in the world.

Ripley probably brought home more artifacts from China than from any of the other countries he traveled. He furnished a lavish upstairs suite near his studio at BION Island in an outlandish red-and-gold-laquered riot of carved dragons and loud silks which his friend Hazel Storer swore no Chinese person would be caught dead in. In 1940 he bought a curious New York apartment primarily because it looked like the inside of a pagoda: the perfect excuse to cram every square inch of it with amazing Asian artifacts. And in 1946, Ripley delightedly purchased the Mon Lei, an authentic Foochow fishing junk, with which he startled other water travelers on the Hudson River for 2 1/2 years.

China's exotic mystery and Ripley's itchy-footed, restless nature were a perfect match. Ripley was fortunate enough to live in an era when China was still largely "undiscovered country" to the majority of westerners. In fact, something seemed to happen deep inside Ripley at the end of World War II. As soon as travel was permitted again, Ripley hurried to his beloved China, only to find that the untarnished beauty he remembered was gone forever. When he returned home, he sank into a deep depression.

Ripley began yet another new career with the advent of television. Ripley signed on to host a new weekly TV series of Believe It or Not! stories. On May 24, 1949: Ripley was making what was to be his thirteenth and last television appearance, prophetically including a dramatized sequence on the origin of "Taps," when he collapsed. Two days later, he admitted himself to Columbia Presbyterian Hospital. On May 27, Ripley called his best friend Bugs Baer to tell him he was just in for a check up and would be out to see him tomorrow. He hung up the phone, succumbed to a heart attack, and died.

Ripley was buried in his home town of Santa Rosa, California, leaving behind him a legacy of strange facts and bizarre items, and a beloved cartoon read by milions the world over. Ripley's Believe It or Not! has outlived its creator, expanding into the worlds of museums, aquariums, books, television series, and educational programs: a tribute to the man who lived his life in a tireless quest for the bizarre.

Over the course of this book, you'll encounter Believe It or Not images from the earliest days of Ripley's, through the "Golden Era" of the 1930s and the 1940s, and beyond into more recent times. The images gathered here are grouped into some of Ripley's favorite topics, including the Nutty Names he loved to collect and the Queer Customs he traveled thousands of miles to observe. The sources vary: some of these items come from previous Ripley books, others directly off the cartoon pages, still others are photos of Odditorium performers and museum displays. But the bulk of what you are about to see comes from you, Ripley's fans: the photos and stories you, and generations of fans before you, sent in out of that wonderful sense of the bizarre that lives in all of us.

Amazing ANATOMY

Robert Ripley nursed a passion for discovering people with strange anatomical attributes and bizarre abilities. Inspired by a 1928 photo of a Manchurian farmer—known only as Wang—who had a 13-inch horn on the back of his head, Ripley offered a large sum of money to anyone who could find Wang and convince him to come to America to appear in his Odditorium. No one ever claimed the reward. After briefly exhibiting himself among a group of fakirs in Fuchtiatien, Manchuria, Wang vanished without a trace. But the "human unicorn" left a permanent impression on Ripley. As he traveled the world, he continued to search for people with unusual features and abilities. He invited them to entertain at his parties, hired them to perform at his Odditoriums, filmed them, introduced them on his radio show and of course, featured them in his famous Believe It or Not! cartoons.

Ripley's Believe It or Not! cartoon, June 10, 1945, featuring Wang "The Human Unicorn", a major source of inspiration for Robert Ripley.

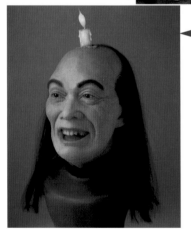

The **"Lighthouse Man"** of Chungking, China, who plugged a hole in his skull with a candle! He is shown here as a wax figure Odditorium exhibit. The Lighthouse Man was known to hire himself out to travelers at night to light their way down dark streets! Author Stephen King claims that this Ripley classic inspired his work.

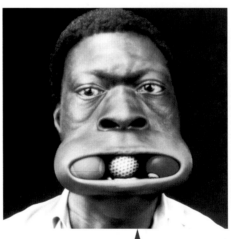

Cuban Ringling Brothers star **Antonio Galindo's** amazing ability may have been due in part to a punctured eardrum, which would allow air to pass from the throat through the ear canal.

Empress Marie Louise could fold her ears inside out at will.

! Ellen Matthews of Collingwood, Australia lost the use of her voice in an accident. She recovered it seven and a half years later, but thereafter spoke with a Scottish accent.

"Three Ball Charlie", of Humbolt, Nebraska, a famous side show performer in the 1950s and 1960s. This photograph is displayed in a number of Ripley's Odditoriums.

This 1934 Odditorium performer could whistle with a mouthful of balls.

Mother Said I Was Special

Ripley was particularly fascinated by an unusual citizen of Chungking, Sechuan Province, China, who came to be known as "The Lighthouse Man." Dr. J. J. Kaveney of the U.S. Navy examined him, and found that a hole had been made in the top of the man's skull through the hard outer layer of bone and the soft bone tissue beneath it, leaving only the internal plate above the membrane that covers the brain. The man kept a seven-inch red candle stuck in this hole with sealing wax, and would often guide visitors around the dark streets of Chungking by its light.

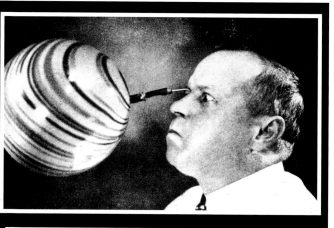

Alfred Langevin of Detroit, Michigan could blow up balloons, smoke a cigarette, and play a recorder—through his eye! He was featured in a 1930 Believe It or Not! cartoon, appeared at Ripley's Odditoriums from 1933 to 1940, in a 1931 compendium and on a postcard. Circa 1940.

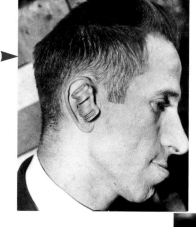

Max Calvin of Brooklyn, New York could fit twenty-five quarters in his ear! (July 15, 1933.)

Rosa Barthelme, the human slate, could raise temporary welts on her skin by drawing on it with a blunt instrument. This photograph was taken at Ripley's Chicago Odditorium during one of Barthelme's performances in the summer of 1934.

Human Bend'ems

Ezechiel Eads of Athens, New York was born without ears. The sides of his head were smooth, without even any holes where his ears would have been. Yet he could hear through his mouth, which he would open wide when he was listening to something.

Where'd his guts go? **Ed Anato Hayes** of Mountainair, New Mexico could displace his muscles and organs and could completely flatten his abdominal cavity, so that his backbone could be seen from the front!

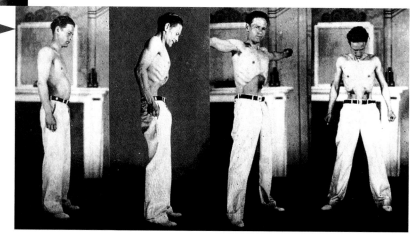

Martin Joe Laurello, "The Human Owl." His amazing 180 degree head-twisting contortion turned heads in Ripley's Odditoriums throughout the 1930s.

In 1929, Ripley received a letter from John T. Bowers of Chicago, Illinois, who claimed to be able to speak with his stomach. Bowers' larynx, windpipe, and vocal cords had been removed in an operation, yet he had taught himself to speak by forcing air from his stomach through an opening in the lower part of his throat. As his doctor testified, Bowers had worked hard to perfect his ability to speak this way. His voice was clearly audible, and he hoped that the publicity he gained through Ripley would encourage countless others who had been deprived of natural speech. Bowers' remarkable achievement won first prize in the *Chicago Herald-Examiner's* Believe It or Not! contest. He donated his $1,000 cash prize to the *Herald-Examiner's* Christmas Fund.

F. Velez Campos, contortionist, from Fortuna, Puerto Rico...if he's in pain, he's hiding it well. (August 23, 1933.)

These teeth knew neither brush nor toothpaste for twenty years, yet **John M. Hernic** of New York, New York could lift a 180 lb. man with them! (December 8, 1935.)

! ● *Lui Ch'ung of Shansi, China was born in 955 A.D., with two pupils in each eye. His unusual anatomy did not deter him from a successful life—he served as Governor of Shansi and Minister of State. Chung was one of Ripley's all-time favorite "human oddities," and is one of the most popular wax figures at a number of Ripley's Odditoriums.*

! ● *Hsieh Hsuan of Cihli, China (1389–1464) was born with transparent flesh. The organs and bones of his body were plainly visible. Despite this unusual trait, Hsuan led a productive life, and became an avid scholar—so devoted to his books, in fact, that when he was sentenced to die for bribery, he continued to read on the way to his execution.*

Contortionist **Charlie Romano** claimed that he slept in this position. He was featured in a cartoon on December 5, 1931, and performed at various Ripley's Odditoriums in the 1930s.

Charlie Romano "L'Homme désarticulé". 0126

Chou Kung, the inventor of the compass, had a swivel wrist and could turn his hand completely around.

William D'Andrea of Waterbury, Connecticut could stick his foot in his pocket... let's hope he could also take it out again!

Lorraine Chevalier of Philadelphia, Pennsylvania could sit on her own head! This amazing feat of gluteo-cranial repose can only be accomplished by a talented few. The famous Chevalier family of acrobats claims that only one person is born into their family every two hundred years who is capable of attaining this position. (October 24, 1937.)

Illustrated Men

His wife's name forever on his lips: **William Lucas** of St. Paul, Minnesota had his wife Mabel's name tattooed on the inside of his lower lip. The tattooed letters on his knuckles spell out "Holy Ghost". (December 19, 1936.)

OMI – OH, MY!
STRANGEST LOOKING MAN in the WORLD
COMPLETELY TATTOOED FROM THE TOP OF HIS HEAD TO THE BOTTOM OF HIS FEET

The Great Omi the Tattooed Man appeared in Ripley's Odditorium in 1940.

Charles Wagner's lavish tattoos included a rendering of Rosa Bonheur's horses on his chest, and a scene entitled 'Child Christ and a Trip to Mars' on his back.

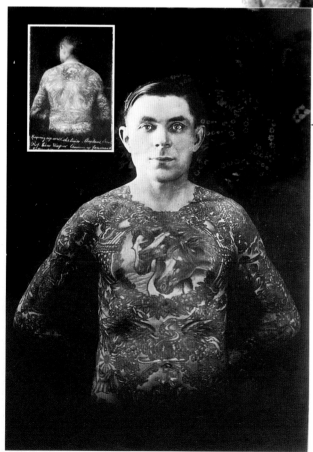

The Human Autograph Album: former boxer **Dick Hyland** was "signed" with the tattooed names of over 600 celebrities, friends, and acquaintances. Note Ripley's name in the center of his chest—right above Pancho Villa! (July 12, 1939.)

Yogi Haridas, a Hindu ascetic, could touch his forehead, where the caste mark lies, with his tongue. In order to accomplish this feat, Haridas had numerous operations on the root of his tongue and endured many years of painful practice.

Deeds of Dexterity

Lena Deeter of Conway, Arkansas could write with both hands simultaneously—backwards, forwards, upside-down, even upside-down backwards! She could write in a different direction with each hand simultaneously. Deeter was featured in a Believe It or Not! cartoon on April 1, 1942.

Toe-painting! **Anthony Cicale** of New York, New York created abstract paintings using only the toe, heel, and ball of his right foot.

Pierre Mahieux of Paris, France, although born without arms or legs, was highly skilled at making miniature wooden furniture with tools he gripped between his teeth! He was the subject of a Believe It or Not! cartoon on March 13, 1951.

! **Magdalena Strumarczuk** of Tobolsk, Russia had her breasts on her back. In spite of their unusual placement, they appear to have functioned normally—Strumarczuk successfully breast fed all three of her children.

This 1936 Dallas Odditorium performer could draw three different cartoons simultaneously—with both hands and a foot!

George Stall of Kansas City, a turn-of-the-century sideshow 'wildman.' One of the oldest images in the Ripley collection, this photo was taken in 1898

Naomi Thorne, whose stage name was 'Santa Fe Kate', could play clearly recognizable tunes while blindfolded and wearing gloves, and with a thick blanket covering the keyboard! Her cartoon was published on January 22, 1936.

It took pianist **Arthur Schultz** of Hamtrack, Michigan ten years to train himself to play the piano with his hands upside-down. He claimed he had to wait five minutes after doing this before he could play normally again! (March 1, 1939.)

A Manicurist's Worst Nightmare

This unknown patient was photographed at Soochow Hospital in China in 1935. His shorter nail measures a mere 15 inches; the longer nail, an incredible 33 inches! He claimed the nail took 44 years to grow. What the world may never know: how long it would take to chew it off! (January 15, 1934.)

Here's Lookin' At You

J.T. Saylors of Memphis, Tennessee, perhaps the world's most famous 'girner.' Saylors 'swallowed' his nose before Odditorium visitors in 1933, and has been featured in numerous Ripley's Believe It or Not! museums ever since! (September 8, 1933.)

Joseph Green, 5'5" 148 lb, of Brooklyn, New York could pull three automobiles weighing a total of 21,000 lbs with his hair! Because of his great strength and his 5' 5" stature, Green was nicknamed "The Mighty Atom." (July 1, 1931.)

Hair to Eternity

Hair suite: Three women display their floor-length tresses. The first photograph features Lydia McPherson, whose 7' 4" cascade of red hair once held the world's record. The second and third photographs are part of a collection of more than 900 'circus freak' images purchased by Ripley's in the 1970s.

Tip O'Neil of Minneapolis, Minnesota, inspired by a performer he saw impersonating a well-known spinach-chomping sailor at the Cleveland Odditorium, sent Ripley this photo of himself to show that he could look just as convincing as the man on Ripley's payroll. Circa 1937.

Margaret Hayes 'girned' for visitors of Ripley's Odditorium in 1933. The real secret to girning is to knock out all your teeth—or wait until they fall out.

Every male in the Colombiere family of Nancy, France was born with two left hands: both their hands had thumbs on the right side. They were perfectly normal in every other way. This trait only appeared in Colombiere males; females of the Colombiere family had normal hands.

Leopard 'Popeye' Perry, from Richland, Georgia, appeared as an Odditorium performer in 1933. He could 'dislocate' both his eyes simultaneously or individually.

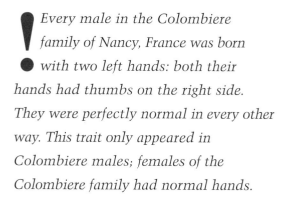

'Whisker King' **Hans Langseth** (above right) greets 'Whisker Prince' **Zach Wilcox** (above left.) While Wilcox sports an 11-foot beard, Langseth's beard measures an incredible 17 feet! Langseth's beard today resides in the Smithsonian. They were featured in a Believe It or Not ! cartoon on December 30, 1953.

HAIR RAISING

PIERRE MESSIE, of Nantes, France, a provincial actor, was able to move his hair at will, cause it to stand on end, fall or curl. According to Dr. Auguste Cabanes (*Les Cinq Sens*) this ability—rare in human beings—is due to an extraordinary development of the muscles of the hair (erectospilae) which modern man possesses in a rudimentary form.
Messie was able to move any part of the hair as he wished, and could make one side curl while the other side lay flat.

Messie Hair! French actor **Pierre Messie** could move his hair at will, causing it to stand, fall, or curl- and could even curl one side while leaving the other flat. This ability may have been due to an unusually high level of development in Messie's erectospilae, or muscles of the hair- a rare trait in modern human beings.î

LONELY AT THE TOP:
The Life of Robert Wadlow, the World's Tallest Man

Robert Pershing Wadlow, at his full height of 8 feet 11 inches, stands beside his father Harold.

When Robert Pershing Wadlow was born in Alton, Illinois on February 22, 1918 weighing 8 pounds, 6 ounces, he appeared to be a normal, healthy child in every way. A respectful, quiet lad, Robert seemed ideally suited to the goodhearted family that Addie and Harold Wadlow were raising. If all had remained as it seemed at his birth, Robert Wadlow would probably have lived out his life in relative obscurity as a fine lawyer in a small Midwestern town.

But when Robert was six months old, his parents noticed that there was something different about their son. Where most babies at six months weighed between 7 and 14 lbs, Robert tipped the scales at a whopping 30 lbs. A year later, 18-month-old Robert weighed 62 lbs. By the time he was eight years old, he weighed 195 lbs and stood 6 feet 2 inches tall.

Addie and Harold were determined to protect their son from unkind attention, and they did all that they could to give him as normal a life as possible. Robert was a good student in school and was well-liked by his classmates. He enjoyed the usual boyhood pursuits: photography and stamp collecting, and at the age of 13, when he measured 7 feet 4 inches, he became the world's tallest Boy Scout.

But when you're head and shoulders above the crowd, it's hard not to be noticed. By the time he was nine, the press had started taking an interest in him. The Wadlows began a battle to keep their son from being exploited that would continue for the rest of his life. One rainy night a man claiming to be a doctor appeared unannounced on the Wadlow's doorstep, invited himself in, and proceeded to ask Robert a number of embarrassing, intrusive questions. The report this so-called doctor published made Robert out as a freak, calling him 'slow-moving and thick-witted.' The Wadlow family sued, but lost.

The taller Robert grew, the harder his body had to work to maintain itself. A common symptom of the overactive pituitary gland, which caused Robert's tremendous growth, was a loss of sensation below the knees. Medically speaking, the impulses from the nerves in his lower extremities had to travel so far to reach his brain that the taller he grew, the fainter the signals became. Robert's explanation was simply that his legs were growing 'too fast for the nerves to keep up.' As Robert continued to grow, the signals from his lower legs and feet grew dimmer and dimmer, until he could hardly feel them at all.

Robert became prone to injuring his feet. Because he could not feel them, even minor blisters and chafing often became seriously infected. By the time he had grown to 8 feet tall, Robert needed leg braces in order to support his massive frame. He often had to lean on family and friends in order to walk.

Robert's dream was to become a lawyer. He was determined not to allow his unusual height to stand in his way. After he finished high school, Robert began studying law. But after a while he began to realize that his huge size would affect the way a judge and jury would react to him in court.

At age 18, Robert measured 8 feet 4 inches, and wore a size 37AA shoe. Two years later, he struck a deal with the International Shoe Company: he would become their spokesman; they would provide his shoes for free. Robert and his father began traveling across the country, promoting International's shoes. Harold modified the family car to fit Robert. He removed the front passenger seat so that Robert had room for his long legs. Father and son traveled to over 800 towns and 41 states.

Robert enjoyed working for the shoe company. He decided that instead of towering over his clients in courts of law, he would open his own chain of shoe stores. In order to raise the money to start his shoe company, Robert agreed to hire himself out for a short time with Barnum and Bailey's circus. He refused to wear the tall hats and platform shoes most circus giants wore, and he would not allow anyone to photograph him from an angle that exaggerated his height.

In the summer of 1940, when Robert was 22, he was scheduled to ride in a 4th of July parade. That morning, Robert felt ill and had no appetite. During the parade, Robert complained of a fever. His father was immediately concerned; Robert almost never complained about anything. When Harold examined his son's feet, he discovered that one of Robert's braces was cutting into the flesh. A massive infection had set in. Robert had not felt a thing.

On July 5, doctors confined Robert to bed. He was placed in a hotel bed, because local hospitals had no beds that would fit him. A few days later, Robert's infection had worsened. He was rushed into surgery and given blood transfusions, but his temperature continued to rise. At 1:30 AM on July 15, 1940, Robert died in his sleep.

He was taken home to Alton to be buried. On the day of his funeral, all of Alton's businesses closed their doors. 40,000 people attended the funeral. His casket required 12 pallbearers. His grave was sealed with steel cables and cement, as protection against any who might try to steal his remains. His gravestone simply reads, "At Rest."

When Robert died at age 22, he measured 8 feet, 11 inches—the tallest man who ever lived. He exceeded the previous record of an 8 feet 4 inch Irishman who had died in 1877. But those who knew Robert would not only remember him for his height. Because of his quiet, affectionate manner and his generous, uncomplaining nature, Robert was dubbed the "Gentle Giant" of Alton. During his lifetime, he gained many loyal fans and friends across the country, and was even affectionately dubbed "Tall Pine" by a neighboring Native American tribe. In 1984, the town of Alton erected a bronze statue in his honor.

Prague, Oklahoma, 1937: Robert Wadlow poses outside Peters' Shoe Company during a promotional tour. Seven-year-old Morris Blumenthal and his mother, whose family owned the store, stand beside him.

Robert Ripley kept track of Wadlow's astonishing growth, featuring him twice in Believe It or Not! cartoons and once on his radio show.

Baffling BALANCE

Bill Fontana, professional "birler" from Fort Frances, Ontario, and his dalmatian, Peppy, could roll their log a full mile in one hour (September 15, 1953.)

At the age of 17, **Jacqueline Terry** of Montgomery, Alabama could sit on her head while balanced in the air on her jaw! (October 5, 1948.)

Mighty-jawed **Jackie Del Rio** of Chicago, Illinois could lift two tables and six chairs using only his teeth! (February 17, 1938.)

James Paul, "The Greek Titan" of Brooklyn, New York could lift six people, weighing a total of 735 pounds, with his teeth! The 5′6″, 140-pound titan claimed that a "weak condition" of the teeth forced him to visit a "quack" doctor in Cypress, Greece, who gave him a special dental paste that had startlingly powerful results! (August 14, 1951.)

Charles C. Russell, inspired by the Believe It or Not! cartoon of Mr. Hugo, hoisted 12 cups of coffee with one hand and his sister with the other hand—while on ice skates! Russell, an ice skating and barbell instructor at the South Chicago "Y", could also hoist a bar over his head with a woman seated at either end—a total of 265 pounds. Again, he did all this on ice skates—but this time, the two women he hoisted were playing ukeleles!

Robert Fern of Dallas, Texas could balance a quarter upright on his nose for 30 seconds. (June 28, 1933.)

❗● Cornish immigrant *"Uncle Billy" Hooper* of Lebanon Kansas could stand on his head at the age of 86. (March 12, 1935.)

The Great Johnson, also known as the Silent Entertainer, could still perform this feat well into his sixties (November 6, 1940.)

Mr. Hugo, a waiter at Brown's restaurant in New York City, could not only carry ten coffee cups in one hand, but could take orders for 25 sandwiches at one time and serve everything correctly without writing anything down. (August 13, 1931.)

Bob Jones, Philadelphian gymnast extraordinaire, appeared in numerous Ripley cartoons.

AT LEFT: **Bob Jones** is pictured celebrating his 53rd birthday by standing on his thumbs on a mirror! (November 1, 1959.)

A WELL-BALANCED INDIVIDUAL

Master Equilibrist Bob Dotzauer

Joe Horowitz of Los Angeles, California, "The Man with the Iron Nose", balanced an 18-pound cavalry sword on the tip of his nose. He could also perform this feat with a lighted torch. (December 21, 1934.)

Waitress **Blanche Lowe** of Clayton's Cafe in Tyler Texas, could carry 23 coffee cups in one hand. (April 9, 1940.)

A.C. Johnson of Larned, Kansas balanced an egg atop an ordinary strand of wire...a classic Believe It or Not! feat that begs the question, "But why?..." (December 26, 1929.)

Wally Parker of Cheswick, Pennsylvania could shoot and hit a four-inch target while balancing on one hand. Normally, Wally shot with his right hand, but since he needed his right hand to balance, he had to train himself to shoot accurately with his left. (December 29, 1960.)

Jo Ann Summer of Decatur, Alabama performed a tap dance routine on top of milk bottles (July 8, 1946.

! *Mayne Mullin of Berkeley, California could support her entire weight on her elbows. (January 25, 1948.)*

Dotzauer, partially disabled in one leg and weighing a modest 148 pounds, balanced three lawn mowers weighing a total of 150 pounds on his chin. (December 12, 1953.)

"I have always been interested in balancing things on different parts of my anatomy," master-balancer Bob Dotzauer wrote in 1974 to explain his unusual hobby, "I've always had fun doing things like this." Dotzauer became one of the most frequently featured people in Believe It or Not! history, wowing Ripley's readers with his equilibrial antics over an impressive 33-year span.

Bob Dotzauer took up his balancing hobby after a grim, difficult childhood. Orphaned at age three, He grew up in poverty in Chicago, Illinois and earned his education on the G.I. Bill after serving in World War II with the United States Marine Corps. He moved to Cedar Rapids, Iowa and became a teacher of Social Studies and English. He did volunteer work with teens and special education kids, yet still found time to practice his "equilibrial arts."

Bob Dotzauer was featured a whopping seven times in Ripley's Believe It or Not! cartoons. He appeared in his first Ripley's cartoon in 1941, standing on top of an 18-foot ladder and balancing a 50-pound lawn mower on his chin. He appeared again in 1948 when he broke the world's record for balancing a pencil on his nose for three minutes. In 1950, Dotzauer balanced two 50-pound lawn mowers on his chin. The following year, he topped his own amazing stunt by balancing a total of three lawn mowers—which, combined, weighed more than he did!

But the best was yet to come: In 1956, Dotzauer balanced 20 goldfish bowls on top of a baseball... on the tip of a pencil... on the tip of his chin! In 1958, Dotzauer braved the ice of the Cedar River to balance an 18-foot canoe on his chin. His final stunt in 1974, performed on the grounds of the school where he taught, involved a 24-foot fire ladder, a basket and a disgruntled tomcat. For years afterward, Dotzauer handed out pictures of this stunt to family and friends as mementos.

What gave Bob Dotzauer his amazing aptitude for balance? Maybe it had something to do with the symmetry of the tunes in his head. Although Dotzauer never played an instrument or had formal music training, he claimed he just naturally and spontaneously composed music. He even won a national songwriting contest. A teacher by profession, Dotzauer never performed his amazing stunts for money. "I cannot call myself a professional balancer in the true sense of the word," he explained, "because I have never made my living balancing things." Dotzauer died in 1985 at the age of 62, after a well-balanced life.

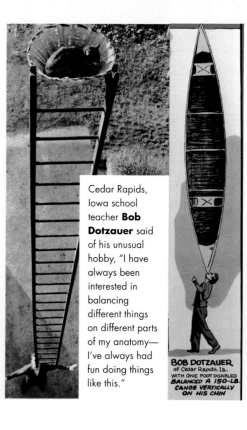

Cedar Rapids, Iowa school teacher **Bob Dotzauer** said of his unusual hobby, "I have always been interested in balancing different things on different parts of my anatomy— I've always had fun doing things like this."

BOB DOTZAUER of Cedar Rapids, Ia. WITH ONE FOOT DISABLED BALANCED A 150-LB. CANOE VERTICALLY ON HIS CHIN

Bizarre BUILDINGS

THE CATHEDRAL of BARCELONA in Spain, WAS STARTED IN 1249 AND NOT COMPLETED UNTIL 1913 — 664 YEARS LATER
© 1998 Ripley Entertain

THE UNCOUNTABLE COLUMNS of KAIROUAN, Tunisia
NO MUHAMMADAN IS ALLOWED TO COUNT THE MANY COLUMNS OF THE GREAT MOSQUE of SIDI-OKHBA UNDER THREAT of BLINDNESS
ALL OF THE COLUMNS WERE TAKEN FROM THE RUINS OF CARTHAGE the EXACT NUMBER IS STILL UNKNOWN

HOUSE BUILT ENTIRELY OF TOMBSTONES
Owned by O. E. YOUNG, Petersburg, Va.

IN THE MIDDLE OF THE Uyuni Salt Flats in Bolivia, THERE IS A HOTEL CALLED The Salt Palace and Spa, WITH WALLS, ROOF, CHAIRS, BEDS, TABLES and FLOORS ALL MADE OUT of SALT!
SUBMITTED BY TOM HIGGINS, SAN DIEGO, CALIF

HOUSE THAT SHELTERS AN ENTIRE VILLAGE
Kwantung, China
ONE HUGE CIRCULAR BUILDING HOUSES ALL OF THE 1800 INHABITANTS OF TSO-CHEN EVERY OCCUPANT IS NAMED TSOU

The sanctuary of Katra Madriganj in the state of Partabgarh, Rajputan, India, is thickly crusted with sugar. The structure was erected over a gushing spring so richly saturated with sugar that it is possible to distill thick molasses from it by boiling. The saccharine spring overflows at regular intervals and drenches the temple with a sugary flood. As a result, the edifice is always heavily coated with sugar and the walls are eagerly licked by sweet-starved children.

THE TREE HOUSE
JOHN MASON HUTCHINGS, BECAUSE HE COULD NOT BEAR TO CUT DOWN A TREE, BUILT HIS INN IN YOSEMITE VALLEY, CA., AROUND THE GIGANTIC CEDAR

WHAT IS IT?
THE MAN WHO MADE IT DIDN'T WANT IT, THE MAN WHO BOUGHT IT HAD NO USE FOR IT, THE MAN WHO USED IT DIDN'T KNOW IT
A COFFIN

THE HOME OF ALFRED REXROTH IN LOHR, GERMANY, IS BUILT AROUND A 241-FT. FIR TREE THAT EXTENDS *THROUGH ITS ROOF*

by Ripley

OUR BOYS IN SERVICE WILL SEE The QUEEREST HOUSE IN AUSTRALIA AT BALLARAT
CONSTRUCTED OF AN ENDLESS MEDLEY of MISCELLANEOUS OBJECTS IN A VAST VARIETY of COLORS. LAMPS, JUGS, DISHES, PLAQUES, SHELLS, ROCKS, ORNAMENTS, STATUETTES, BROKEN GLASS, ETC.

A Sunday Believe It or Not! cartoon from January 11, 1942, featuring Thailand's colorful Wat Arun temple.

TEMPLE OF BROKEN DISHES
The WAT ARUN – 242 FEET HIGH
BANGKOK, SIAM
A MAGNIFICENT AND COLORFUL TEMPLE BUILT OF BROKEN DISHES SALVAGED FROM A WRECKED SHIP

LONDON'S HAUNTED HOLLAND HOUSE
(England) HOLLAND HOUSE, WHERE THE POET SHELLEY AND OTHERS REPORTED MEETING APPARITIONS OF THEMSELVES--*AND THEN EACH DIED SOON AFTERWARD*

The "Mystery House" of Santa Clara Valley, California is one of the strangest testimonials to human eccentricity. The house, which is furnished with gold and silver fixtures and costly stained glass windows, is a maze of walled up entrances, closet doors opening upon blank walls, trapdoors and weird stairways leading nowhere. Its builder, a woman of unlimited means, believed that she would never die, as long as she kept adding rooms to the house. She did so until this rambling mansion became a mystic maze of 144 rooms. She kept carpenters busy for 38 years.

WHICH IS THE 40TH STATE IN THE UNION — Answer Next Sunday

MEXICO'S BEAUTIFUL OPERA HOUSE IS SINKING
THE CITY IS BUILT ON A SWAMP AND THE BUILDING HAS SUNK ABOUT 12 FEET — CAUSING TWO BUILDINGS ACROSS THE STREET TO RISE A FEW FEET
Copr. 1943, King Features Syndicate

Ripley climbs the "Miraculous Staircase" in Santa Fe, New Mexico, so named because it was built without supports of any kind. 1940.

• • • • • • • • • • ➤

Justo Rosito of Alcolea del Pinar, Spain spent 22 years carving a house out of solid rock. The spacious seven-room home includes a fireplace, benches, shelves, even a kitchen. The Spanish government was so impressed with Rosito's feat, they gave him the house and the five acres around it, plus a lifetime pension of one peseta a day! (July 29, 1934.)

The **ALL-GLASS CHURCH**
Tubize, Belgium
THE ENTIRE STRUCTURE CONSISTS OF GLASS ERECTED UPON A GLASS FOUNDATION

UNDERGROUND CHURCH
CARVED FROM SOLID SALT! — WIELICZKA, Poland
A COMPLETE CITY HAS BEEN BUILT IN THESE SALT MINES WHERE **1500** MEN WORK DAILY.

This Miami, Florida Inn is decorated with 300,000 bottle caps. Look closely—they're even in the drapes! (April 16, 1939.)

The **TWO LOWER FLOORS OF A THREE-STORY HOUSE WERE STOLEN!** "APPROPRIATED" FOR KINDLING WOOD, ETC., FROM 51 HERKIMER ST. ALBANY, N.Y.

Pottery Place? Crockery Corners? Dishware Downs?

Raymond Isodore, of Chartres France labored 23,000 hours to make his home and all its furnishings out of 1,000,000 broken dishes.

THE CASTLE THAT REFUSES TO FALL – Bridgnorth England
IT WAS BLOWN UP IN **1651** AND HAS BEEN DEFYING GRAVITY FOR **305** YEARS

THE STEEPLE THAT FULFILLED A PROPHECY
THIS **PROPHECY** WAS QUOTED IN CHICHESTER, ENGLAND, FOR **800** YEARS: "If Chichester Church Steeple ever fall In England there is no king at all." THE STEEPLE COLLAPSED IN FEBRUARY, 1861 — AND AT THAT TIME ENGLAND HAD NO KING ON ITS THRONE – BECAUSE ITS RULER WAS QUEEN VICTORIA

The Cathedral of Notre Dame de la Garde in Marseille, France is located on a mountain several hundred feet above the city and can be entered from its harbor side only by means of cable cars.

This tiny chapel on the Isle of Guernsey is made entirely of sea shells. 1933.

! *Charlotte, North Carolina once boasted a building built entirely of coal.*

The Church of Notre Dame des Mission in Epinay, France bears a facade of mah jongg tiles. (March 24, 1956.)

ATLANTIC CITY'S ELEPHANT HOTEL:
Souvenir of a Bygone Era

Mention the Elephant Hotel to anyone who remembers traveling to Atlantic City, New Jersey before the era of the casinos, and their faces will glow with a wistful smile. "Lucy" has been a beloved landmark to generations of vacationing families since her creation in 1881.

Would-be real estate mogul James V. Lafferty built Lucy in 1881 in an attempt to attract buyers to the tracts of land he hoped to sell as sites for vacation cottages. Over one million hand-carved pieces of wood went into Lucy's construction, whose exterior was covered with a skin of painted sheet tin. The completed building—a true architectural marvel in Lafferty's day—stood six stories tall and weighed 90 tons. Lucy fulfilled her owner's wishes: she quickly became a beloved landmark and a thriving neighborhood grew up around her.

Lafferty made sure his amazing elephant-shaped building would have no competition by acquiring a patent granting him exclusive permission to build animal-shaped buildings for 17 years. After building Lucy, Lafferty built two more elephant buildings: a twelve-story "Elephantine Colossus" on Coney Island and "The Light of Asia", slightly smaller than Lucy, at South Cape May, New Jersey. The "Colossus" burned down and the "Light of Asia" was demolished, leaving Lucy the sole survivor of her very rare family.

After serving faithfully as a real estate office, a restaurant, a hotel, a private cottage and a tavern (closed down due to Prohibition from 1920–1933) a dilapidated Lucy came perilously close to demolition in 1969, only to be saved in the nick of time by public outcry and loving donations. She was tenderly restored by the "Save Lucy" Foundation in the 1970s, designated a National Historic Site and reincarnated as a museum.

Today, Lucy is alive and well and living in Margate, New Jersey. She stands cheerfully gazing out at the Atlantic, with a souvenir store and the "I Love Lucy" sandwich shop to keep her company. Visitors can climb the spiral staircases in Lucy's back legs to view the historical exhibits in the main room in her belly, or ascend another stairway to her howdah (the seat that rests on her huge back) to look out to sea, where it is said that on a clear day, ships as far as eight miles out are greeted by the astonishing sight of an enormous wooden elephant!

Atlantic City, New Jersey's famous Elephant Hotel, beloved landmark to vacationing families in the era before the casinos. (October 15, 1933.)

"Lucy", fully refurbished in the 1970s, is open to the public daily in Margate, New Jersey.

Creature CURIODDITIES

A BULL CAN WHIP A TIGER! THEY HAVE BEEN MATCHED IN THE BULLRING AND THE TIGER HAS ALWAYS LOST

The Believe It or Not! cartoon for September 12, 1965 features a canine hero.

THE DOG THAT SAVED 92 LIVES! THE S.S. ETHIE, A COASTAL STEAMER OF 414 TONS, AGROUND ON MARTIN'S POINT OFF CURLING, NEWFOUNDLAND, AND BREAKING UP IN A VIOLENT STORM AND HEAVY SEAS, WAS UNABLE TO FIRE A LIFELINE OR LAUNCH ITS BOATS, AND NO MEMBER OF THE CREW DARED ATTEMPT TO SWIM ASHORE A NEWFOUNDLAND DOG MADE THE SWIM WITH A LIFELINE GRIPPED IN ITS TEETH AND ALL 92 PASSENGERS AND CREW MEMBERS WERE PULLED TO SAFETY ON A BOATSWAIN'S CHAIR (DEC. 10, 1919)

THE AUSTRALIAN COCKROACH (Panesthia Laevicollis) WHICH NEEDS NO WINGS BECAUSE IT LIVES IN THE GROUND BITES OFF ITS OWN WINGS WHEN IT REACHES MATURITY

! *A seal only sleeps at one and one-half minute intervals.*

! *The Earl of Glasgow, who had lost millions betting on his own horses, announced that he would shoot the next one that lost. That afternoon, on October 30, 1852, all six of his horses won!*

The Fish that Climb Trees

Periophthalmus Schlosseri is a species of fish native to Malaysia that likes to climb trees. When the tide is out these frisky fish squirm playfully in the mud and frequently wriggle up nearby trees in search of tasty insects. Propelling themselves with unusual agility by means of two leg-like fins, these fish are able to ascend good-sized trees, where they often look down on surprised travelers.

! *Flamingos can only eat with their heads upside down! (September 9, 1991.)*

The Roman Emperor Caligula, 12–41 AD, is remembered as The Horse Emperor because he bestowed the rank of Consul and Co-regent upon his favorite horse, Incitatus. The horse was accorded every honor of the office, and was provided with an ivory manger and a golden drinking goblet from which he drank wine.

THE MARINE ANIMALS WHO PAY FOR TRANSPORTATION MELIA TESSELLATA, A CRAB, TRANSPORTS IN ITS CLAWS 2 ANEMONES WHICH RETURN THE FAVOR BY PERMITTING THEIR HOST TO STEAL THEIR FOOD AND BY USING THEIR STINGING CELLS TO PROTECT THE CRAB FROM PREDATORS

The LARGEST AND STRONGEST ANIMALS ON EARTH ARE VEGETARIANS! ELEPHANT, GORILLA, HIPPOPOTAMUS, GIRAFFE, RHINO, WATER-BUFFALO, MUSK-OX, ETC.

HUFF HUFF

Believe It or Not! A PENGUIN CAN RUN AS FAST AS A MAN!

The Hen that became a Rooster

For many years, there was no reason to believe that the hen belonging to Dr. M.S. Gillespie was unusual. She laid eggs and clucked around her home in a Pennsylvania poultry yard just like any other normal chicken. One day, however, Dr. Gillespie noticed that the hen was sprouting bright new feathers, hackles, and a long drooping tail. She even sported three sharp spurs on each leg. Dr. Gillespie brought the bird to the Natural Science Halls of the Brooklyn Museum, where it was displayed for some time. Certain physiological changes are known to bring about this bizarre sex change—frequently, it is caused by abdominal tuberculosis.

HEADLESS CHICKEN
LAID AN EGG!
Owned by MRS. CLARA MEREDITH
Elizabethtown, Ky.

The Headless Hen

On November 12, 1904, **Herbert V. Hughes** of Sault St. Marie, Michigan was preparing chickens for Sunday dinner at the Belvedere Hotel. The chickens had been killed in the usual manner, by holding the birds by their feet on a block and chopping their heads off with an axe. A kitchen maid was picking and cleaning the chickens when she suddenly dropped one of the hens and fled screaming in terror.

A black Minorca chicken, entirely headless, had refused to die and was walking slowly around the room. The Sault St. Marie newspapers carried the story, and for more than two weeks, great crowds thronged the Belvedere Hotel to see the unbelievable sight of a living headless hen.

Mr. Hughes fed the freak by means of a syringe injected into the raw end of the food pipe, and she seemed to relish it. At times she would walk about slowly, stretch up and flap her wings, going through the motions of trying to adjust and smooth her ruffled feathers as though her head was still in place. At other times she would turn on her perch, sit down and get up again; sometimes she would try to croak or sing.

She appeared not to suffer pain and was as happy as any other hen. The chicken lived seventeen days after her head was cut off, and might have lived longer but for the fact that a careless attendant allowed the end of the neck to heal over the windpipe so that she suffocated.

The Marquise de Maintenon, second wife of Louis XIV of France, lived to become queen thanks to a kitten. When she was only three years old, she was pronounced dead at sea, and sewn up in a sack to be pitched overboard. Her pet kitten had crawled inside the sack, and began meowing during the funeral service. Knowing that cats hate corpses, the mourners opened the sack, and discovered that the little girl was still alive. She lived to marry the Sun King, and died in 1719 at the age of 84.

"GYP" a German Police Dog OWNED BY HERBERT NEFF RAN AWAY FROM HOME -BUT RETURNED TO SPEND CHRISTMAS WITH THE NEFFS EACH DEC. 25 FOR 9 SUCCESSIVE YEARS - Knoxville, Tenn.

AN ANIMAL THAT CAN EAT THROUGH METAL. THE PIDDOCK, A TYPE OF MOLLUSK, CAN BORE HOLES RIGHT THROUGH CAST IRON.!

THE BLACK COWS OF VALAMO
Russia
WILL NOT PERMIT
WOMEN TO MILK THEM!

! *Frogs hear with their eyes. Behind each eye is a small aural nerve connected to the brain.*

A mummified Egyptian cat, purchased in 1989, on display at the St. Augustine, Florida Odditorium. Mummified cats were once found in such profusion at archaeological digs that they were ground up as fertilizer.

A BRIGHT RED 12-INCH LONG SQUID THAT LIVES 3,300 feet UNDERWATER AND IS COVERED WITH TINY LIGHTS and SPINES WAS NAMED "VAMPYROTEUTEUTHIS INFERNALIS" or "VAMPIRE SQUID from HELL" BY THE SCIENTISTS WHO DISCOVERED IT.!

THE CALF OF A BLUE WHALE IS 23 FEET LONG AT BIRTH, CONSUMES HALF A TON OF MILK A DAY FOR 6 MONTHS AND GAINS 220 POUNDS EACH DAY

Anabas scandens, the crawling fish, is a species of fish native to Asia that can actually leave drying streams, ascend the banks, and make its way over dry land to a better water source. It can cover a distance of a mile or more and can remain out of water for up to a week. The bones of its head are enlarged and modified into a series of cavities which are capable of retaining water to help keep the gill membranes from drying out.

KANGAROO MEANS: "I DON'T UNDERSTAND"

WHEN ASKED THE NAME OF THIS ANIMAL A NATIVE REPLIED:- "KAN GA ROO"

What Talent!

Inspired by the Mark Twain tale, *The Celebrated Jumping Frog of Calaveras County*, Bill Steed of Oakland, California founded Croaker College in the early 1970s. Steed uses hypnosis to train frogs to perform amazing feats. One of his frogs was featured in the opening credits of the 1980s Believe It or Not! television series starring Jack Palance.

• • • • • • • • • • • • • • • ►

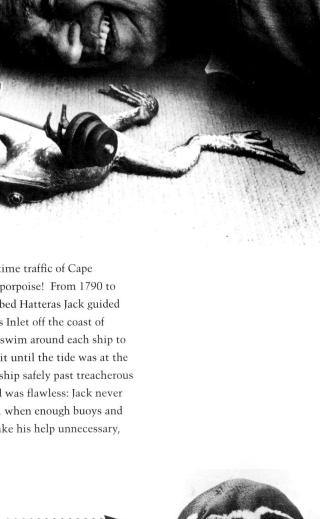

◄ • • • • • • • • • • • • • •

Canned possum—almost as good as fresh! Jake Thomasson of Arlington, Texas discovered this possum, which had wedged itself into a one-quart oil can! (July 1, 1951.)

Sea World's Chester the Chimp overcame his natural fear of water to allow Donna the Dolphin to pull him along at ten miles per hour on six-foot-long custom-built waterskis! (September 22, 1972.)

For twenty years, the maritime traffic of Cape Hatteras was directed by a porpoise! From 1790 to 1810, a white porpoise dubbed Hatteras Jack guided ships in and out of Hatteras Inlet off the coast of North Carolina. He would swim around each ship to gauge its size and draw, wait until the tide was at the proper level, then lead the ship safely past treacherous shoals and reefs. His record was flawless: Jack never lost a vessel. Then in 1810, when enough buoys and bells had been rigged to make his help unnecessary, Hatteras Jack disappeared.

• • • • • • • • • • • • ►

Rollie, Sea World San Diego's rollerskating Humboldt penguin, was a member of the National Rollerskating Association. (April 30, 1972.)

THE **GLASS EEL** of Australia IS SO TRANSPARENT THAT THE PAGES OF A BOOK CAN *BE READ THROUGH ITS BODY*

Ginger, a cocker spaniel, was able to carry three balls in her mouth at once! (April 8, 1951.)

Black Dog, Mascot of Airship Squadron Two

In the 1940s, Airship Squadron Two at the Naval Air Station in Lakehurst, New Jersey boasted an unusually dedicated mascot. A sleek black Labrador retriever mix, known only as Black Dog, appointed himself the official escort of every flight. He would run ahead of each aircraft on takeoff, regardless of the weather conditions, at any hour of the day or night. Despite this hazardous self-appointed task, Black Dog never sustained an injury while on duty.

3-5

EYEBALL TO EYEBALL THE HORNED TOAD OF MEXICO AND SOUTHERN U.S. DESERTS, REACTS TO ATTACK BY *SQUIRTING BLOOD FROM ITS EYES AS FAR AS 5 FEET*
© King Features Syndicate, Inc., 1977. World rights reserved.

O.J. Plomesen of Luverne, Minnesota owned this Buff Cochin rooster, Golden Duke, who would actually pull a carriage containing his baby daughter down Main Street during parades. The photo is circa 1910.

Riverview Restaurant owner **Frank Jacobs** of Newcastle, Maine owned and trained this remarkable skating pooch. (June 4, 1931.)

Mr. Personality

Sweet smell of success! After a long day bringing home ribbons from poultry shows, this White Australorp rooster enjoyed a hard-earned smoke. (May 28, 1934.)
••••••••••••▶

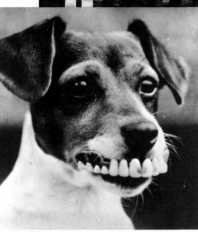

This dog is wearing his owners' false teeth! Whenever Mrs. W. R. Rhodes of Shreveport, Louisiana left her dentures on her nightstand, her dog would steal them and wear them himself! (1936.)
••••••••••••▶

CAT LICKS GOLDFISH. THE FISH SWIMS TO THE TOP AND ALLOWS CAT TO LICK ITS BACK Owned by M. HILL MANCHESTER, Eng.

Cackling Kitty: yep—you feed them, pet them, change their box, buy them little catnip mice... and this is what they do whenever your back is turned. (February 25, 1933.)
••••••••••••▶

◀ •••••••••••
Sammy, the firehouse cat at Fire Station Six in Long Beach, California would slide down the brass pole with his crew at the first sound of the alarm bell! (November 29, 1958.)

Mrs. Joan Wallis, a New South Wales orchard farmer in the early 1900s, was very fond of her affectionate pet, Peter. Peter would come when she called his name. Mrs. Wallis fed Peter cake and bread crumbs in the winter, and allowed him to catch his fill of flies in the summer. Peter had the run of the house, but preferred to spend most of his time behind a picture frame. What kind of pet was Peter? An enormous tarantula!

BOZO THE MIND READING DOG

Unlikely Pals

Yellow kittens with pointy noses: that's what these chicks must have seemed like to Frowzy the cat, owned by **Mr. and Mrs. A. W. Mitchell of Vancouver,** British Columbia. Instead of making a quick meal of the chicks, Frowzy zealously guarded his unusual litter night and day! (July 17, 1957.)

Defying nature! This dog and cat not only got along, they were friends! The dog would even give his kitty pal a lift on his back. Photo circa 1930.

Captain E. C. Lower's uncanny canine telepath, Bozo: a Collie/Chow mix who could correctly bark out the number of rings on audience members' fingers, the denominations and dates of coins, and any number his master thought of. (September 24, 1932.)

A slender dog with bright eyes and a silky coat stands alone on a stage. His ears twitch at the murmurs from the crowd in the darkened room, but his eyes never leave his trainer. The dog is all focus; every muscle poised. "Bozo," asks the trainer, "How many quarters do I have in my hand?" Bozo pauses, gives three ringing, Lassie-like woofs... and the crowd explodes in astonished applause. Right again!

At first the young pup had shown little promise. A neighbor had given Captain E. C. Lower the fluffy Collie/Chow mix when Bozo was only nine days old. An expert judge of dog sense, Captain Lower didn't figure Bozo to be worth training. He almost sold the tiny pup to a friend for $2 when he was five weeks old.

But Bozo was eager to please. By the time he was five months old, he had demonstrated a remarkable aptitude for learning. While still a puppy, Bozo displayed his mastery of 22 commands at a dog show. Shortly afterwards, Bozo's repertoire expanded to 33. He could count, add, and even subtract from a blackboard. But the true measure of his genius was yet to be discovered.

One day while working with Bozo, the captain was thinking of two numbers he was going to have Bozo add, when the young dog began to bark. Lower thought Bozo was barking out of turn, and scolded him. He thought of two more numbers, and Bozo barked again—the correct number of barks for the numbers in Lower's head!

Lower took Bozo to see a long succession of scientists and psychologists. Before every one, Bozo was able to repeat his astonishing mind-reading trick. His performances were so flawless that the captain was soon seating him alone on a stage, while soliciting numbers from the audience. Bozo could locate cards in a shuffled deck, bark the number of rings on ladies' fingers, count the number of coins in his master's hand—and even tell their denominations and dates. Bozo's performance was flawless, even when the dog was blindfolded.

Bozo went on to perform on numerous radio shows and stages across the country. He headlined at Atlantic City's Steeplechase Pier. Throughout his career he was tested, even by the famous detective William J. Burns and the noted magician Harry Thurston. No one could detect hidden signals between dog and trainer, and there didn't seem to be a logical explanation for Bozo's remarkable ability. The verdict seemed to be, as far as anyone could tell, that Bozo was reading his master's thoughts.

Curious COINCIDENCES

Mule deer antlers, a 6 pointer & a 4 pointer found locked together dead on Manzanita Mt. July 30 1938. On display in Wilson Suggetts Bar Room Alturas, Modoc Co, Calif.

Two mule deer found dead, with their antlers entwined, on July 20, 1938, by **Wilson W. Suggitt** of Alturas, California. Suggitt recalled finding bucks with locked antlers before, but was at a loss to explain how these two bucks had managed to get tangled up side by side."

When Vancouver, Washington homesteader **Emile Willard** abandoned a steel wheelbarrow on his land (in the mid-1920s) it became home to a growing alder sapling. This photo was taken in 1974, when the full-grown alder was still wearing the barrow-wheel that had once sheltered it. (January 23, 1974.)

What Are the Odds?

Officer Tapscott's gun, on display in Ripley's Odditoriums since 1936. Police Officer Tapscott was in a shoot-out with a suspect when the suspect fired. Tapscott inadvertently "caught" the suspect's bullet in the chamber of his own gun! Circa 1935.

TAPSCOTT'S BULLET IN CHAMBER OF WEBB'S GUN

JOINED BULLETS FEDERAL AND CONFEDERATE

Union and Confederate bullets that met in midair! **Chief Clerk Colin E. McRae** of the U.S. War Department in Washington, D.C. brought these unique fused bullets to Ripley's attention in 1935.

THE LAKE THAT YIELDS FISH AND CROPS Popovo Field, near Trebinye, Yugoslavia, IS A LAKE 20 MILES LONG AND 200 FEET DEEP EACH FALL, WITH MILLIONS OF FOOD FISH— EACH SPRING THE WATER DRAINS OUT THROUGH FUNNEL-LIKE HOLES AND ITS BED BECOMES A FERTILE FIELD HARVESTED BY 20 VILLAGES

THE STRANGEST GUN FIGHT IN HISTORY! CITY MARSHAL JEFF PACKARD OF BAKERSFIELD, CALIF., AND A FUGITIVE NAMED "OUTLAW" MCKINNEY, DREW AND FIRED SIMULTANEOUSLY AND EACH BULLET ENTERED AND PLUGGED THE OTHER MAN'S GUN!

These two bullets saved a life! During World War II, Pfc. **William A. Ball** was carrying a box of cartridges in his field jacket when he was hit by a sharp-nosed bullet. The enemy's bullet pierced two of the bullets in the box, and was slowed enough that only 1/2 of the bullet entered Ball's body (January 14, 1946.)

Newton Smith of Cuero, Texas killed three deer with one shot! Smith had seen only one deer, but his bullet passed though a second standing behind it, then through a third deer standing in the brush 15 feet away. (August 8, 1965.)

Bye Bye Black Sheep!

During a storm in Lapleau, France, lightning struck into a sheep fold, killing every black sheep but leaving all the white sheep unharmed.

STRANGEST ANNAL OF THE SEA!
THE SAILING SHIP "ECLIPSE" WAS STRUCK BY A METEOR IN MID-PACIFIC. THE MASTS WERE CARRIED AWAY, THE VESSEL WAS ABANDONED WITH A LOSS OF 3 LIVES.

ONCE **A BLUE MOON** APPEARED IN AUSTRALIA
IT WAS CAUSED BY A TREMENDOUS DUST STORM CONTAINING MYRIADS OF SPECKS OF SILICA OXIDE WHICH CUT OUT THE RED AND YELLOW RAYS — LEAVING ONLY THE BLUE

ALL THE BOOKS ON INSECTS IN THE JUNIOR HIGH SCHOOL LIBRARY IN Moultrie, Ga. **WERE DESTROYED BY TERMITES**

3 FROGS WERE FOUND IN A POTATO! by MRS. ED. HANSEN Foley, Minn

PREHISTORIC SEA SHELLS FOUND EMBEDDED IN A ROCK SPELL THE WORD "**SOIL**" FOUND **60** MILES INLAND BY MRS RAY GRUHLKE Olympia, Wash.

Coughlan's Come Home Again

Charles Coughlan of Prince Edward Island died in 1899 and was buried in Galveston, Texas. His coffin was washed out to sea, where it floated 2,000 miles before it finally washed ashore again... on Prince Edward Island, Coughlan's home.

! *Over a century ago, 12 sycamore trees were planted beside the Grace Episcopal Church in Plymouth, North Carolina. Each tree was named after one of Christ's apostles. The tree called Judas was hit by lightning and destroyed.*

! *A hurricane damaged or destroyed 6,923 churches on the eastern seaboard of the United States in 1938. But through some strange chance, all the synagogues and Episcopal churches were spared!*

! *On December 2, 1927, little Marie Finster jumped from the roof of a building in Vienna and was saved from death by falling into the arms of her mother who happened to be passing along the street below at that very minute.*

! *In May 1698, King Louis XIV of France ordered a road to be built through Great Bayard Rock, near Dinant, Belgium. The day before work was to start, a meteorite split the rock, creating a natural roadway that is still used today.*

! *When Vera Czermak learned that her husband had betrayed her, she jumped out of her third story window—and survived. She landed on her husband, who was killed instantly.*

The gun tree

Local legend has it that this 1839 Springfield Flintlock was placed in the notch of an oak tree in Chehalis, Washington as a symbol of a truce between settlers and local Native American tribes. The tree later grew around the gun, with this amazing result. (July 30, 1952.)

"If I died this hour, I should die happy." Thus spoke **John Liston,** celebrated English comedian on Sunday, March 22, 1807, at 10:30 AM, as he was married in the Church of St. Martin-in-the-Fields to Miss Tyrer, an Irish balladeer. Thirty-nine years later, as the clock struck 10:30 AM on Sunday, March 22, 1846, Liston died in his wife's arms.

When **Dennis L. Wheat** of Malvern, Arkansas won this car in a raffle, he discovered that it was the very same 1950 Chevrolet Fleetline sedan he had traded in six years earlier! (May 2, 1963.)

The Luckiest Man Alive

When **Captain J. H. Hedley** of Chicago, Illinois fell out of a plane nearly three miles up in the air on January 6, 1918, he was probably sure he'd had his last plane ride. But no—the plane was making a steep vertical dive in line with his own fall, and Hedley alighted on the tail. He was brought back to earth shaken, but none the worse for wear.

A lost donkey wandering aimlessly over the Idaho hills near what is now the town of Kellogg accidentally discovered a silver/lead mine worth $100 million. The animal was found standing on an outcropping of ore over what became the famous Bunker Hill & Sullivan mine.

"CALAMITY MARY" of SANTA ROSA, California

MARY BERGERE UNDERWENT 13 AUTOMOBILE ACCIDENTS IN WHICH THE CARS WERE DEMOLISHED EACH TIME — SHE WAS THROWN FROM A HORSE - KICKED BY A COW - BITTEN BY A DOG - SCRATCHED BY A WILDCAT, AND SURVIVED AN ARIZONA CLOUDBURST, FLORIDA HURRICANE, KANSAS CYCLONE, MISSISSIPPI FLOOD, CALIFORNIA EARTHQUAKE - A 3000-FOOT FALL FROM A PLANE — ALL THIS WITHOUT A SINGLE SERIOUS INJURY!

Beehive Hairdo!

These bees made their home atop a statue in the St. Francis Cemetery in Taunton, Massachusetts. The bees did such a flawless job making their hive match the style and coloration of the stonework, that at first folks assumed the hive was simply part of the statue! (January 17, 1966.)

Owen's School, in Islington, England, was built by **Alice Owen** on the spot where she had a miraculous escape from death. She had been watching a maid milking a cow and inquired if she might try her hand at milking. As she bent down to the task an arrow whizzed overhead and passed right through the crown of her hat. Had she been erect it could not have failed to kill her. In gratitude for her hairbreadth deliverance, she built a free school in 1613 for 30 boys on the spot. The school is still in use.

On May 3, 1972, **Patrick Donnelly** of Belfast, Ireland stopped his car to pick up a wallet he saw lying in the road. In order to find the name of its owner, Donnelly leafed through the wallet, only to discover that the owner's name was... Patrick Donnelly! The wallet belonged to another Patrick Donnelly who lived in the nearby town of Augher. The first Patrick Donnelly contacted the second, and returned the lost wallet.

Mrs. Harrieta Boyd and Mrs. Lorieta Meloche, identical twin sisters from Detroit, Michigan, appear to have had more in common than mere genetics. Both women contracted measles on the same day, both had their tonsils removed on the same day, both had accidents the first time they drove a car, and both were operated on for cataracts on the same day... in the same eye... by the same doctor!

Geordie Gill Lost His Legs—All Four of Them!

Geordie Gill of Broken Hill, New South Wales, had his legs amputated twice! The first time was when he fell from a moving train, which crushed his legs. Both legs were removed and replaced with prosthetics. Several years later, Geordie fell under a steam tram. The tram's wheels severed his artificial legs. Geordie sat in the road roaring with laughter at the fact that he had lost four legs!

! *After a cyclone swept through Marshfield, Missouri on April 8, 1880, a baby girl was found sleeping peacefully in the branches of a tall elm. The child was never identified and was later adopted by a local family.*

Lady Luck Was Smiling...

BROTHERS REUNITED AFTER 30 YEARS BY THE SMELL OF AN APPLE

A TRAVELER STANDING IN THE R.R. DEPOT IN STILLWATER, OKLA. WAS EATING AN APPLE, WHEN A STRANGER APPROACHED AND SAID, "THAT SMELLS LIKE A NORTH CAROLINA APPLE." "IT IS", SAID THE TRAVELER, "I'M FROM NORTH CAROLINA." "SO AM I," SAID THE STRANGER — AND THEY TURNED OUT TO BE BROTHERS WHO HAD NOT MET IN 30 YEARS!

BROTHERS MEET HUNTING EACH OTHER'S GRAVE

GRANT AND KARL WINEGAR Marines - HADN'T SEEN EACH OTHER FOR 20 MONTHS BUT KNEW THAT EACH WAS IN THE PACIFIC AREA. WHEN FIGHTING ON IWO JIMA - EACH THINKING THAT THE OTHER MIGHT HAVE BEEN KILLED — WENT PROWLING THRU A CEMETERY READING THE INSCRIPTIONS ON THE GRAVE MARKERS - WHEN SUDDENLY THEY MET FACE TO FACE

BUMPED OFF!

AN ITALIAN SAILOR WAS SLEEPING ON THE DECK OF AN ITALIAN DESTROYER WHEN IT ACCIDENTALLY COLLIDED WITH AN AMERICAN ROCKET SHIP — THE IMPACT BUMPED THE SAILOR OFF THE ITALIAN SHIP AND ONTO THE DECK OF THE AMERICAN SHIP! BOTH SHIPS CONTINUED ON THEIR RESPECTIVE WAYS

THE BABY THAT WAS BLOWN 70 FEET BY GUNPOWDER - AND LIVED!

AN INFANT SLEEPING IN ITS CRADLE ON GREAT TOWER STREET, LONDON, ENGLAND, WAS HURTLED TO THE ROOF OF A NEARBY CHURCH BY AN EXPLOSION THAT DEMOLISHED ITS HOME -YET THE BABY WAS FOUND SLUMBERING PEACEFULLY IN ITS UNDAMAGED CRADLE!

THE CHILD'S PARENTS WERE AMONG THOSE KILLED AND ITS IDENTITY WAS NEVER DISCOVERED   (Jan. 4, 1649)

No Way!

The twin girls in the top two photographs are **Lorraine and Loretta Szymanski** of Pittsburgh, Pennsylvania. So are the girls in the bottom two photos! Both sets of Szymanski twins lived near each other, attended the same school and even had the same classroom, yet were not related in any way!

One Pair Fits Both!

Albert Farler and his son **Albert Farler Jr.** of Kildonan, Manitoba, Canada both lost a leg and both wore the same size shoe. The father was missing a right leg; the son was missing a left, so they only needed to buy one pair of shoes between them!

James B. Williams, born on leap year, became the father of a daughter born on leap year! Williams was born on February 29, 1944. His daughter, **Moneyn Lynn,** was born on February 29, 1968.

Father and son were struck by cars at the same moment—a block apart! In Reading, Pennsylvania on May 14, 1970, **Carl A. Waldman,** age 34, was struck by a truck while crossing an intersection at 11th and Spring streets. At the same time, his son Michael, age 11, was hit by a car at the intersection of 10th and Spring. Neither knew that the other had been hit until they met at the entrance to the emergency room of St. Joseph's Hospital. Both father and son were treated for minor cuts and bruises and released.

Too Weird!

In New Zealand, a grieving widow whose husband had died two days earlier got the shock of her life when she received a telegram addressed to her, which read:

"Arrived in Paradise today. Everything lovely."

The telegram was signed with her dead husband's initials!

It turned out that the telegram had been sent to her in error. It was actually meant for a woman of the same name, but at a different address. The other woman's daughter, who coincidentally had the same initials as the dead husband, was writing to tell her mother that she had just arrived at the town of Paradise, on Lake Wakatipu.

THE **STATUE** OF A CHAINED WATCHDOG MOLDED FROM THE IMPRESSION MADE BY A DOG STRAINING TO ESCAPE THE **DESTRUCTION OF POMPEII** (79 A.D.)

SID WOLINSKY
Chicago
WAS BORN IN A HEARSE!
HIS MOTHER ENROUTE TO A HOSPITAL IN A STREET CAR REQUIRED *FASTER* TRANSPORTATION AND WAS PLACED IN A PASSING HEARSE

WINNER OF A TRIP TO BERMUDA
1939 *BELIEVE IT OR NOT CONTEST*

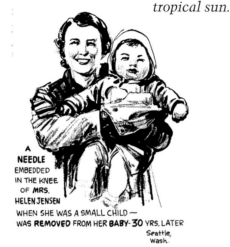

A **NEEDLE** EMBEDDED IN THE KNEE OF MRS. HELEN JENSEN WHEN SHE WAS A SMALL CHILD — WAS **REMOVED** FROM HER BABY—**30** YRS. LATER
Seattle, Wash.

! *Near the Equator in 1908, a caravan of travelers was found frozen to death beneath a brilliant tropical sun.*

The **PRIZE-WINNING CARTOON** of 1939

STABBED TO DEATH BY A BASEBALL!
STANTON WALKER ATTENDED A BALL GAME AND WAS SEATED BETWEEN 2 FRIENDS WHEN ONE ATTEMPTED TO PASS AN OPEN POCKET KNIFE TO THE OTHER. *JUST AS THE KNIFE PASSED IN FRONT OF WALKER IT WAS STRUCK BY A FOUL BALL AND DRIVEN INTO HIS HEART - KILLING HIM*
MORRISTOWN - BETHESTA - MORRISTOWN, OHIO, 1902.

THE **PROPHET OF DOOM**
Ned Pearson
GRAVEDIGGER of Grimsby, England, FOR A PERIOD OF **22 YEARS** ALWAYS VISITED THE HOME OF HIS NEXT CLIENT **24 HOURS BEFORE THE PERSON DIED**!

ONE SNAKE BITE KILLED **3 GENERATIONS** OF THE **SAME FAMILY**
Kingwald Family - Austria 1928

A VIPER BIT THE GRANDFATHER AND THE FANG REMAINED IN HIS BOOT. HIS SON AND GRANDSON WORE THE BOOTS AND WERE POISONED ALSO

© 1961, King Features Syndicate, Inc., World rights reserved.

There's Something About That Date

Historically, September 1 is not a good date to be in Japan. Severe earthquakes devastated Japanese cities on:

September 1, 259
September 1, 827
September 1, 867
September 1, 1185
September 1, 1649
September 1, 1923

William Blake (1757–1827) the mystic poet, artist and musician, quit his job the first day that he was apprenticed to William Rylands, England's foremost engraver. The reason that Blake, who was 14 at the time, quit, was that when he looked at his employer, he had a chilling vision of Rylands hanging dead on a gallows. 12 years later, the vision became a reality when Rylands was hanged for forgery.

Alone and broke on Christmas Day, 1977, artist **John Helms** flung himself off the 86th floor of the Empire State Building in New York City. Half an hour later, he woke up, only to find himself on a narrow ledge on the 85th floor. He knocked on the window of the offices of a TV station and crawled to safety. Hundreds of families called to offer him a home for the holidays.

Tragic Turns

Little **Mickie Kennedy** lived with his parents in the Western District of Victoria in the 1940s. He seemed an ordinary child, until he began to speak. His first words were, "Mummy dead and Daddy gone." He repeated this phrase over and over for three years, much to the surprise and horror of his parents, until one night, on his parents' ninth wedding anniversary, his father murdered his mother. At the exact same moment that his father was sentenced to death, Mickie stopped repeating the phrase, and suddenly, inexplicably died.

On November 26, 1703, the great Eddystone Lighthouse, off Plymouth, England, was demolished by a tempest. Henry Wistanley, the builder of the lighthouse, perished in the disaster. At the same time in Wistanley's home in Littlebury—200 miles away—a small replica of the lighthouse fell from a shelf and was smashed to bits.

! *John Howard Payne, author of Home, Sweet Home never had a home! He wandered the globe all his life, until he died penniless in Tunisia.*

! *Each of the five husbands of Frau Irmgard Bruns of Berlin committed suicide.*

THE MAN WHOSE LIFE WAS SAVED BY A GHOULISH JEST!
Sir Hugh Acland of Killerton, England, WAS PRONOUNCED DEAD IN 1770, BUT WAS REVIVED WHEN A FOOTMAN SITTING WITH THE "BODY" POURED A DRINK OF BRANDY DOWN THE "CORPSE'S" THROAT. HE LIVED ANOTHER 18 YEARS

This man's grisly but miraculously non-fatal wound has been featured in several of Ripley's Odditoriums in their "Accident Survivors" galleries. Circa 1940.

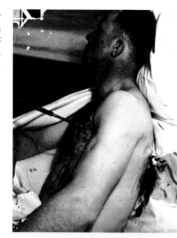

Skeleton Crew

"While cruising near the coastline off Punta Arenas, Chile, the British sailing ship *Johnson* sighted what appeared to be a boat with sails floating in the wind. When British signals elicited no response, the craft was approached. The crew noticed that the ship's masts and sails were covered with some kind of green moss, and that the vessel seemed abandoned by its crew. Upon boarding it, the skeleton of a man was discovered beneath the helm. The deck was decayed to such an extent that it gave under the footsteps. Three more skeletons were found near a panel, ten were found in the crew's quarters, and six on the bridge. Upon the ravaged prow of the vessel, the words *Marlborough Glasgow* could still be discerned. The *Marlborough* left Littleton, N.Z. in January, 1890 with a cargo of wool and frozen mutton, and a crew of 23 men under Captain Hird... In April of 1890 an unsuccessful search for the vessel was made... "

—Wellington, *New Zealand Evening Post*
November 13, 1913 and *Agence Havas*

PAUL HUBERT of Bordeaux, France WAS CONVICTED OF MURDERING HIMSELF! He served 21 years in solitary confinement before it was discovered that his supposed victim was none other than himself.

DUKE TARRELL THREW OUT 8 PLAYERS TRYING TO STEAL IN ONE GAME

YOU CAN SEE BOTH THE PACIFIC AND ATLANTIC OCEANS FROM THE TOP OF MT. IRAZU COSTA RICA

In June, 1908, a massive explosion jolted the remote Tunguska forest in Siberia. The blast occurred about four miles above the earth. It leveled trees for several thousand square miles. Horses more than 400 miles away were knocked to the ground. The night sky glowed for weeks afterwards. A number of scientists believe the explosion was caused by a meteor, which must have weighed more than 5 million tons, carrying the explosive equivalent of 300 million tons of TNT. Others believe that it was a chunk of ice and dust that broke off from Encke's comet, which circles the earth every 3.5 years. Wilder theories include the idea that it was a rock of antimatter from another universe, a black hole that hit Siberia and passed through the earth, or a nuclear blast, caused when an alien ship blew up.

Drag Race

Jockey Ray Selkrig was thrown from his horse, Hot Chestnut, during a 1973 race at Kembla Grange, New South Wales. He became tangled as he fell, and crossed the finish line literally dangling from the horse's reins. Judges later decided that the horse had transported Selkrig's body across the line, and awarded him the victory!

In January of 1945, **Ernest Young** of Pasadena, Texas was hit by a German machine gun bullet in the right shoulder as his unit fought the Germans in the aftermath of the Battle of the Bulge. Twenty-eight years later, Young went into a violent coughing fit, and spat out the bullet!

EARNEST YOUNG OF PASADENA, TEXAS. WHO WAS WOUNDED IN THE CHEST BY A MACHINE GUN IN WORLD WAR II, COUGHED UP THE BULLET 28 YEARS LATER.

"The Little Bastard"

This was what James Dean called his hot new little sports car. Sir Alec Guinness warned Dean that the powerful little car would kill him. Guinness was right—Dean died at the wheel of "The Little Bastard". After his death, the car continued to leave death and injury in its path: Within a few years of its owner's death, the demon car killed two more people and caused the injury of half a dozen others before it vanished in 1959.

James Dean was killed in the Bastard in a head-on crash at 80 miles per hour. Investigators were baffled by evidence that suggested that Dean, an expert driver, did nothing to avoid the crash. The death car immediately became a grisly trophy, but fans who arrived on the scene and tried to help themselves to souvenir pieces of the wreckage were injured while trying to remove them.

When a friend tried to sell the car, it fell on a garage mechanic and broke his legs. Two doctors bought parts from the car to reuse in their race cars. One was killed and the other seriously injured. The only two undamaged tires were sold to a man who was sent to a hospital after they both mysteriously blew at the same time. Later inspection failed to find fault in either tire.

After these grim developments, the California Highway Patrol planned to use the remains of the car in an auto show, but the night before the show opened, a fire broke out, destroying every vehicle—except Dean's car, which escaped the blaze without a smudge. The car was later loaded on a truck to be driven to Salinas, Dean's destination the day of the crash; the driver lost control of the truck and was thrown from his cab and crushed. The Dean car rolled safely off the truck.

In 1959, another attempt was made to display the vehicle. This time, the car inexplicably broke into eleven pieces, even though it had been carefully welded back together.

Finally, the Florida police offered to take the vehicle for a safety display in Miami. After it was crated and hoisted onto a truck, the "Little Bastard" disappeared, and has not been seen since.

Unexplained Phenomena

A RAILWAY TRAIN WAS STALLED BY THOUSANDS OF CRABS WHICH MADE THE RAILS SO SLIPPERY **THE TRAIN WAS UNABLE TO MOVE** Manzanillo, Mexico

ON October 9, 1892, A YELLOW CLOUD HOVERED OVER THE TOWN of Paddehorn, Germany, THEN A RAIN of 'LIVE' MUSSELS FELL IN THE STREETS!

! *Peter Barr of St. Faiths, England, totally blind for ten years, suddenly regained his sight when he pounded his hands together in an argument.*

! *Captain Joseph G. Belain dedicated his life to attempting to save the carrier pigeon from extinction. During his funeral service at Gay Head, Massachusetts, a single carrier pigeon flew in from the sea, alighted on his bier, and stayed until the service was concluded.*

A Philadelphian Committed Suicide and Left the Following Note:

I married a widow with a grown daughter. My father fell in love with my step-daughter and married her, thus becoming my son-in-law, and my step-daughter became my mother because she was my father's wife. My wife gave birth to a son, who was of course my father's brother in law, and also my uncle for he was the brother of my step-mother. My father's wife became the mother of a son, who was, of course, my brother, and also my grandchild for he was the son of my daughter. Accordingly, my wife was my grandmother because she was my mother's mother—I was my wife's husband and grandchild at the same time—and as the husband of a person's grandmother is his grandfather—I AM MY OWN GRANDFATHER!

-MARK TWAIN

Cow Winds Watch

"Seven years ago a farmer in Iowa hung his vest on a fence in the barnyard. A calf chewed up a pocket in the garment in which was a gold watch. Last week the animal, a staid old milk cow, was butchered for beef. The timepiece was found in such a position between the lungs of the cow that respiration—the closing in and filling of the lungs-kept the stem winder wound up, and the watch had lost but four minutes in the seven years."

—*The Torch*
Hastings, Minnesota
December 18, 1927

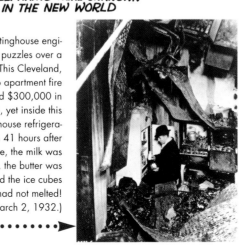

2 ELEPHANTS ARE PORTRAYED IN A MAYA SCULPTURE ON THE TEMPLE OF COPAN, HONDURAS -YET THE SCULPTURE PRE-DATES COLUMBUS' VOYAGES, AND ELEPHANTS WERE UNKNOWN IN THE NEW WORLD

A Westinghouse engineer puzzles over a mystery: This Cleveland, Ohio apartment fire caused $300,000 in damage, yet inside this Westinghouse refrigerator, even 41 hours after the fire, the milk was fresh, the butter was firm, and the ice cubes had not melted! (March 2, 1932.)

"May Pure White Pigeons Nest in the Beams of Your House"

This was the traditional blessing of **Ali ben Abu Talib**, son-in-law and successor of the prophet Mohammed. Ali, who died in 661, is believed to be buried in the mosque of Mazar-i-Sharif in Afghanistan. Shortly after Ali's death, thousands of pure white pigeons took up residence near his grave, and have lived there ever since. If a pigeon with even a single black feather tries to join the flock, the white pigeons attack it and drive it away.

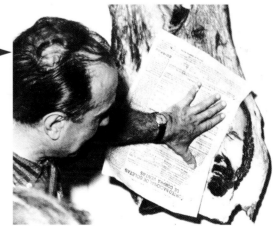

Butcher **Oscar H. Ibarra Guzman** of San Bernardo, Chile was startled to see this human face staring back at him from a leg of veal! (July 7, 1963.)

The World's Weirdest War Stories

In 1945, Robert Ripley held weekly contests to find the most unusual Believe It or Not World War II stories. Fans across the country sent in astonishing tales of coincidence and bravery, and received prizes of $1,000 grand prize, $100 cash, an autographed *Believe It or Not!* book, or honorable mention. The following are among the best:

Merchant Marine **Roy Dikkers** was Bombed to Safety: The First torpedo that hit his tanker blasted the door to his quarters shut. The second torpedo broke it open. He reached the deck only to find himself engulfed in burning oil. There seemed to be no hope until a third torpedo blew him into the air, over the fire and deposited him safely in clear water beside a life raft. After drifting for three days, he was rescued by a Norwegian ship.

-submitted by Mrs. G. W. Grant of Bingham Lake, Minnesota- Dikkers' grandmother. Winner: $100 prize.

Special Delivery: Sgt. Joseph Charles was in a foxhole in New Guinea when the mail boys called him to come out for a letter. He had crawled out about 10 feet when a Japanese plane flew over and dropped a bomb that completely destroyed the foxhole he had just left.

-submitted by his aunt, Mrs. Marion Harrison of Chicago, Illinois, who wrote the letter that saved his life! Winner: $100 prize.

Saved by a Hand Grenade! PFC Allen Fuehrer of the 100th division, Lembach, France, was struck with an armor-piercing bullet that passed completely through a hand grenade in his pocket without exploding it, then passed through his Bible. Fuehrer was only slightly wounded.

-Honorable Mention

Miracle at Sea! Lt. Commander Robert W. Goehring was swept off the Coast Guard cutter *U.S.S. Duane* by a mountainous wave during a storm. The ship was turned around to rescue him, when suddenly another giant wave tossed him back on board to safety!

The Remarkable Dog of Sgt. Robert W. Ferling: The mascot of his battalion was left behind when the troops embarked from Oran, Algeria for Italy. But miraculously, he found his way to a port and crossed the sea to Italy, and made his way back to his master.

-submitted by Kathryn Wetzel, Honorable Mention

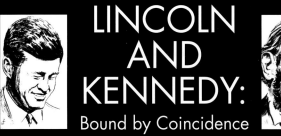

LINCOLN AND KENNEDY:
Bound by Coincidence

Two of America's greatest and most beloved presidents are linked by an eerie set of coincidences. A pattern runs through the circumstances of their presidencies and brutal assassinations that hints at some unknown, unexplained connection. Consider the following:

- Both Kennedy and Lincoln were deeply involved in the civil rights issue of the era—in Lincoln's day, the issue was slavery; in Kennedy's, it was segregation.
- Lincoln's assassin, John Wilkes Booth, was born in 1839. Kennedy's assassin, Lee Harvey Oswald, was born in 1939.
- Lincoln had a secretary named Kennedy who warned him not to go to the theater that night. Kennedy had a secretary named Lincoln, who warned him not to go to Dallas.
- Both were shot on a Friday.
- Both were shot from behind.
- Both wives were present.
- Booth shot Lincoln in a theater and ran into a warehouse; Oswald shot Kennedy from a warehouse and ran into a theater.
- Both were succeeded by men named Johnson.
- Both Johnsons were Democrats from the South.
- The Johnson who succeeded Lincoln was born in 1808; the Johnson who succeeded Kennedy was born in 1908.
- Both presidents' names contain 7 letters; their successors' names contain 13; their assassins have 15.

Different DUDS

Bank officer **E. W. Brown Jr.** of Orange, Texas sported bow ties made of $20.00 bills! Brown collected retired bills from the era when banks issued their own currency. Note that the signature in the lower left-hand corner of Brown's tie is his own! (April 17, 1963.)

A vest made of human hair, by barber **Bill Black** of St. Louis, Missouri. Black began saving hair to see if the nitrogen in it could be used as fertilizer. Rather than let it all go to waste, he created an entire line of clothing: this vest, hats, scarves, pants and even bathing suits.

Believe It or Not!, Pard'ner: Ripley sports a broad-brimmed ten-gallon hat and cowboy duds at his Dallas, Texas Odditorium in 1936. He was presented with the hat when he was named an honorary Texas Ranger.

5-16

THE **TALL** FEATHERED HEADDRESS WORN BY THE BOYS of the Booli Tribe, in the Congo, IS ANCHORED AGAINST THE HIGH WINDS *BY A STRING ATTACHED TO ONE OF ITS WEARER'S TEETH* THE WIND EVENTUALLY CAUSES THE STRING TO WEAR A GROOVE IN THE YOUTH'S UPPER LIP-WHICH IS BELIEVED TO ENHANCE HIS MANLY APPEARANCE

The chiefs of the Bashilele tribe in the Republic of Congo wear an extremely long wrap-around dance skirt called a lupungu, made of the fiber of raffia palm leaves. When dressing for a dance, the chief orders two attendants to hold up the 18-yard-long skirt at either end, then spins into it by performing 18 pirouettes. On one occasion, a chief named Lekhomale demonstrated his nimbleness by performing a total of 58,000 pirouettes, thereby spinning in and out of his elongated skirt 2,200 times in succession. This feat took him 18 solid hours.

BOOTS MADE FROM THE LEGS OF A BEAR WERE WORN BY AMERICAN INDIANS TO CONFUSE TRACKING PURSUERS

TURTLE SOUP

A WIDOW in the VUGUSSU TRIBE, So. Africa AS MOURNING GARB WEARS HER DECEASED HUSBAND'S CLOTHING

LIVING CALENDARS
GIRLS on the island of Helgoland CELEBRATED NEW YEAR'S DAY IN 1866 BY WEARING DRESSES ON WHICH WAS PRINTED *!TIRE CALENDAR OF THE YEAR*

YOUNG ABORIGINES OF CENTRAL AUSTRALIA PLEAT THE HAIRS OF THEIR BEARD AROUND *THE CURVED TAIL OF A THALGOO -- AN AUSTRALIAN MAMMAL*

"FRANKLIN" WIRES ADORNED THE HATS OF CHIC PARISIAN WOMEN IN 1776 IN HONOR OF BENJAMIN FRANKLIN'S INVENTION -- *THE LIGHTNING ROD*

TRICK RIDERS OF THE BRITISH ARMY WHO CALLED THEMSELVES "THE DEATH OR GLORY BOYS," *DRESSED AS SKELETONS*

It took **Mrs. Willis N. Ward** and **Mrs. John Hoppemath** seven years and 1400 yards of thread to make these "Eskimo Suits" from editions of the *Florida Times Union* newspaper (August 17, 1936.)

•••••

••••••••••••••••••➤

Owen Totten of Mt. Erie, Illinois models his unique 5,600-button formal wear—no two buttons alike! (March 31, 1936.)

Corn Gown

◀ ∙∙∙∙∙∙∙∙∙∙∙∙∙∙

Virginia Winn of Mercedes, Texas stitched 60,000 grains of corn onto this evening dress. The completed garment weighed 40 pounds! (August 4, 1947.)

THE BLUE PEOPLE of MOROCCO
BERBERS of the Draa Valley, USE A BLUE INDIGO DYE ON THEIR CLOTHING WHICH GRADUALLY TURNS THEIR ENTIRE BODIES **AN INDELIBLE BLUE!**

CHARLES BRONSON
FAMED FOR HIS MOVIE TOUGH-GUY ROLES, WORE HAND-ME-DOWNS AS A CHILD OF 6 -- OFTEN GOING TO SCHOOL IN, *A DRESS INHERITED FROM AN OLDER SISTER*

THE JADE FUNERAL SUIT OF PRINCESS TOU WAN OF CHINA, WHO DIED IN THE 1ST CENTURY B.C., IS COMPOSED OF 2,000 PIECES OF JADE--KNITTED TOGETHER WITH GOLD AND SILK-COVERED WIRE

High in Vitamin C, fiber, and fashion!

Wilma Beth Shulke of Mission, Texas models an outfit made of cross-sections of corncobs and orange peels. (May 23, 1940.)

THE MAN WHO WORE IRON UNDERWEAR
Sir William de Lacy
A NORMAN BARON WHO BECAME A HERMIT IN 1100 WORE HIS COAT OF ARMOR AS UNDERCLOTHING *DAY AND NIGHT FOR 21 YEARS!*

THE FIRST SEE-THROUGH FASHIONS
DANCERS IN THE NEW HEBRIDES, IN THE SOUTH SEAS, WEAR WEB COSTUMES *WOVEN BY SPIDERS ON SPECIAL CONICAL FORMS*

THE ATTIRE
SOUTHERN WOMEN WORE TO CHURCH IN THE U.S. DURING THE 1700's DETERMINED HOW MUCH THEIR HUSBANDS WERE REQUIRED TO PUT INTO THE CHURCH COLLECTION PLATE --*THE MOST ELEGANT CLOTHING REQUIRING THE HIGHEST PAYMENTS*

SWISS PEASANT WOMEN
IN THE MID-17TH CENTURY WRAPPED THEIR BRAIDS AROUND *THE CROWN OF THEIR HAT*

THE CLOAK THAT WAS WORN FOR 885 YEARS
KING CHARLES of Hungary WAS CROWNED ON DEC. 20, 1916 IN THE MANTLE OF ST. STEPHEN --WHICH HAD BEEN WORN AT THE CORONATION OF *EVERY HUNGARIAN MONARCH SINCE 1031!*

ROBERT RIPLEY

Fashion Mogul?

Ripley travels Afghanistan clad in a native ghoutra.

Ripley, in Greek military attire, kicks up his heels in front of the bar at his home on BION Island. Circa 1935.

Not only was he the champion of the strange and unusual, Robert L. Ripley was himself something of a walking Believe It or Not!. From the very earliest beginnings of his empire, Ripley adopted a unique style of dress which was considered peculiar even among the free-spirited circles in which he traveled. He was, in a word, "colorful."

Ripley's best friend, Bugs Baer, once exclaimed, "He looks like a paint factory that got hit by lightning!"

Ripley's standard outfit consisted of shiny two-toned spat shoes, a black and white hound's tooth check suit, pink pleated shirt and a multicolored bat-wing tie. A typical variation on this basic dress scheme might include a blue shirt, orange tie, plaid jacket and fawn-colored slacks. During the golden era of his ca-

reer, Ripley added a pith helmet to his ensemble, perhaps to encourage the world-wise, "Great White Hunter" image he sought. Ripley was seldom parted from his pith helmet. He even wore it with formal suits!

Ripley was also fond of the various forms of exotic dress he observed in his travels. He owned a collection of traditional Chinese outfits for use aboard his Chinese junk, the *Mon Lei*, as well as for guests who stayed in his upper-floor Chinese suite at BION Island. He also kept a collection of flowing mirrored costumes for moonlit rides aboard his Shikara boat.

Of course, Ripley's legendary parties often included costumes of various sorts. 1930s- and 1940s-era photos of his shindigs reveal the champion of the strange in false mustaches, beards and noses, and in a number of burlesque outfits. Ripley may not have been exactly the fashion plate of his time, but he inevitably stood out in any crowd!

Ripley dons a wide-lapel plaid suit and fake mustache for a party in honor of the 30th anniversary of the first Believe It or Not! cartoon. The fourth woman from the left is Louise Baer, wife of Ripley's best friend Bugs Baer. Second from the right is Milly Considine, wife of Ripley's first biographer, Bob Considine. Toots Shor restaurant, 51st Street, New York City, December 14, 1948.

Ripley in Chinese garb at his Manhattan apartment. He kept a number of such outfits for guests to wear while sailing on his Chinese junk, the *Mon Lei*.

Eccentric EPITAPHS

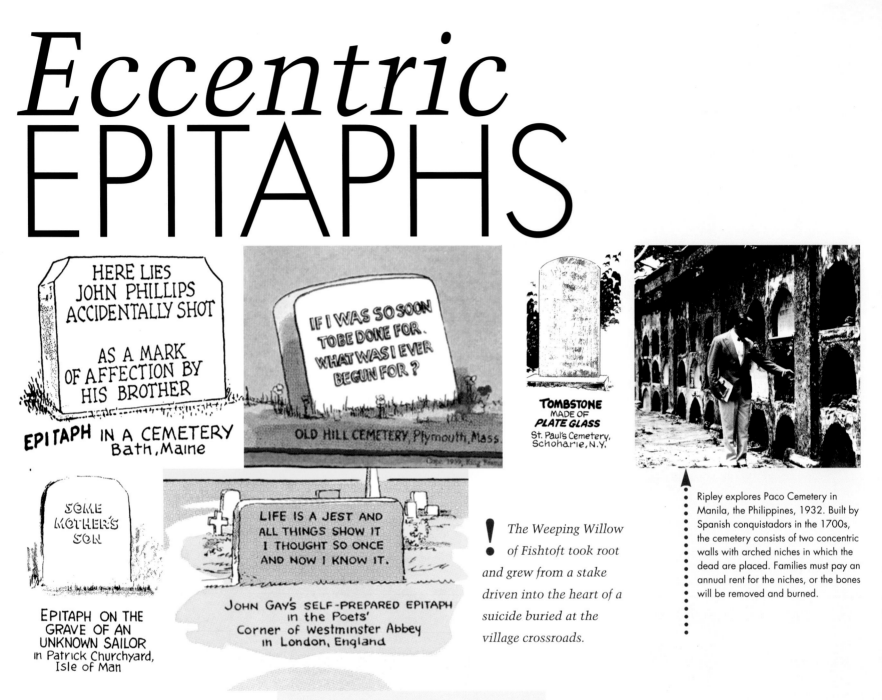

HERE LIES
JOHN PHILLIPS
ACCIDENTALLY SHOT

AS A MARK
OF AFFECTION BY
HIS BROTHER

EPITAPH IN A CEMETERY
Bath, Maine

IF I WAS SO SOON
TO BE DONE FOR.
WHAT WAS I EVER
BEGUN FOR?

OLD HILL CEMETERY, Plymouth, Mass.

TOMBSTONE
MADE OF
PLATE GLASS
St. Paul's Cemetery,
Schoharie, N.Y.

SOME
MOTHER'S
SON

**EPITAPH ON THE
GRAVE OF AN
UNKNOWN SAILOR**
in Patrick Churchyard,
Isle of Man

LIFE IS A JEST AND
ALL THINGS SHOW IT
I THOUGHT SO ONCE
AND NOW I KNOW IT.

**JOHN GAY'S SELF-PREPARED EPITAPH
in the Poets'
Corner of Westminster Abbey
in London, England**

! The Weeping Willow
of Fishtoft took root
and grew from a stake
driven into the heart of a
suicide buried at the
village crossroads.

Ripley explores Paco Cemetery in
Manila, the Philippines, 1932. Built by
Spanish conquistadors in the 1700s,
the cemetery consists of two concentric
walls with arched niches in which the
dead are placed. Families must pay an
annual rent for the niches, or the bones
will be removed and burned.

! Eulogy given in the Western
Australian town of Sandstone in
1908, by a Jewish prospector: "There lies
the body of the first Jew to die in
Sandstone. Please God may he be the
last, because I'm the only other one in
this district, and I'd hate to die in a place
like this."

Here Beneath this Stone We Lie
Back to Back my Wife and I
And when the Angels' Trump shall Trill
If She gets Up, then I'll Lie Still
—Barlinine Cemetery, Glasgow

In Memory of
ELLEN SHANNON
Aged 26
FATALLY BURNED
1870
BY THE EXPLOSION
OF A LAMP FILLED
WITH DANFORTH'S
NON-EXPLOSIVE FLUID.

**EPITAPH IN CEMETERY
AT GIRARD, PA.**

Here Lies
A.P. Sisson
God only knows
What will become of him
In the future
　　　　—Gravestone in Red
　　　　　Oak, Louisiana

The grave of **E. H. Johnson** in London Cemetery, London, Kentucky. The gravestone to Johnson's left reads: "Molly R., wife of E. H. Johnson. 1878–1917. No Better Woman Ever Lived." The gravestone to his right reads: "Sarah E., wife of E. H. Johnson. 1874-1906. No Better Woman Ever Lived." (May 15, 1983.)

Here lies Fred
Who was alive
And is dead
There's no more to be said
　　—Grave of Prince Frederick

Owen Moore
Is gone away
Owin' more
Than he could pay
　　　　—Epitaph in
　　Surrey, England

Watch your step! **R. E. Bahm's** grave in Husser, Louisiana is studded with Native American arrowheads! Bahm began collecting the arrowheads as a child and carried his beloved collection with him throughout his life. His family had his collection embedded in the cement covering his grave to honor his request. (June 11, 1947.)

IN RURAL CHINA, WEDDINGS ARE OFTEN PERFORMED IN WHICH *DECEASED SINGLE GIRLS and BOYS ARE WED IN GRAVESITE CEREMONIES* SO THAT THE GIRL CAN SERVE HER *"HUSBAND"* IN THE AFTERLIFE!

Here lies John Higgs
A famous man for killing pigs
For killing pigs was his delight
Both morning, afternoon and night
　　—Epitaph in Cheltenham
　　　Cemetery, England

Will Rogers America's beloved humorist unwittingly wrote his own obituary. Before he was killed in a plane crash in 1935 he had been working on with some of his last words which read: "Well, I must stop now. The horses are coming in..."

Here lies the body of Solomon Peas
Under the daisies and under the trees
Peas is not here-only the pod;
Peas shelled out; went home to God.

　　　　—Wetumpka, Alabama

FINIS
MAGINNIS

     —Witchurch graveyard,
     Dorsetshire, England

Here Lies an atheist
All dressed up and no place to go

     —Epitaph in Thurmont, Maryland

The Living Tomb

In the beautiful little village of Noebdenitz, Germany, there stands an aged oak tree in solemn majesty. Wrapped in its heart are the mortal remains of Germany's great romantic poet, Hans Wilhelm von Thummel. It is a living tomb, for the old tree is still very much alive, despite its age of more than 1,000 years.

It was von Thummel's wish that this great oak which he admired so much in life should, serve him after death as a tomb. The day of his death, March 1, 1824, a sad procession stopped under its branches, while the body of the poet was wrapped simply in linen cloth and placed upright in a narrow hollow in the center of the tree.

One-hundred and seventy-five years later, the aged oak has slowly and kindly wrapped itself around him: The breach in its side has gradually healed and von Thummel sleeps on in peace and privacy.

A gambler's grave

Mr. and Mrs. Vieira's tombstone is a tribute to gambling. The headstone is Canadian-quarried pink granite, which gives the polished hearts a realistic pinkish hue. (June 24, 1981.)

GRAVES of CHUKCHE NATIVES of Siberia ARE DECORATED WITH REINDEER ANTLERS—WITH AN ADDITIONAL SET ADDED EACH YEAR

GRAVESTONE TO A HAND
Blandon, Pa., Cemetery
C.T. ALBRIGHT LOST HIS HAND IN AN ACCIDENT AND PUT UP THIS STONE

God does do wonders now
and then
Here lies a lawyer who
was an honest man

     —St. Peter's Exon,
          England

Here lies the father of twenty-nine
He would have had more but he didn't have
time

     —Moultrie, Georgia

In Fairplay, Colorado stands a tombstone that marks the grave of a burro. The burro, named "Prunes", died in 1930 at the age of 63, after having worked in all the mines of the district for a continuous period of 62 years.

Epitaph ON THE TOMBSTONE OF AN UNKNOWN MAN near the Molyneux River, N.Z.

SOMEBODY'S DARLING LIES BURIED HERE 1865 ERECTED 1903

! A tombstone erected by disappointed heirs in the New Church at Amsterdam, Holland:

Effen Nyt
(Exactly Nothing)

HERE STANDS OLD BRITT BAILEY

EPITAPH TO JAMES BRITTON BAILEY— WHO WAS BURIED STANDING UP BECAUSE HE REFUSED TO *LOOK UP* TO ANY MAN

Cemetery in Brazoria County, Texas

OH LORD SHE IS THIN!

GRAVESTONE IN COOPERSTOWN, N.Y.
SUPPOSED TO READ "OH LORD SHE IS THINE"
BUT THE STONE CUTTER FOUND THE STONE TOO NARROW

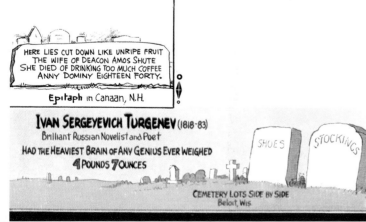

HERE LIES CUT DOWN LIKE UNRIPE FRUIT
THE WIFE OF DEACON AMOS SHUTE
SHE DIED OF DRINKING TOO MUCH COFFEE
ANNY DOMINY EIGHTEEN FORTY.

Epitaph in Canaan, N.H.

IVAN SERGEYEVICH TURGENEV (1818-83)
Brilliant Russian Novelist and Poet
HAD THE HEAVIEST BRAIN OF ANY GENIUS EVER WEIGHED
4 POUNDS 7 OUNCES

SHOES   STOCKINGS

CEMETERY LOTS SIDE BY SIDE
Beloit, Wis.

COGNAC AND ROSES:
The Mysterious Poe Toaster's Annual Homage Before Poe's Grave

THE GRAVE of EDGAR ALLAN POE in Baltimore, Md., HAS BEEN VISITED BY AN UNKNOWN PERSON FOR OVER 35 YEARS ON JANUARY 19th, POE'S BIRTHDAY, WHO PLACES ON THE FAMED 19th CENTURY MYSTERY WRITER'S TOMBSTONE A BOTTLE OF COGNAC AND A BOUQUET OF ROSES. Submitted by Kevin Rutter, Ellicott City, Md.

Oddly enough, Edgar Allen Poe's grave site in Baltimore's Westminster Cemetery bears no epitaph. Poe was due to get a headstone with an epitaph in 1849, but before the stone could be placed, it was crushed by a train that jumped its tracks. Some might say that Poe's stone needs no epitaph, because Poe's memory is served by a unique, mysterious "living epitaph" known affectionately as "The Poe Toaster."

Every January 19, since 1949, a mysterious individual has commemorated the anniversary of Poe's birthday by placing a bottle of cognac and three roses upon his grave. The cognac bottle is always open and one drink has been taken, hence the notion that the stranger toasts the great writer before leaving his or her tribute. The significance of the cognac is unknown, as there is no reference to it in Poe's works. Several bottles from previous years are on display in Baltimore's Poe House, the curator of which first brought the tradition to Ripley's attention. The three roses, it is believed, honor the three people buried in the grave: Poe himself, his wife Virginia and his mother-in-law Maria Clemm.

The identity of the "toaster" is unknown to this day. Some speculate that as so much time has passed since its beginning, the tradition may have been taken over by a successor. A number of intriguing mysteries surround Poe's death and grave. Poe fans speculate as to the causes of his death (one theory has it that he died of rabies) and debate among themselves whether his remains really do lie beneath his gravestone (a controversy still lingers that the exact whereabouts of Poe's body is unknown). Amid the mysteries Edgar Allen Poe has left behind, the identity of the Poe Toaster remains unsolved.

Effort and ENDURANCE

A Sunday Ripley's Believe It or Not! cartoon dated July 11, 1965, depicts **Frank Tower,** the man who survived the sinking of the *Titanic,* the *Lusitania* and the *Empress of Ireland.*

Trick-Riding Grandmother! **Tad Lucas**, world champion trick rider, rode in the same rodeo at Madison Square Gardens, New York, as her daughter and granddaughter! (November 18, 1947.)

Joyce Hart of Barrington, New Jersey could do a back somersault through two hoops at the age of ten. Trained by the famous gymnast Bob Jones, Hart first appeared in a Ripley cartoon walking on her hands with stilts on April 24, 1953. (June 15, 1955.)

! **Elijah the Gaon,** *Chief Rabbi of Lithuania, never forgot a book once he read it. Gaon committed to memory 2,500 volumes. He knew by heart the Bible, Midrash, Mekilta, Sifre Tosedfta, Seder Olam, the Talmud, the Zohar, the Code, Rashi, Rambam and many others, and could quote any passage at will.*

Two thousand-five hundred and three pounds of human cargo: The Victor McLaughlin Motorcycle Corps of Colorado Springs, Colorado packed **fourteen men on a single motorcycle.** (August 28, 1939.)

Internationally known clown **Kenneth Waite** walked a total of 4,177 miles in three-feet- long leather clown feet. He would circle a 450- foot track inside a circus tent six times in each performance. He performed twice a day for 30 weeks every year for 25 years. (November 8, 1931.)

Fred Steinlauf, age 18, cycles blindfolded down a Chicago street on a ten foot unicycle built by his father, Joseph Steinlauf, a builder of whimsical bicycles. (July 8, 1940.)

For a higher purpose: **Angelo Corsaro** of Catania, Italy walked from Catania to the Vatican—a total of 558 miles—**on ten-foot-high stilts!** Upon his arrival, the pope granted him an audience! (February 13, 1958.)

Four-year-old **Billy Crawford** leapt over the Municipal Building in Cleveland, Ohio, harnessed to a balloon just large enough to render him not-quite-lighter-than-air. He spent several hours leaping around the city. (June 1, 1934.)

Alexandre Patty had a unique way of getting up-stairs. (February 15, 1931.)

! Senora **Salomea Wolf** had the portrait of her husband tattooed on her tongue to atone for nagging him to death. Jerez, Spain, 1927.

DIANDRA SALVIATTI
WIFE OF BARTOLOMEO FRESCOBALDI
Florence, Italy
GAVE BIRTH TO **52** SONS BEFORE SHE WAS **38**
SHE HAD **13** SETS OF TRIPLETS · **2** SETS OF QUADRUPLETS
AND ONE SET OF QUINTUPLETS AND NEVER A DAUGHTER

Pierre Defournel of Barjac, Vivarais was the father of three children, each born in a different century! The first boy was born in 1699, the second was born in 1738 and the third was born in 1801, each to a different wife. Defournel married his third wife when he was 120—she was 19. He died in 1809 at the robust old age of 129. The *Magasin Pittoresque* dated May 1877 has a reprint of the original birth certificates of the three children.

SMILING BILLY BURTON
HANDCUFFED TO WHEEL
DRIVING 126 HOURS CONTINUOUSLY
C.E.TYSON CO.

Smilin' Billy Burton, professional endurance driver, did 26 long-endurance drives while handcuffed to the wheel, between 1926–1931: a total of 2,915 hours and more than 55,000 miles. This 126 hour drive in Schenectady, New York was sponsored by a local newspaper. (September 12, 1931.)

! Madame de Maldmeure gave birth to one child the first year, twins the second year, triplets the third year, quadruplets the fourth year, quintuplets the fifth year and sextuplets in the sixth: a total of 21 children in six years. She died as a result of her last confinement.

On December 28, 1949, gymnast Glenn Sundby became the first person to ever walk down the 898 steps of the Washington monument **on his hands.**

! On July 19, 1955, nineteen-year-old **Giuseppe de Ponti** of Melzo, Italy arrived in Venice—after floating in an inner tube for 122 hours, paddling 210 miles with only his hands. Ten miles of his journey was on open ocean.

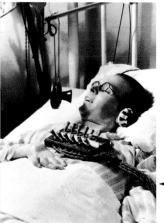

Bill Carpenter of Boise, Idaho was rendered paralyzed and blind by an accident, yet with no experience and no money, he built a magazine subscription business that made a living for three people (March 23, 1939.)

Lifetime Ripley fan **Dr. Ralph B. Williams** of Juneau, Alaska was shot in the head five times by thugs in May of 1968. All five bullets remained embedded in his head, yet he continued to live normally with no loss of function!

In the "Chronique Publique dans la Revue Retrospective sous la Regne de Louis XV" (1742-1743) there appears an account of La Belle Paule Fieschi of Rue del la Perle, Paris, who became a mother at the age of ninety. The child, a boy, was born on December 1, 1742.

GALAHAD GRANT N.Y.U. LOST 22 POUNDS IN A SINGLE GAME OF FOOTBALL THE TEAM LOST 267 POUNDS THAT DAY Oct 1, 1927

DR WILLIAM C. GORGAS —Famed Surgeon OPERATED ON A SOLDIER BY THE LIGHT FROM A JAR OF FIREFLIES ! Cuba-1898

THE MARTYR WHO GAVE HIS LIFE FOR STRANGERS YUAN CH'ANG CHINESE GOVERNOR OF HANGCHOW DURING THE BOXER REBELLION RECEIVED A TELEGRAM FROM THE CHINESE EMPRESS ORDERING HIM TO EXTERMINATE ALL FOREIGNERS— HE SAVED THE LIVES OF THE EUROPEANS BY CHANGING THE WORD "EXTERMINATE" TO "PROTECT"—BUT WAS HIMSELF SAWED IN TWO AS PUNISHMENT

THE ANIMAL WOMAN of HOWE, Ind. WHO LIVED WITH SKUNKS AND DID NOT CHANGE HER CLOTHES OR TOUCH WATER IN 25 YEARS SHE WAS GIVEN A BATH—AND DIED 10 DAYS LATER.

THE MOST SENSELESS DUEL IN ALL HISTORY! BODO von EGISHEIM and RUDOLPH LOSTIER, KNIGHTS IN THE SERVICE OF EMPEROR SIEGMUND of GERMANY, QUARRELED OVER THE AFFECTIONS OF A GIRL IN 1425 —BUT WERE ORDERED BY THE EMPEROR TO POSTPONE THEIR DUEL FOR 70 YEARS THE DUEL WAS ACTUALLY FOUGHT AND BOTH MEN WERE WOUNDED IN 1495 —WHEN THEY WERE 94 YEARS OF AGE

The Man Who Was Seen to Death

Wei Chieh, son of Wei Huan (286-312) was popularly known as "The Jewel" on account of his great beauty. At the age of five, his handsome face and graceful form caused the populace to regard him as a supernatural being. He joined the entourage of the heir-apparent of China, but during political troubles it was necessary for him to flee to the city of Nanking where people crowded around him in such numbers and stared at him so hard that he was literally "seen to death."

Stephen Pozdzioch was the father of seven children—each born in a different country.

Rama V, or **King Chulalongkorn** of Siam, who died in 1910, had 3,000 wives and 370 children—134 sons and 236 daughters.

Crocodile Tears

•••••••••••••••••••••➤

Attorney **Carl Harper** of Bedias, Texas, to gain sympathy from the jurors, always filled his handkerchief with onion shavings! It worked—he may not have smelled very good, but his streaming tears helped him win most of his cases! (January 29, 1965.)

THE MAN WHO WAS IN LOVE WITH HIS SHADOW
WILLIE BEYER a businessman of Halberstadt, Germany, TO VIEW THE BROCKEN SPECTER, AN ENORMOUSLY MAGNIFIED SHADOW CAST UPON THE CLOUDS FROM MOUNT BROCKEN WHEN THE SUN IS LOW CLIMBED **3,733** FEET TO THE TOP OF THE MOUNTAIN **650** TIMES

Death Takes a Coffee Break

THE MAN WHO WAS DEAD FOR 3 DAYS! SAI BABA (1856-1918) of Shirdi, India, WAS PRONOUNCED DEAD IN 1886, WITH BOTH CIRCULATION AND BREATHING STOPPED COMPLETELY. AS PREPARATIONS FOR HIS FUNERAL WERE BEING MADE 3 DAYS LATER, IT WAS OBSERVED THAT HE WAS BREATHING--AND HE LIVED ANOTHER 32 YEARS

87 INCHES IN CIRCUMFERENCE AND WEIGHING 122 LB. Grown by SAMUEL DAVIDSON Barnegat, N.J.

EDWARD DUMARESQ (1802-1906) a Surveyor for the East India Company WAS PENSIONED AT THE AGE OF 19 WHEN DOCTORS PREDICTED HE WOULD DIE IN LESS THAN ONE YEAR-- YET HE LIVED TO THE AGE OF 104 AND DREW HIS PENSION FOR 85 YEARS!

> **!** For the last 28 years of his life, German poet Baron Oskar von Redwitz (1823–1891) complained of a new illness every day. He described more than 10,000 ailments—each of them unknown to medical science!

THE HUMAN CORK! CASIMIR POLEMUS of Ploërmel, France, WAS INVOLVED IN 3 SHIPWRECKS - AND EACH TIME WAS THE SOLE SURVIVOR! HE WAS THE SOLE SURVIVOR OF THE "JEANNE CATHERINE" WRECKED OFF BREST ON JULY 11 1875, THE "TROIS FRÈRES," WRECKED IN THE BAY OF BISCAY ON SEPT. 4 1880, AND "ODEON," WRECKED OFF NEWFOUNDLAND ON JAN. 1, 1882

U.S. SKYDIVER Bob Hall JUMPED from A PLANE WITHOUT A WORKING PARACHUTE AND FELL 3,300 ft. TO THE GROUND. BUT GOT UP AND WALKED AWAY WITH HIS ONLY INJURY BEING A BROKEN NOSE! (1972)

The First Hundred Years Are the Hardest

Jean Baptiste Mouron of Toulon, France served a full sentence of "100 years and a day" as a galley slave! In 1684, when but 17 years of age, Mouron was arrested for incendiarism and sentenced to the depths of a galley ship to slave his life away. Exactly one hundred years and a day later, a tottering old man shambled unsteadily ashore in the town of Toulon. Mouron had served his sentence in full and was a free man. Fortunately, Jean Baptiste had not been pulling an oar the whole time. As slaves were generally used to row war galleys, the ships were simply chained together as prison hulks during peace time. During most of Mouron's sentence, France was at peace. Mouron learned to accept and even cherish his imprisonment. In fact, when Luis XV offered to let him go free early, Mouron refused to leave until one day after a hundred years had passed. He died six years later.

THE MAN WHO BIT A CROCODILE! A SWIMMER NAMED HANOCK, SEIZED BY A HUGE CROCODILE IN THE KAFUE RIVER IN NORTHERN RHODESIA CLAMPED HIS TEETH ON THE TIP OF THE REPTILE'S TAIL – FORCING THE CROCODILE TO RELEASE HIM AND RETREAT INTO DEEP WATER! HANOCK HIMSELF HAD BEEN SEVERELY BITTEN BUT RECOVERED IN THE HOSPITAL AT LUSAKA (1940)

TRAINED HIS OWN EXECUTIONER

Now Why Didn't I Think of That?

J. G. Levack of Williamsville, New York could drive a golf ball 150 yards with the stock of a rifle. (1938.)

Ernie and Dot Lind's bullet-hole-art is now part of Ripley's museum collection. (August 22, 1939.)

1,000 STUDENTS at The University of Guelph, Ont., Canada, ROLLED A SURFBOARD ACROSS THEIR BODIES WITHOUT LETTING IT TOUCH THE GROUND!

Feature Syndicate, Inc.   www.comiczone.com

Anything to Keep You Entertained...

Entertainer **Judith "Sparky" Roberts** of Eugene, Oregon could manipulate puppets with her feet while standing on her head and whistling. (July 17, 1988.)

Connie Phares of Marion, Indiana rollerskated five miles an hour **on her toes!** (October 23, 1945.)

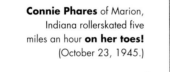

Musician **Anton Pagani** of La Salle, Illinois could whistle "The Piccolino" while playing an accordion with his hands and a cello with his feet... and he was blind! (April 29, 1940.)

These three musicians wandered the floor of a New York City club in the position you see here. The names of the top two musicians are unknown, but the trombonist on the bottom, **Jack Trimble**, could play the trombone with his foot... while smoking! (October 28, 1940.)

54

Frank Damek of Chicago, Illinois compiled a complete deck of cards by picking them up from time to time in the street. After ten years he was 15 cards short. It took twenty more years before he finally completed his deck, in 1890.

Julius B. Schuster could hold 10 billiard balls, 20 baseballs or 25 tennis balls in one hand. He named himself "professor of ball-ology" and had his hands insured for $1 million. (August 5, 1933.)

Ed Kottwitz poses with the thirty cobs of sweet corn he gnawed clean in order to win the title of World Champion Corn Eater. Kottwitz held the corn-eating record from 1931–1934.

Berk Motley, a band leader and emcee in Norfolk, Virginia played two-part harmony on two clarinets while standing on his head. His son, **Berk Jr.,** could play "Carry me Back to Old Virginny" upside down on the trumpet at age four. (March 2, 1945.)

Tex Tyrell won a "tall tale" contest in Alice Springs, Australia, by telling incredible stories continuously... **for eight hours!**

Leuben, a famous German lunatic, bet that he could turn up an entire pack of cards in a certain order. He turned the cards ten hours a day for 20 years—exactly 4,246,028 times-before he succeeded.

"Scuba" Osborne of Myrtle Beach, South Carolina's famous Bowery Tavern, could carry 34 mugs of beer at once! Scuba was one mug shy of Pittsfield, New York's Clement Piehl's 35-mug record, featured February 23, 1935.

KUDA BUX'S AMAZING TRIAL BY FIRE

August 16, 1938, 10:00 PM: A fire rages in the center of the parking lot beside Radio City Music Hall and half of New York City has turned out to watch. This is an intentional blaze, set in a trench 25-feet-long, 4-feet-wide and 3-feet-deep. It has been burning since nine o'clock this morning and is now so hot that no one can get within 6 feet of it.

In a few minutes, a mysterious "holy man" from India is going to walk barefoot through the entire length of this searing inferno. Some will cover their ears to keep out the sound of burning flesh. Others will hold their noses to keep from smelling the odor of charring human tissue. But Robert L. Ripley will watch it all, broadcasting live to a rapt nation, as he witnesses an event so enthralling that for once he even forgets to be nervous in front of the microphone.

At the center of tonight's performance is a small, dark-eyed Hindu named Kuda Bux, who at the age of ten was found to have supernatural powers. He could stop his own heart, suspend his breathing for extended periods of time and read through a blindfold. He became a "holy man" in order to develop his powers fully.

Ripley's has had to take out a million dollar insurance policy from Lloyd's of London, covering all contingencies from 8:00 AM to midnight. Fire engines and an ambulance stand at the ready. The fiery pit has eaten up more than five cords of oak wood and an hour before performance time, 26 bags of charcoal have been shaken out on top. The pit's temperature reads 1220°F.

Ripley appears with a police escort through the huddle of media people. He tells his audience, "In my travels to the Orient, I have always been fascinated by the unexplainable miracles that the holy men of India perform. It has been one of my fondest hopes to some day present one of these miraculous feats on my program. Tonight I have the great pleasure of realizing this ambition..."

At the stroke of ten, Kuda Bux arrives in a dark business suit, turban and tunic. He seems cool and unruffled. He removes his shoes and socks and presents his feet to four doctors, Dr. John Hudson Storer, Dr. John L. Rice, Dr. Van Alstyne Conrell and New York City Health Commissioner Haralson, for their inspection. His feet are officially declared normal: no heat-resistant callouses or growths. Bux's feet are then washed thoroughly to rid them of any possible heat-repelling chemical.

Ripley steps to one side of the pit, announcer Graham McNamee steps to the other. McNamee declares, "He can't survive... It's like a blast furnace. That poor guy's going to be incinerated."

August 16, 1938: The pit dug for Kuda Bux's performance in the parking lot at Rockefeller Center, 25-feet-by-4-feet-by-3-feet-deep. At 9:00 AM the morning of the performance, oak logs were laid in the pit and ignited. At 9:00 PM, an hour before the performance, 26 bags of charcoal were spread over the logs.

The pit reached a blistering 1220°F by the time of the performance, yet Kuda Bux showed no discomfort during his walk, even when sinking up to his ankles in hot coals.

Kuda Bux pauses, gathers up the hem of his tunic, raises his face to the sky in a brief, silent prayer, then steps forward into the burning pit. The crowd gasps. Bux walks briskly down the length of the pit, at times sinking almost to his knees in the coals. When he reaches the other side, cameramen scream, "Do it again! Do it again!" So he does.

The battery of doctors literally grab him as he arrives at the end of the pit. They examine his feet a second time. One live coal still clings to the sole of his foot. Dr.Haralson flicks it off. There is a tiny red patch where the coal had stuck. Otherwise, his feet are completely unharmed.

Skeptics have offered various explanations of how the "trick" was accomplished, none of them satisfactory. It has been suggested that Kuda Bux could have treated his feet with aluminum and potassium to protect them from heat, that he deliberately prepared the fire so that it would burn from the center out, leaving a cooler trench down the center, that the charcoal formed a layer of protective ash that insulated his feet from the hottest part of the fire, that his "primitive" feet were tougher and could take the heat better or that Kuda Bux's feet should have been examined again 30 minutes after his walk, because blisters take time to form.

Yet, Kuda Bux's feet were washed thoroughly prior to his performance to ensure that they were not treated with a chemical. Whether the fire's center or the layer of ash on top might have been cooler than other parts of the fire is a moot point, because no part of the fire was cool enough for normal human contact—no one could get within six feet of it without feeling the heat.

Whether Bux's feet were primitively tough, or whether they should have been examined again later in the evening are irrelevant questions, because at 1220°F (indeed, at temperatures anywhere near it) the toughest flesh would have been incinerated. There should have been nothing left to blister. And whatever means Kuda Bux used to resist the blaze, he alone appeared to posses it. In a previous demonstration, a skeptical young medical student had attempted to follow Bux across the coals and had collapsed with severe burns after taking just one step.

If not by some trick, then how did Kuda Bux accomplish this feat? When Robert Ripley asked him how he did it, the holy man replied, "It is faith, Mr. Ripley. It is faith I have that allows me to do it." Then the smiling Hindu removed his tunic, put on his shoes and socks, thanked the spectators and left. As though satisfied that he had proven his point, he never walked through fire again.

The soles of Kuda Bux's feet were completely unharmed.

Doctors examined Kuda Bux's unsinged feet in disbelief.

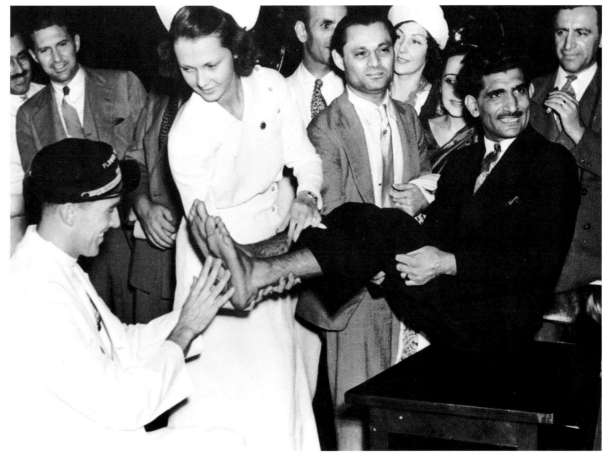

Fabulous FOODS

HORSE MILK, WHICH SELLS FOR UP TO $17 A LITER, IS A POPULAR HEALTH FOOD IN EUROPE!

THE KARIMOJONG - A TRIBE IN UGANDA, AFRICA, DRINK THE MILK AND BLOOD OF THEIR CATTLE -BUT RARELY EAT THE MEAT

MILK IS SOLD IN SHEETS IN DENMARK. The Dehydrated Milk Is Restored to Liquid Form by Dissolving in Hot Water

Ripley demonstrates his skill with chopsticks to friends Anna May Wong (left) and Ann Sheridan (right). Circa 1940.

SHARK SAUSAGE and SHARK CHEESE ARE POPULAR DELICACIES IN COLUMBIA, SOUTH AMERICA!

THE FRUIT OF THE AKEE TREE IS DELICIOUS -BUT IT CONTAINS 3 BLACK SEEDS THAT ARE DEADLY POISONOUS

FRESH ALLIGATOR STEAKS RESTAURANT

ALLIGATOR MEAT TASTES GOOD

IN Kisakata, Japan, YAKITORI- A TRADITIONAL JAPANESE DISH- USES CROW MEAT!

I'll Have the Curried Fruit Bat and Cockroach Tea, Please... ...oh, and Tuna Eyeballs on the Side.

Believe It or Not! A POPULAR DISH in Burma IS PORK-STUFFED CRICKET!

CURRIED FRUIT BAT IS A POPULAR DISH IN THE SEYCHELLES ISLANDS!

IN Hong Kong, PRE-COOKED TUNA EYEBALLS ARE CONSIDERED A DELICACY!

❗ *If you eat 20 caterpillars a day, you will meet the adult daily requirement of phosphorus calcium, riboflavin and iron! Submitted by Tracy Wiser, Atlantic City, New Jersey. (December 28, 1998.)*

OUR CRICKET MEAT LOAF IS SUCCULENT!

IN Washington, D.C., THERE IS A RESTAURANT CALLED "THE INSECT CLUB" WHICH SERVES CRICKET MEAT LOAF and MEALWORM WONTONS!

Hungry? Australian Aborigines enjoy snacking on the witchetty grub, a moth larva found among the roots of the witchetty bush. The fat, 3-inch-long grub is lightly crunchy when baked, soft and buttery-flavored when eaten raw...

IN 1991, DELEGATES TO A CONFERENCE in South Africa WERE GIVEN A MEAL CONSISTING of LOCUSTS, TERMITES, WATER LILIES and CATERPILLARS IN PUFF PASTRY!

❗ *Up until the 1930s Finnish peasants regularly ate bread made from the bark of pine trees. (February 17, 1990.)*

A FOOD DELICACY in Newfoundland is seal flipper pie

LION STEAK WAS ON THE MENU OF A N.Y. CITY RESTAURANT IN FEB. 1980 AT $20 A SERVING

AT MEDIEVAL BANQUETS IN EUROPE, MEAT-BALLS AND SMALL BIRDS WERE FREQUENTLY PAINTED WITH *EDIBLE GOLD AND SILVER LEAF!*

"ORCHID ICE CREAM" In Turkey, A FAVORITE DELICACY IS ICE CREAM *MADE from THE DRIED TUBERS of WILD ORCHIDS!*

! *Wild rats weighing up to four pounds are a delicacy sold in public markets in parts of Africa. (August 10, 1990.)*

AT THE 1994 WINTER OLYMPICS in Lillehammer, Norway, FOOD WAS SERVED ON PLATES MADE OUT OF POTATO STARCH and EATEN WITH CUTLERY MADE OUT OF STIFFENED MAIZE! CRUNCH 6-25

DURING WORLD WAR II, MANY PEOPLE IN HOLLAND SURVIVED THE WINTER OF 1944-45 BY EATING OVER 140 MILLION TULIP BULBS!

A **SPECIAL CAKE** BAKED IN HESSEN, GERMANY, ONLY FOR A CHILD ENTERING SCHOOL FOR THE FIRST TIME

THE **SPINY-TAILED IGUANA** IS EATEN IN THE SIERRA MADRE MOUNTAINS OF MEXICO AS A CURE FOR DEPRESSION

PEACOCKS BAKED, AND WITH ALL THEIR PLUMAGE INTACT, WERE ONCE A POPULAR CHRISTMAS DISH IN ENGLAND

WHEN FRIED, THE WHITE of A MURRE'S EGG TURNS BRIGHT BLUE, WHILE THE YOLK BECOMES RED!

Locusts, lizards, ants, and deep-fried scorpions are all on the menu at the Imperial Restaurant in Singapore! (November 2, 1997.)

An Appetite for Adventure

DR. WILLIAM BUCKLAND, THE FIRST PROFESSOR of Geology at England's OXFORD UNIVERSITY, ATE THE HEART OF FRANCE'S KING LOUIS XIV AT A DINNER PARTY!

POLYSTYRENOMANIACS ENJOY EATING POLYSTYRENE CUPS. SURGEONS AT THE TRUMAN MEDICAL CENTER IN MISSOURI, REMOVED A POLYSTYRENE "HAIR BALL" FROM THE STOMACH OF A PATIENT WHO SUPPLEMENTED HIS DIET WITH STYROFOAM CUPS Submitted by John Turner, St. Augustine, FL. 4-29

THE DIET OF **DURGA** (Michigan's Man of Iron) HE ATE THE FOLLOWING MENU

- 5 RIFLE SHELLS
- 3 JACK-KNIVES
- 4 DOOR KEYS
- 17 HORSE SHOE NAILS
- 4 SIX-PENNY NAILS
- 1 FISH HOOK
- 18 COINS
- 175 PIECES OF BROKEN GLASS
- 1 KNIFE HANDLE
- 2 JOINTED RODS

AND **LIVED!**

HARRIET LASKY of Denver, Colo AGE 40, HAS BEEN CHEWING THE SAME PIECE of BUBBLEGUM for **33 YEARS**! SUBMITTED BY TOM HIGGINS, SAN DIEGO, CALIF.

SCHOOLBOYS in Morocco ARE FED THE ROASTED LIVERS of HEDGEHOGS TO HELP IMPROVE THEIR STUDIES.

RURAL POST BOX NEAR BROCKPORT, N.Y.

KOKICHI MIKIMOTO, AGE 94, WHO DEVELOPED THE *CULTURED PEARL*, ATTRIBUTES HIS LONGEVITY TO *THE FACT THAT HE EATS* TWO PEARLS *EVERY DAY!* SUBMITTED BY ROB CURTISS, SCHENECDAY NV

! *In 1991, Llewellyn Diamond, a British fisherman, raised $1,100 for a charity by eating a bucket of live worms! (February 26, 1992.)*

! *An 18th-century French entertainer named Dufour once ate a meal of snakes, rats and toads, garnished with thistles, spider webs and butterfly wings. He later drank flaming brandy and ate four large candles for dessert. (January 3, 1990.)*

Care to Sample These Tasty New Products?

Nicholas A. Ruggieri has invented a sealed cup of wound spaghetti that is eaten with a straw! (June 23, 1994.)

CONSTANTIN BOYM and Laurene Leon of New York City, INVENTED EDIBLE ALMOND and HAZELNUT FLAVORED PENCILS!

"EDIBLE BOOKS"
Josie Holton PUBLISHED 100 COPIES of "The Rime of the Ancient Mariner" PRINTED ON EDIBLE SEAWEED!
MUNCH MUNCH

Manuel Oliveira of Merida, Venezuela has created over 567 different flavors of ice cream including chicken with rice and spinach! (August 29, 1994)

"Hotlix"
TEQUILA-FLAVORED LOLLIPOPS WITH WORMS EMBEDDED IN THEM ARE A POPULAR TREAT IN CALIFORNIA!

! *When the Russian-Japanese war began in 1904, a Moscow guild merchant named Lomakin bet that the Japanese would sue for peace before July 1, 1904, or he would eat his boots. They didn't...so he did.*

MICHEL LOTITO OF GRENOBLE, FRANCE, WHO EATS 2 LBS. OF METAL EACH DAY—ONCE ATE A SUPERMARKET CART, 7 TV SETS AND A CESSNA LIGHT PLANE!
11-24

Mrs. Harriett Russell of Woodbury, Connecticut kept her wedding cake for more than seventy years! As of 1949, it was still intact and in perfect condition, bearing the year of her wedding: 1879! (March 28, 1950.)

The average Irish peasant of the 17th century consumed about 8 pounds of potatoes a day, which accounted for 80% of each person's caloric intake. (March 20, 1989.)

! In a village near Accra, Ghana, five thousands tons of rock are mined every year, then crushed and mixed with water and turned into an edible dough! (May 8, 1997)

John Rowers bet $10 that he could eat a more expensive breakfast than his friend. He then put $100 between two pieces of cake–and ate it.

John W. Horton, the Iron Duke of Wellington, Kansas had what you might call an unusual appetite. He could put away whole cases of soda pop, egg shells, glass, a bunch of bananas (including the stalks) a forty pound watermelon, a raw cow's liver, newspapers, catalogs... He was known to eat 10 pounds of raw beef at a single sitting, 11½ dozen eggs at another. Once, for dessert, he actually ate a sack of Portland cement. (He admitted later that this was the only meal he'd ever eaten that had made him sick.) An eater both by trade and by appetite, John made a fair amount of money from skeptics who would place bets on his ability to eat (or not to eat.) Some of the bets were harder than others to win, but win he did, whether he had to devour a dozen 2-pound fried chickens or eat a dozen large lemons without sugar. He was a renowned pie-eating champion as well, gobbling up 27 pies to his opponent's 19.

And for Those with Hearty Appetites...

IN LOUISIANA, IN THE 1800s, A TEA MADE OF **COCKROACHES** WAS A REMEDY FOR TETNUS, AND COCKROACHES FRIED IN OIL WITH GARLIC WERE USED TO CURE INDIGESTION!

6-28

If That's the Cure, I'll Stick With the Illness

A COMPANY in Woodlands, Texas, MAKES **GRASSHOPPER**- and **BEETLE**-FLAVORED LOLLIPOPS!

SUBMITTED BY CHESTER TUMIDAJEWICZ, AMSTERDAM, N.Y.

Pat Crowther of Sheffield, England drinks 70 cups of tea a day with five spoonfuls of sugar in every cup! (Submitted by Tom Higgins, San Diego, California. December 6, 1997.)

The average person eats 66,133 pounds of food in a lifetime–equal to the weight of six elephants. (March 21, 1998)

Eat Like the Animals!

Believe It or Not, visitors to the San Diego Zoo can take the "Incredible Edibles" tour and sample the food that the pandas, parrots, iguanas, and tree kangaroos usually eat! (November 17, 1998.)

Ever wonder what a mile of brownies looks like? The **Plantation Baking Company** in Lake Bluff, Illinois produces 1 million brownies per day. If a day's worth of their brownies were laid end to end, they would stretch more than a mile! (January 2, 1988.)

"THE BIGGEST CAESAR SALAD IN THE WORLD"

Believe It or Not! 10 CHEFS in Tijuana, Mexico, MADE A GIANT CAESAR SALAD IN A 30-YARD LONG TROUGH USING 1,200 HEADS of LETTUCE, 1,200 BOILED EGGS, 75 LITERS of OLIVE OIL, 53 Kg. of LEMONS and 99 Kg. of PARMESAN CHEESE!

THE RIJSTTAFEL
A POPULAR JAVANESE DISH
REQUIRES 20 WAITERS TO SERVE IT!

Rip

Hotel des Indes
BATAVIA - 1925

RIJSTTAFEL:

Dinner is Served...
　　...and Served
　　　...and Served
　　　　...and Served....

Not surprisingly, Ripley was known to be a connoisseur of exotic edibles. For the house-warming banquet at his luxurious new Asian-style apartment in 1939, Ripley served rattlesnake and locusts in honey. At a garden party on BION Island, Ripley's guests picked their luncheon from the trees: Ripley had cleverly hung the trees and bushes with bread, sausage and eggs, as if they had grown there.

When asked to name his favorite dish, Robert Ripley gave numerous answers over the years, everything from spinach with chopped bacon to oxtail soup and deviled crabs. But once Ripley experienced the full-blown splendor of a Indonesian *rijsttafel* dinner, his answer never wavered again.

In 1932, during one of his first journeys to the Far East, Robert Ripley visited the Indonesian town of "Djokjarta" (Jakarta.) "All Java is a great show," Ripley wrote of the colorful stream of humanity he saw on the streets. On March 11th, Ripley and his entourage made their way up to the mountain resort of Garoet, where they filmed a lavish *rijsttafel* dinner being served at an outdoor banquet table. As the cameras rolled, 22 waiters in sarongs and white jackets appeared, each bearing a different dish. The dishes were paraded past the diners one by one, then the serving began:

The first waiter lined the bottoms of the diners' dishes with boiled rice. The second ladled a vegetable curry over the rice. The third spread a layer of fried bananas, the fourth, eggfruit. The fifth waiter dotted the diners' plates with potato balls, the sixth covered these with curried chicken. Fried duck was heaped on after the chicken, followed by ten varieties of dried fish. Next came *rissoles*, *croquettes*, pastries, sausages, fried eggs, baked eggs, and liver. These were covered in pancake strips, atop which were placed meat skewers, cucumbers, chopped onions, grated coconuts, chilies, *zuurjes* (tiny pickles), chutneys, and peas. The last waiter passed out *kroepoek,* crinkly rice-flour biscuits as large as a plate.

Rijsttafel refers more to the way of serving than to the actual ingredients of the meal. Although the contents of the individual dishes may vary, it takes at least twenty people to serve a proper *rijsttafel,* which can take several hours to eat. As Ripley discovered that day in Jakarta in 1932, it's time well spent. Ripley finished filming the meal that same day, but the following evening, he left his cameras behind and went back for another round!

Feats of FAITH

Ripley's Believe It or Not! cartoon for Sunday, December 23rd featured the birthplace of Jesus Christ.

THE MAN WHO BURNED HIS TONGUE WITH A RED-HOT IRON 25,000 TIMES!

BAIRAGI GYURI of Badrinath, India, SAID HIS PRAYERS 5 TIMES A DAY FOR NEARLY 52 YEARS AND EACH TIME PLUNGED HIS IRON STAFF INTO A FIRE AND LICKED ITS HOT TIP WITH HIS TONGUE!

GYURI WAS CREMATED AT HIS DEATH AT THE AGE OF 62 IN A PURPLE SHROUD WHICH HE HAD WORN THROUGHOUT HIS LIFETIME

THE PATIENT PILGRIMS TO THE LAMASERY OF LABRANG TIBETANS, VISITING THE SACRED LAMASERY OF LABRANG (China) CIRCLING THE ENTIRE MOUNTAIN ON WHICH IT STANDS BY FALLING FORWARD ON THE GROUND, THEN RISING AND FALLING AGAIN — A PAINFUL JOURNEY THAT REQUIRES 7 DAYS THEY WEAR SANDALS ON THEIR HANDS BECAUSE OF THE ROCKY TRAIL OVER WHICH THEY MUST DRAG THEMSELVES FORWARD

! *The 13th century church of Chateloys, France was built on top of a lofty and inaccessible crag. Parishioners earned special merit by making the arduous climb up the rocks to attend services.*

The Sun Gazer

Ripley was especially galvanized by the naked fakir he observed at the Daashwamedh Ghat. For fifteen years, this man had sat every day staring at the blazing sun. The fiery rays of the sun had burned his eyes out long ago, yet he continued to gaze upon it. Each morning, Ripley observed the man being carried down the steps by his brothers to his accustomed place; his legs had withered away years ago from inactivity. They gently placed him down and turned his face to the east. There he would remain all day, following the sun with sightless eyes as it made its way across the sky.

Buried Alive

In his enthusiasm for Hindu mysticism, Ripley collected numerous accounts of individuals achieving Samadai, or suspended animation. The best known account was recorded in the summer of 1837, when a Yogi named **Haridas** was buried in the ground for forty days, after which he was dug up and revived. Before the Maharajah Rujneet Singh in Lahore, Haridas fell into a trance. His assistants stopped his nose, mouth, ears and eyes with wax, wrapped him in a cloth and buried him in a grave. A guard was placed on the spot to prevent trickery. When the Yogi was disinterred 40 days later, he was slightly emaciated, but was otherwise none the worse for wear.

BENJAMIN SCHULZE (1689-1760) COPIED THE BIBLE IN LONGHAND 3 TIMES—*EACH TIME IN A DIFFERENT HINDU LANGUAGE.* HE KNEW 100 FOREIGN ALPHABETS, AND COULD RECITE THE LORD'S PRAYER IN 215 LANGUAGES

THE MOST DEDICATED PILGRIMS IN THE WORLD Mount Minobu, Japan BUDDHISTS PAYING HOMAGE AT THE GRAVE OF NICHIREN, FOUNDER OF A JAPANESE SECT, REMAIN MOTIONLESS AND SILENT WHILE 5 CANDLES PLACED ON EACH OUTSTRETCHED ARM BURN DOWN INTO THEIR FLESH

THE DOOR of the MOSQUE of SHEIKH SELIM CHISTI in Fatehpur Sikri, India IS STUDDED WITH HORSESHOES - HUNG THERE BY THE OWNERS OF AILING HORSES WHO FELT THIS WOULD MAKE THE ANIMALS WELL

RANGANATHA of Allahabad, India COUNTED EACH HAIR IN HIS HEAD EVERY DAY FOR 36 YEARS! IT TOOK 9 HOURS EACH DAY— YET HE PUNISHED HIMSELF BY A SEVERE FAST IF HE ERRED BY EVEN ONE HAIR

Fakir Agastiya of Bengal willed himself to go through life with his left arm raised in the air. He belonged to a Hindu sect which believes that the physical qualities we perceive as belonging to the human body are merely an illusion. After three months in this excruciating position, the joints in Agastiya's arm became so rigid that he was unable to lower it. After ten years, a small bird built a nest and took up residence on his immobile palm.

THE LIVING CANDLES of the ANDES PUYA RAIMONDII A PLANT THAT GROWS TO A HEIGHT OF 33 FEET IS SO SATURATED WITH RESIN THAT SHEPHERDS USE IT AS A CANDLE IT WILL BURN FOR DAYS

THE FIRST BOOK DIGEST

DUBASH MEGHJI of Zanzibar ATE ONE PAGE OF THE KORAN EACH DAY FOR 30 YEARS!

THE STRANGEST PRINTER IN ALL THE WORLD! A LAMA near Ra-gyrya, China, CONSTANTLY DIPS IN THE HWANG HO RIVER A FONT OF INKED TYPE CONTAINING A PRAYER, IN THE BELIEF HE IS INFLUENCING THOUSANDS DOWNSTREAM BY *IMPRINTING HIS PRAYER ON THE RUNNING WATER!*

The members of the Shah Dawal Temple in Berar, India are the only sect in the world that must attend religious services while wearing iron handcuffs. They are believed to put the wearer in the proper mood for fervent supplications.

Ripley examines the Footprints of Buddha.

Christo Rey, the floating church

THE TEMPLE OF ALL FAITHS BIRLA TEMPLE in New Delhi, India, INCLUDES SEPARATE AREAS FOR WORSHIP *FOR EVERY KNOWN RELIGION*

FROM ITS HEART Grown by CHARLOTTE RINALDI Van Nuys, Calif.

THE RAVEN OF ST. BENEDICT 1400 YEARS AGO A RAVEN SAVED THE LIFE OF ST. BENEDICT BY SNATCHING A POISONED SLICE OF BREAD FROM HIS HANDS! AS A RESULT - FOR 14 CENTURIES - THE BENEDICTINE MONASTERY AT SUBIACO, Italy, HAS NEVER BEEN WITHOUT A TAMED RAVEN AS A PET

A Sabbath Day Journey, 3,675 feet and 9 inches, is the longest distance a Jew may walk on the Sabbath Day as prescribed by the Talmud Berachoth. Orthodox Jews observe this Rabbinical rule to the present day.

Ripley received a letter and some snapshots from a young English army officer stationed in Bombay, who had witnessed a remarkable feat. A juggler carrying two baskets had approached him on the street and offered, for a small handful of coins, to demonstrate that he could lift a snake with his eyeballs:

"...The juggler took the larger of two baskets, containing a python and placed it upon a large cloth, the four corners of which he knotted together with a strong, thin rope. At the end of this rope were affixed two little hollow leaden cups. These cups the man placed over his eyeballs in such a manner that a vacuum was created, then he shut his eyelids firmly over the outside of the cups and, rising up from his former squatting position, he lifted the heavy basket containing the snake by the grip of his eyelids and the suction on his eyeballs alone. After the feat was finished and the cups had been removed, to the accompaniment of a horrid sucking sound, I examined the man's eyes, which were horribly bloodshot; moreover, he seemed to have difficulty in seeing for a few minutes and the tears streamed down his cheeks."

The Ever-Standing Men

Ripley writes of his experience with a rare sect of Hindu ascetics who had resigned themselves to remain standing for the rest of their lives:

"They were standing by the river not far from the Khali-Ghat in Calcutta. They had been standing for ten years or more without once sitting down and were apparently prepared to remain upright the rest of their lives. I doubt if there be two more homely objects. Their bodies and faces were smeared a dirty sickly white leaving two black spots for their eyes, which were divided by perpendicular red and yellow caste marks. They had forced two poles into the sand from which were suspended arm rests on which they leaned now and then, but never at any time did they take their weight entirely off their feet, or attempt to sit down in any manner.

Sankal-Walah, the Man of Chains

Many years ago, a fakir known as the **"Man of Chains"** was familiar sight on the streets of Lahore, India. He was dressed entirely in a mass of heavy chains, which he had begun collecting piece by piece when he was a young man and had welded together painstakingly bit by bit. At the time of his death, the load was 670 pounds.

THE MAN WHO REPEATED ONE WORD NIGHT AND DAY FOR 20 YEARS MAHARAJA SHEO RAO BHAO RULER OF JHANSI, INDIA, FOR 21 YEARS, GAVE UP HIS THRONE TO BECOME A SAINT AND SAT ON THE SHORE OF THE GANGES RIVER FOR ALL THE REMAINDER OF HIS LIFE FOR 2 DECADES HE SPOKE NO WORD BUT "RAMA" (GOD) - AND THAT WORD HE REPEATED WITH EVERY BREATH HE DREW!

RIPLEY'S FASCINATION WITH MYSTIC INDIA

ABOVE. Ripley contemplates the Bho Tree, pilgrimage site for Buddhists the world over, where Gautama Buddha received enlightenment. Bodh Gaya, India, 1936.

OPPOSITE PAGE. An installment of Ripley's 1923 "Ramble 'Round the World", the daily journal he published in the New York Globe as he made his first journey around the world.

"Strange is Man when he seeks after his gods," Ripley wrote in his first "Believe It or Not!" book in 1929, "therefore the strangest places on earth are the holiest." Ripley spent a considerable amount of his life traveling to the most exotic parts of the globe, yet of all the places he traveled, none held his fascination like India. Ripley may have been in love with the romantic enchantment of China, but India gripped him with a mixture of horror and attraction that deeply affected his life's work.

What follows are excerpts from Ripley's first visit to India in 1923, during his globe-trotting expedition which he dubbed his "Ramble 'Round World" and published in the New York Globe in daily installments. The India Ripley saw in the 1920s is not what we would perceive today, but in the era of Ripley's travels, it seemed to the average westerner a mysterious, deeply exotic land. Ripley's awe is well reflected in his writings:

*BENARES, Feb. 10: We arrived at the cantonment (military) station of this ancient city before the golden sun had cast a shadow on the holy Ganges. I am now standing on a spot believed by millions of people to be the center of the earth. It is the religious center of Hinduism and the central fountain from which has emanated the religious tenets of more than half the nations of the world. Benares, called "Kashi" by the natives, is the holy city of India. It is held sacred alike by Muslim, Hindu and Buddhist and is so old that all idea of time has been lost in antiquity.

More people die in Benares than are born: the death rate has exceeded the birth rate since antiquity, yet the city grows in size each year until today it has nearly half a million human beings crowded into a labyrinth of narrow alleys, rich with crumbling shrines and balconies over which sacred monkeys cling and clamber and winding streets along which a chattering multitude elbow their way among the thousands of sacred cows wandering aimlessly and contentedly.

The holy city of Benares is the most remarkable in the world. I have traveled 20,000 miles and have seen no place which so baffles description as this.

BENARES, India, Feb. 12: Crowding my way down the steps of the ghat among the weirdest collection of humanity on the face of the earth—demented, delusioned and devout—all struggling after their gods. At last I clambered aboard a boat and floated slowly down the Ganges before all this pagan panorama, all the while wondering if leprosy was contagious and if that one-eyed beggar with spots and both hands and feet eaten away had tainted me with that unmerciful malady with the red stump of his hand when he nudged me as I passed.

Each ghat (steps leading to the Ganges) and each temple is different. Each is built and dedicated to a different deity and each spot is peculiarly holy to a Hindu—from the Assi Ghat, built at the junction of a river not visible to anybody but the Hindu, down past several hundred ghats to the Prahlad Ghat, the last of all.

Five of the Ghats are particularly holy and the millions of pilgrims must immerse in each successively on the same day: the Assi, Dasashwamedh, Barna-sangam, Panchganga and the Manikarnika. Some are built in honor of monkeys, others to "Ganesh", a red idol with three eyes, a silver cap and an elephant's trunk, riding on a rat. Another was built for the "Dandis", ascetics who always carry long sticks upright, never putting them down. The Sitla Ghat was built in honor of "Mother Smallpox," and the Dasashwamedh Ghat means "the ghat of the ten-horse sacrifice."

All the ghats are thronged with multitudes which swarm down in multicolored waves to the filthy—but purifying—water.

BENARES, India, Feb. 13: I have seen burning ghats before, if you remember. I was not particularly anxious to see this one at

Jalsain

Ghat. However, when I

learned that more than a million

human beings offer up a daily prayer that

they be burned on this very spot I decided to

witness the entire ceremony.

I have seen many dead people in India—it is a

common thing to die here—and frequently I have seen the

bodies being wrapped in winding sheets of thin gauze as they

lay on the ground in front of a hut. When a death occurs the body

is immediately taken out of the house. If it is that of a woman, she is

wrapped in red, if it is that of a man, he is covered over with white.

Children are not wrapped at all and neither are those who die of leprosy

and smallpox, but are simply taken down to the Ganges and thrown in.

I stood for a few minutes watching the ghastly fires of several corpses

leaping viciously to the sky, when behind me came the chanting of a funeral

procession I had passed near the Chowk. Down the crumbling steps they went

to the edge of the sacred water and advancing out, gave the body its last bath in

the holy Ganges, for without that bath any shadow which might fall upon the de-

ceased would convey impurity. Then, resting the feet of the white-robed figure in

the water, the two bearers set about to build the funeral pyre.

The body was placed on top and several cakes of cow dung laid on its chest. As

I waited, a sacred cow came wandering down the steps and calmly proceeded to eat

the grass strands that bound the winding sheet to the corpse. The widow returned

with shaven head and snow-white garments and waited for the cow to finish. Then

she placed a handful of meal on her dead husband's mouth, walked five times around

the pyre and without the slightest sign of emotion set fire to the pile at her husband's

throat.

When the fire died away the widow threw the remaining parts into the Ganges.

The relatives led her to the water's edge and broke the jewelry from her wrists and

ankles and threw them into the water also. Then filling an earthen jar with the sa-

cred water, the widow placed it on her shoulder, ascended the smoldering pyre and

tipped it backward over her shoulder onto the glowing ashes of her master.

Straightaway she walked on up the steps and will never again look backward

toward the spot. You are never so dead as when you die in India.

BENARES, India, Feb. 15: Tonight we leave Benares! The bustle of bag-

gage is annoying as it constantly reminds me that I am soon to see no

more of Benares—and Benares is so weirdly fascinating that it has a

hold of me.

The Ganges riverfront is the most interesting sight in the

world. It is ever changing and ever fascinating. I walked along

and almost imagined it was all a dream, until I stumbled

over a "suttee" stone and was aroused to conscious-

ness by the odor of burning flesh which warned

me that a burning ghat was near.

Suttee stones, short, small

markers about two feet

high,

'ROUND THE WORLD WITH RIPLEY

WE SEE OUR FIRST **HINDU**

HIS TURBAN IS 30 FEET LONG

RIP—CALCUTTA

By ROBERT L. RIPLEY.

HOOGHLI RIVER, India, Feb. 5.—We have been sailing through flat muddy water for half a day—a sign that we were approaching the many mouths of the holy Ganges through which are spewed the sins and sediment of India. We picked up the pilot at the mouth of the Hooghli River, which is about 100 miles from Calcutta, the metropolis of the Near East, and proceeded up the stream by high tide as far as Diamond Head.

The Hooghli is the most dangerous river in the world and the most diffi-cult to navigate. Apart from the dan-ger of cyclones, which occur in any month except this one, there is the normal danger of shoals and tides and quicksands which, Captain Brown in-forms us, are so powerful as to wreck a ship the size of the Laconia. New shoals are forming continually and only a daily experience on the river will qualify a pilot to handle a ship safely. Naturally the status of the Calcutta pilots is higher than that of any of their profession anywhere.

The anchor splashed down in the mud and a lop-sided old ferryboat transferred the passengers to the shore. We set foot on India, the land of dreams and were immediately searched for firearms. The English are careful that no weapons of any sort enter the country.

We walked nearly a mile along the shore through small villages of native mud huts to a small railroad station where a train awaited us. Hindoos fol-lowed with our baggage on their heads the only way anything is carried in this country and after a long delay, which I learn is quite common in the East. Time is very cheap out here. When a Hindoo misses a train he never worries. There is another one to-mor-row, he says, and folds himself up in slumber.

India's trains are different from ours, of course. The cars are divided into compartments which open only at the side and have no connection between. It is impossible to go from one compart-ment to another without stopping the train.

We clambered aboard. Jack and I. and rode bumpingly along stopping every few minutes—until finally our compartment door was unlocked and we were dumped out in Calcutta.

"Visit the Taj by moonlight," Ripley recommended in his "Ramble 'Round the World", 1923.

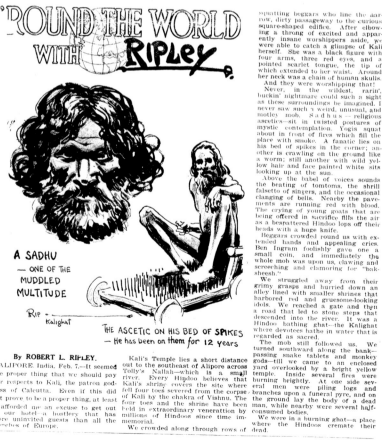

RIGHT. Ripley mingles with bathers on the banks of India's sacred Ganges River, 1936.

BELOW. An installment of "Ripley's Ramble Round the World" written in Calcutta, India, February 6, 1923.

'ROUND THE WORLD WITH RIPLEY

A SADHU
— ONE OF THE MUDDLED MULTITUDE

RIP Kalighat

THE ASCETIC ON HIS BED OF SPIKES
— He has been on them for 12 years

By ROBERT L. RIPLEY.

ALIPORE, India, Feb. 7.—It seemed the proper thing that we should pay our respects to Kali, the patron goddess of Calcutta. Even if this did not prove to be a proper thing, at least it afforded me an excuse to get out of our hotel—a hostlery that has more uninvited guests than all the trenches of Europe.

Kali's Temple lies a short distance out to the southeast of Alipore across Tolly's Nullah—which is a small river. Every Hindoo believes that Kali's shrine covers the site where fell four toes severed from the corpse of Kali by the chakra of Vishnu. The four toes and the shrine have been held in extraordinary veneration by millions of Hindoos since time immemorial.

We crowded along through rows of squatting beggars who line the narrow, dirty passageway to the curious, square-shaped edifice. After elbowing a throng of excited and apparently insane worshippers aside, we were able to catch a glimpse of Kali herself. She was a black figure with four arms, three red eyes, and a pointed scarlet tongue, the tip of which extended to her waist. Around her neck was a chain of human skulls.

And they were worshipping that!

Never, in the wildest, rarin', buckin' nightmare could such a sight as these surroundings be imagined. I never saw such a weird, unusual, and motley mob. Sadhus — religious ascetics—sit in twisted postures of mystic contemplation. Yogis squat about in front of fires which fill the place with smoke. A fanatic lies on his bed of spikes in the corner; another is crawling on the ground like a worm; still another with wild yellow hair and face painted white sits looking up at the sun.

Above the babel of voices sounds the beating of tomtoms, the shrill falsetto of singers, and the occasional clanging of bells. Nearby the pavements are running red with blood. The crying of young goats that are being offered in sacrifice fills the air as a bespattered Hindoo lops off their heads with a huge knife.

Beggars crowded round us with extended hands and appealing cries. Ben Ingram foolishly gave one a small coin, and immediately the whole mob was upon us, clawing and screeching and clamoring for "baksheesh."

We struggled away from their grimy grasps and hurried down an alley lined with smaller shrines that harbored red and gruesome-looking idols. We reached a gate and then a road that led to stone steps that descended into the river. It was a Hindoo bathing ghat—the Kalighat where devotees bathe in water that is regarded as sacred.

The mob still followed us. We turned southward along the bank—passing snake tablets and monkey gods—till we came to an enclosed yard overlooked by a bright yellow temple. Inside several fires were burning brightly. At one side several men were piling logs and branches upon a funeral pyre, and on the ground lay the body of a dead man, while nearby were several half-consumed bodies.

We were in a burning ghat—a place where the Hindoos cremate their dead.

---

line the shore of the holy river. They are silent sentinels indicating the spots where the widows were burned alive on the funeral pyres of their husbands.

Before the British government stopped it, the Hindus burned widows alive in order that they might join their husbands in the future life. Suttee—as this is called—is undoubtedly still practiced today in remote parts of the country. Suttee was never exactly compulsory. However, every good wife considered it a privilege and an honor to give up her life in this horrible manner. These stoical women were famed for the courageous way they calmly walked into the flames and lay down in the burning arms of their dead. If the lord and master possessed more than one wife, the unfortunate widows joined hands and slowly walked into their fiery fate together, willingly and unflinchingly. It is a proud Hindu who can boast that his mother was burned alive.

FATEHPUR-SIKRI, India, Feb. 18: I am in the heart of India—a heart that beats but faintly now, but in ages gone by it throbbed with glory unsurpassed. I spent today at Fatehpur-Sikri, the deserted city of the mightiest mogul of all India. Here the ruins of a magnificent city lie sleeping—a city built on the whim of a king and deserted at the whim of a son for whom it was built.

Three centuries ago the great Akbar wanted a son and heir. A hermit living in a cave outside the city told him that his wish would come true if he changed his court to a place twenty-two miles from Agra. Akbar at once commenced building a magnificent city, complete with palaces, baths, buildings, streets and all the appurtenances of royalty and moved there with his court. The prophesy of the hermit came true: a son was born. But after Akbar's death this very son—Jahangir—abandoned the city and moved to Agra. From that time to the present day, silence has reigned in Fatehpur-Sikri.

DELHI, India, Feb. 19: arrived last night from Agra. Delhi—pronounced "Delly"—is the present capital of India. Like Agra, it was also the ancient capital at various times and retains the mute monuments of former glory when India boasted the highest civilization in the world, while Europe was wallowing in the morass of the Middle Ages.

We are coming to the land of

Mohammed. Along the streets come the white-robed figures of the faithful, looking for all the world like the Ku Klux Klan. The white gown completely envelopes them from head to foot, with small openings for the eyes. This costume enables the devotee of Mohammed to keep the word of the prophet who said that they should not look upon any other woman than their own wife.

JAIPUR, India, Feb. 24: Jaipur is the most interesting city since Benares. You would like Jaipur. Its streets are flowing rainbows. It is a colorful kaleidoscope of real Indian life. The streets teem with animals, people and birds. Dense flocks of pigeons darken the streets, brilliant peacocks strut about, monkeys clamber up the bright-hued walls of ancient buildings and the hump-backed cows browse peacefully alongside the sidewalks and poke their noses into bazaars.

All animals are sacred here. A merchant considers himself lucky if a holy cow chooses to saunter in and eat his stock of green-stuffs and he rewards bossy with a kiss, not a kick.

Processions seem to start without provocation—and such colorful affairs they are. All the children in town must be getting married. Funerals and weddings are continually passing each other. A gaudy, tuneful, clinking wedding procession just wound its way around a corner as a lone Hindu approached, carrying in his arms the dead body of his small child wrapped in a thin piece of red gauze. The huge elephant with the eight year old bridegroom on top crowded the solitary mourner upon the sidewalk, where he stood wedged in among the laughing mob until the parade had passed. Then he continued down to the river bank and threw the body into the muddy water.

BOMBAY, India: This island city of fine architecture is the queen of modern cities in the East. Bombay is called the "Gateway of the East" and to prove it they are building a huge arch-like gate on the Apollo Bunder, facing the sea. The city is cluttered up with the usual dumb-looking statues of Queen Victoria, which must please the natives immensely. How the English can expect peace in India with such statuary around is a mystery. It would cause a rebellion anywhere.

The Buddhist temple at Bodh Gaya, India, near the sacred Bho Tree where Buddha was enlightened. 1936.

ARABIAN SEA, March 3: India, that enchanting land of squalor and splendor, is gone from sight. I stood at the rail and kept an eye on weird old India to the very last speck. What a strange land! Folks at home who joggle up and down in ruts will find it difficult to believe how this half of the world lives. I know that I never would.

Robert Ripley would feel the lure of India for the rest of his life. He made it his life's work to deal in the bizarre and the exotic; for more than three decades, the strange was his daily fare. Yet in India, this champion of the peculiar met his match. India's mystical juxtaposition of poverty and splendor haunted him for a lifetime.

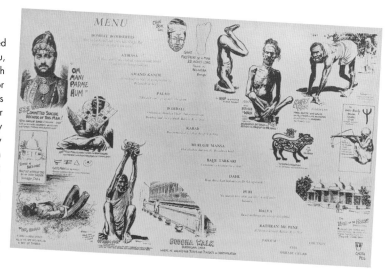

Ripley designed this menu, festooned with Believe It or Not! cartoons about India, for the press party given at New York's Ceylon India Inn after firewalker Kuda Bux's performance, August 16, 1938.

Fishy FABLES

George C. Reedy of Orange, Virginia caught a fake minnow while using a live minnow as bait! The minnow lure that snagged on his line was a lucky catch—he later used the artificial minnow to catch many more live fish! (September 3, 1938.)

A RAIN of FISHES TAKES PLACE EVERY JULY IN YORO, Honduras.

IN 1939, GEORGE STOFFLET OF READING, PENN., WAS STRUCK ON THE HEAD BY A COOKED TROUT *THAT FELL FROM THE SKY!*

Fish Eye Lenses

This spectacle-sporting rock cod was caught wearing glasses belonging to **Ira D. Erling**, a fisherman who had lost them overboard not long before this fish was caught. (April 9, 1940.)

When **James Price** of Locust Grove, Arkansas accidentally dropped his dentures into Bull Shoal Lake, he wrote them off as a loss. But 10 days later, he got them back-when he caught the 20 pound catfish that had swallowed them! (November 15, 1961.)

Two for the price of one

These two bass were hauled out of Herrington Lake, Kentucky on the end of **E. Bramlett's** line-the smaller fish's head became lodged in the larger fish's mouth when both lunged for the same bait at the same time. (June 15, 1933.)

Good thing this one didn't get away!

An accurate 60 foot cast by fisherman **Jack Arnott** saved the life of canoeist **Harry Richardson** when Richardson's canoe capsized. Arnott cast his fly line within Richardson's reach and carefully reeled him in. (October 22, 1949.)

Believe It or Not! A RAIN of FRESHWATER CARP ENCASED IN ICE FELL FROM THE SKY! (ESSEN, GERMANY, 1896)

LIVE TROUT WITH 6-PENNY NAIL ONE INCH IN ITS HEAD Caught by DON DESSIEUX Lewiston, Idaho

...Not!

THE RANUNCULUS (BUTTERCUP) WHICH GROWS IN THE ARCTIC IS THE ONLY BUTTERCUP THAT HAS A SCENT

THE RING THAT WAS RETURNED BY A FISH!
MADAME EDWIGUE REBEIT, of Paris, France, LOST HER RING WHILE WORKING IN HER KITCHEN AND RECOVERED IT A FEW DAYS LATER FROM *A FISH SHE HAD BOUGHT IN THE PUBLIC MARKET* THE RING HAD SLID DOWN THE KITCHEN DRAIN, BEEN WASHED INTO THE RIVER -- AND WAS SWALLOWED BY A FISH THAT WAS PURCHASED BY MADAME REBEIT HERSELF IN THE MOST AMAZING EXAMPLE OF COINCIDENCE IN MODERN TIMES (1903.)

DO YOU BELIEVE IN MERMAIDS?

Robert Ripley's Encounter with the Famous Fijian Hoax

Brandishing a Fiji mermaid, Ripley startles an usherette at the New York City Odditorium, 1939.

New York, 1842: The *New York Herald* shocked the world with astonishing headlines: MERMAIDS ARE REAL! The very distinguished Dr. Griffin of the London Lyceum of Natural History had written the Herald to announce this astonishing discovery on behalf of the scientific community! Dr. Griffin claimed to be in possession of a genuine mermaid cadaver. He had studied it, authenticated it, and after careful research, had proclaimed to be a rare species of Nereids, of the genus Herbivorous Cetacea. Furthermore, the good doctor was prepared to display his rare specimen to the general populace at only twenty-five cents a peek... at the museum of one Phineas T. Barnum.

Americans flocked to see this amazing zoological discovery. Of course, decades later, the truth came out that Dr Griffin was none other than P.T. Barnum's assistant, Levi Lyman, and that the London Lyceum's scientific papers were pure fiction. The cadaver? Real enough, but nothing more than the front half of a dessicated monkey carcass sewed to the back half of a fish. Barnum didn't even own the creature-it was a rented mermaid. Yet the hoax tripled Barnum's income within one month. Mermaids have been swimming around in European folklore and legend for centuries. Accounts of mermaids, dead and alive, are scattered throughout ancient texts. But what sets Barnum's legendary Fiji Mermaid apart from the others is the willing audience it found in modern times, scarcely a century and a half ago. In the mid-1800s, some enterprising South Sea Islander made the discovery that when you join the front

half of a monkey together with the back half of a fish, you get... money. European and American money. Lots of it.

Mermaids have made their home in the South Seas ever since. There must be something in us that wants to believe. Even after Barnum's ruse was uncovered and widely publicized, Fiji Mermaids of all shapes and sizes still found a ready market. One mermaid for sale in a remote shop in Macao, a Portuguese settlement on the China coast, found a buyer in Robert L. Ripley. Ripley claimed that there were fewer than a dozen authentic Fiji mermaids in existence, and that those which remained were priceless. Today, Ripley's owns an impressive collection of Fiji Mermaids.

One of several authentic Fiji Mermaids in Ripley's collection. Made from the front halves of monkey corpses sewn onto the back halves of fish, the mermaids range from 13 inches to 30 inches in length.

Not a bad haul for one cast!

Lawrence Massey of Carlisle, Pennsylvania tossed his line into the surf at Broadkill Beach and snagged a flying seagull. Then to his amazement, a shark lunged for the gull and was snared on his line too! (December 27, 1967.)

! *Carl Moore of Forgan, Oklahoma caught an eight inch trout- without his hook touching the fish! The trout had been hooked some months before, and the hook had remained in its mouth. Moore's hook went through the eye of the other hook!*

For strange catches, this one surely holds the record! When **Bobby Cunningham** of Belfast, Maine caught this 9½ inch speckled trout, it was wearing a 45 rpm record around its middle (June 7, 1966.)

Historical HIJINX

Whisker War

The most fateful whiskers in history belonged to King Louis VII of France. He was the husband of Eleanor, daughter of the last Duke of Guyenne and Poitou, two provinces of Southern France which she brought with her as her dowry. After the King returned from the Crusades, he decided to spruce up and shave off his whiskers. The result was that the Queen declared she had lost her affection for him. She divorced him, reclaimed her two provinces, and presented them as a dowry to her new husband, King Henry II of England. But in 1152, Louis declared war upon Henry, a war which continued between England and France until 1453, 301 years after the King's fateful rendezvous with a razor.

King George!
"Kromprahrachawangbowawnbawarasabtanmongkon" sounds remarkably like "George Washington" if you pronounce it upside-down, and sideways. (Sunday, December 15, 1940.)

Deadly Pun

Napoleon once killed over a thousand people with a single cough. In 1799, he was in the midst of deciding whether or not to release 1,200 Turkish prisoners of war. He was just about to give the order to set them all free, when he coughed. He exclaimed, "Ma sacrè tough!" (My darned cough!) which sounded to his officers like "Massacrez tous!" (Kill them all!) So they did.

During the Civil War in the United States, Julia Ward Howe was visiting Washington and saw soldiers returning from the war. She went to sleep for the night, but when she awoke at dawn, she found herself sitting at her desk. She discovered that she had written a poem of five verses entitled, "The Battle Hymn of the Republic." To her death, Julia wondered if she really wrote the masterpiece or was merely an "instrument" of something bigger.

France, May 28, 1738: an expectant mother witnesses an execution. She is so horrified at what she sees, she goes into labor and gives birth prematurely. Her baby grows up to become a part of history for introducing a highly efficient invention to France. He was Dr. J. I. Guillotin, the inventor for whom the guillotine is named!

Pope Formosus' Posthumous Trial

For some reason now lost to history, Pope Stephen VII (896-897) had the body of Pope Formosus exhumed and arraigned for trial. A legal defender was appointed, and the entire trial was conducted according to the laws of the living. Pope Stephen appeared as the prosecutor and won his case, whereupon the body of Formosus was stripped of its papal robes and insignia, mutilated, and thrown into the Tiber River.

El Cid, the famous Spanish warrior, led his troops into battle after his death. In the eleventh book of the "Chronicle of the Cid", Southey relates that the warrior's embalmed body was placed in the saddle according to his wish, and at the head of his army advanced to battle against King Bucar and his host of Moors... winning a great victory. ily to this day.

Lentil Rental

Archbishop Englebert of Berg built the Cathedral of Cologne in 1225. The magnificent cathedral stood on grounds which belonged to the Lords of Doyme, who offered the use of the land, in exchange for an unusual annual rental fee: the aroma of a dish of baked beans. The building lasted for 600 years. From the 13th to the 17th century, this aromatic rent was paid faithfully every year.

! *The mayor of Grand Lemps, France issued an ordinance that any inhabitant may enter a saloon and drink his fill and then leave without paying... he was a prohibitionist.*

! *Mother Goose was a real person, not an imaginary character. Her maiden name was Elizabeth Foster. She was born in Boston in 1665. She married Isaac Goose in 1693, and wrote her famous, timeless rhymes for her grandchildren.*

The town of Shirhatti in Sangli, India was traded for a cupful of melted butter. In 1607, the owner of the town, an Indian magnate named Anushkar, was playing chess with his wife by the light of an oil lamp, when suddenly the light began to sputter. Alarmed lest he would be unable to finish the engrossing game, Anushkar offered to trade the town for a cup full of oil. A woman named Desai heard the remark, poured a cupful of purified melted butter on the lamp, and claimed her reward. Shirhatti, population 4,000, was owned by the Desai family for years after.

The Comma that Saved a Life

! *Calchas the Greek died from laughter when the day that was predicted to be his death day came around and the prediction did not seem to materialize.*

Maria Feodorewna accidentally caught sight of the following note appended to the bottom of a death warrant. It was the handwriting of her husband, Alexander III. It read as follows:

"Pardon impossible, to be sent to Siberia."

Maria transposed the comma so that it read:

"Pardon, impossible to be sent to Siberia."

The convict was released a free man.

THE PORTRAIT THAT DIED WITH NERO!
A MAMMOTH PAINTING OF NERO!
120 FEET HIGH – IN THE GARDENS OF MAIUS, IN ROME WAS DESTROYED BY A BOLT OF LIGHTNING *ON THE VERY DAY* NERO TOOK HIS OWN LIFE IN A VILLA 4 MILES AWAY

The Roman general Zopyros literally cut off his nose to spite his enemy. His king, Darius the Great, had laid siege to the city of Babylon, but even after 20 months, the city showed no sign of surrender. Zopyros decided that enough was enough. He cut off his own nose and ears, and had himself delivered to Babylon's commanding general. The general believed Zopyros's story that he was a victim of Darius's inhumanity and that he was thirsting for vengeance. He appointed Zopyros the chief defender of Babylon. Zopyros's first deed in his new position was to surrender Babylon to Darius. When Darius beheld Zopyros's mangled features, he shuddered and exclaimed that he would have preferred Zopyros intact to 20 Babylons.

❗ *In Oklahoma it was once against the law to take a bite out of someone else's hamburger! (June 10, 1997.)*

CYRANO de BERGERAC
FAMOUS 17TH CENTURY WRITER & ROMANTIC HERO
FIRST SUGGESTED THE ROCKETSHIP TO THE MOON MORE THAN **300** YEARS AGO!
IN **1640** HE WROTE A BOOK CALLED "*VOYAGE TO THE MOON AND SUN*" IN WHICH HE EXPLAINED THE POSSIBILITIES OF TRAVEL TO THE MOON BY ROCKETSHIP

❗ *Ignacio Camonfort, Former President of Mexico, headed a revolution—against himself! On February 5, 1858, he deposed himself and drove himself into exile.*

In the 16th century, Archie Armstrong of Stubholm Scotland was convicted of sheep stealing and sentenced to decapitation. Fortunately for Armstrong, his king was the affable and accessible James VI. Armstrong appealed to the king for a postponement of the execution until he finished reading the Bible. The king agreed. Then Archie announced that he would henceforth only read one line a day. When James heard this, he was so amused that he not only granted Archie a 300 year postponement of execution, but appointed Archie to be his court jester for the duration of his reprieve.

THE **JEWEL** BEYOND COMPARE!
AT THE CORONATION OF GEORGE III, THE GREAT DIAMOND IN THE CROWN FELL OUT. THE ARCHBISHOP OF CANTERBURY PICKED IT UP WITH THE REMARK THAT "A JEWEL BEYOND COMPARE WILL BE LOST TO THE CROWN" THUS PROPHETICALLY PREDICTING THE LOSS OF THE AMERICAN COLONIES!

The **TABLETS** of **HISTORY**
EMPEROR CHIN SHI HUANG TI (BUILDER OF THE GREAT WALL OF CHINA) ORDERED THE DESTRUCTION OF ALL LITERATURE AND THE EXECUTION OF ALL HISTORIANS SO THAT HISTORY MIGHT BEGIN WITH HIM!
HOWEVER—HE WAS UNSUCCESSFUL, BECAUSE HE OVERLOOKED THE STONE TABLETS OF PEIPING, ON WHICH CHINESE HISTORY WAS ENGRAVED.

Can You Say, "Shibboleth?"

If you can't, be thankful you didn't live in Israel in Biblical times. Judges 12:5 and 6 state that the Hebrew word "shibboleth," meaning "ear of corn" was used as a test on the rebellious Ephraimites who could not pronounce a "sh" sound, but said "sibboleth" instead:

"..and he said sibboleth: for he could not frame to pronounce it right. Then they took him and slew him at the passages of Jordan: and there fell at that time of the Ephraimite forty and two thousand."

Believe It or Not
By Robert L. Ripley

Built a 158 Miles Canal at His Own Expense
SUNDAY, MARCH 14, 1937

P.P. RIQUET
—of Bonrepos, France, 1604–1680
BUILT THE "CANAL du MIDI"—**158** MILES LONG
COSTING **340,000,000** FRANCS –AT HIS **OWN** EXPENSE
THE LARGEST ONE-MAN JOB EVER ATTEMPTED

CANAL du MIDI
TOULOUSE TO NARBONNE
LINKING THE MEDITERRANEAN AND THE ATLANTIC

RIQUET–WHO BORE THIS INCOMPREHENSIBLE FINANCIAL BURDEN– DIED 4 WEEKS BEFORE THE CANAL WAS COMPLETED

IS THE DONKEY COMING OR GOING?
Drawn by E.G. Schneider Rochester N.Y.

THE OPTICAL ILLUSION THE SQUARE IS PERFECT

ATILIUS
ROMAN CONSUL
PRONOUNCED HIS OWN **DEATH SENTENCE!** –AND TRAVELED FROM ROME TO CARTHAGE TO HAVE IT EXECUTED! 255 B.C.

The FLOATING CHURCH
108 FT. LONG–PERFECTLY EQUIPPED–USED ON THE PARANA RIVER, ARGENTINA

THE FIGHTING MEN WHO WERE CARRIED TO SAFETY BY THEIR WIVES!
KING KONRAD III
HAVING CAPTURED THE BESIEGED TOWN OF WEINSBERG, GERMANY DECLARED ITS WOMEN COULD DEPART UNHARMED **WITH ANYTHING THEY COULD CARRY!**
THE WOMEN LEFT THE TOWN **CARRYING THEIR HUSBANDS**
Dec. 21, 1140

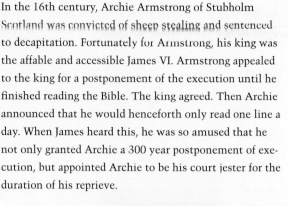

RIPLEY MAKES HISTORY
A BION Cartoon Launches Public Demand
for an Official National Anthem

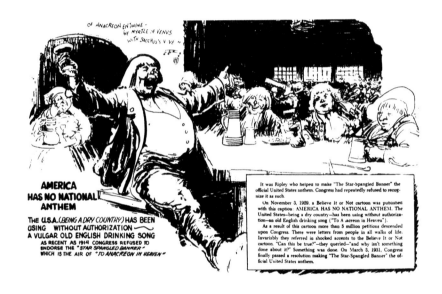

Believe It or Not, the man who started the movement to make "The Star Spangled Banner" the official anthem of the United States was none other than Robert L. Ripley! On November 3, 1929, Ripley published a cartoon with the the the caption, "Believe It or Not, AMERICA HAS NO NATIONAL ANTHEM!" Ripley claimed that Francis Scott Key had borrowed the melody to "The Star Spangled Banner" from a vulgar English drinking song entitled, "To Anachreon In Heaven," and that by refusing to recognize the "Banner" as the country's official Anthem, Congress was dooming millions to take their hats off to a mere drinking song.

Ripley's cartoon galvanized the public's attention. At the time, Congress had repeatedly ignored the public's requests to recognize "The Star Spangled Banner" as the United States' official anthem, despite public support for the measure. After the cartoon was published, Congress received no less than five million demands that the "Banner" be legitimized.

Not all of the response to Ripley's claim was positive. Later that same month, a scathing denouncement of Robert Ripley was published, claiming that Ripley had been irresponsible in his research, and was merely repeating a lie that had been spread in the 1870s by a bitter Englishman who sought to discredit the United States.

Nevertheless, Ripley's cartoon had the desired effect. On March 3, 1931, hardly more than a year after the cartoon first appeared, Congress passed a resolution making "The Star Spangled Banner" the official anthem of the United States of America.

Incredible INVENTIONS

THE "GREEN LADY"
A ROBOT AT THE FRANKLIN INSTITUTE IN PHILADELPHIA, PA. THAT CAN WRITE 3 POEMS AND DRAW 4 PICTURES, WAS MADE IN 1805

VACUUM CLEANERS of the 1800s REQUIRED **2** PERSONS TO OPERATE THEM--*ONE TREADING A BELLOWS THAT SUCKED UP THE DUST*

SCREAM MUFFLER
A NEW INVENTION ENABLES STRESS-RIDDEN PEOPLE TO RELIEVE THEIR TENSIONS BY SCREAMING INTO A SMALL SPHERE PACKED WITH ACOUSTICAL FOAM THAT MAKES THE LOUDEST SCREAM SOUND LIKE POLITE CONVERSATION

ORIGIN of "WEDGIES?"
MUSICIANS OF ANCIENT GREECE WORE SHOES THAT **PLAYED MUSIC** WHEN THEY WALKED

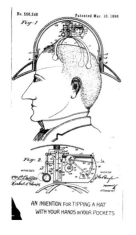

AN INVENTION FOR TIPPING A HAT WITH YOUR HANDS IN YOUR POCKETS

IN THE 1930s HOLLYWOOD MAKEUP ARTIST **MAX FACTOR** INVENTED A HAND-OPERATED *KISSING MACHINE* WITH RUBBER MOLDED LIPS THAT WERE PRESSED TO-GETHER TO TEST *LIPSTICK!*

A **MUSTACHE PROTECTOR** DEVISED BY ELI J.F. RANDOLPH, OF N.Y., IN 1872, WAS A HARD-RUBBER DEVICE WITH PRONGS THAT FITTED INTO THE NOSTRILS TO KEEP **THE MUSTACHE DRY WHEN EATING AND DRINKING**

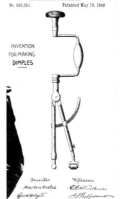

INVENTION FOR MAKING DIMPLES

THE **FIRST ARTIFICIAL LIMB**
AN IRON HAND ORDERED BY KING ROBERT the BRUCE of Scotland FOR A KNIGHT NAMED De CLEPHANES **MORE THAN 650 YEARS AGO** *EACH FINGER COULD BE MOVED BY PRESSING A BUTTON*

In 1933, Monopoly inventor Charles Darrow gave cash-poor Americans, still smarting from the stock market crash, a way to ease their craving to control some capital. Darrow based his game's neighborhood on the vacation town of Atlantic City, New Jersey. Although Parker Brothers, the game's producers, sent him back to the drawing board numerous times to shake out the flaws, Darrow eventually came up with the famous design familiar to Monopoly players around the world. Darrow, who was broke when he first created the game, died a multimil-lionaire in 1970.

THE **ELECTRIC CHAIR** WAS FIRST USED FOR EXECUTIONS IN NEW YORK STATE IN 1890 --AFTER A CITIZEN HAD UN-SUCCESSFULLY OFFERED TO TEST IT FOR A FEE OF $5,000 — TO *BE PAID TO HIS FAMILY IF THE CURRENT WORKED*

BOTTOMS UP!
TO HELP BEGINNERS, THE LAID-BACK SKIERS' ASSOC. HAS DEVELOPED SPECIAL POSTERIOR REGION SKIS FOR THOSE WHO SPEND A LOT OF TIME ON THEIR DERRIÈRES Submitted by Chester A. Tumidajewicz, Amsterdam, N.Y.

IN 1948 GEORGE deMAESTRAL, A SWISS SCIENTIST, INVENTED VELCRO AFTER STUDYING BURS HE FOUND CLINGING TO HIS TROUSERS WHILE WALKING IN THE WOODS!

"GILLS" FOR HUMANS
THE HEMOSPONGE, AN EXPERIMENTAL DEVICE BEING DEVELOPED WITH SUPPORT FROM THE U.S. OFFICE OF NAVAL RESEARCH, MAY MAKE IT POSSIBLE FOR DIVERS TO REMAIN SUBMERGED FOR SEVERAL DAYS, *EXTRACTING OXYGEN FROM THE WATER*

A HELMET GUN
INVENTED BY ALBERT PRATT OF VERMONT IN 1916, WAS FIRED WHEN THE WEARER *BLEW INTO A MOUTHPIECE*

Dr. RICHARD JORDAN GATLING (1818-1903) INVENTOR OF THE GATLING MACHINE GUN, IS RESPONSIBLE FOR THE UNDERWORLD'S SLANG NAME FOR ANY HANDGUN --A "GAT"

A MILITARY TANK
WAS DESIGNED BY LEONARDO DA VINCI IN THE 15th CENTURY

A ROBOT
USED BY THE UNIV. OF SOUTHERN CALIFORNIA'S SCHOOL OF MEDICINE, SHOWED THE REACTIONS OF A HUMAN PATIENT--*INCLUDING SIMULATED HEARTBEATS, BREATHING, BLOOD PRESSURE AND EYE DILATIONS*

THE OZOPHONE
A HEARING AID INVENTED IN THE 1920s WAS SUPPOSED TO HELP THE DEAF TO HEAR THROUGH *THEIR TEETH*

ALEX NIEMIN AGE 47 - of NANTKOKE, Penna., HAS NEVER USED A HANDKERCHIEF. HE HAS NEVER HAD THE OCCASION TO BLOW HIS NOSE IN HIS LIFE

CLOTHES BRUSH IN USE 80 YEARS Owned by MRS.F.J. BRIDGER Ivanhoe Vic Australia.

PLATO'S ALARM CLOCK
WATER
SYPHON
WHISTLE
WATER TRICKLES FROM UPPER VESSEL INTO SECOND VESSEL - WHICH WHEN FILLED EMPTIES ITSELF BY SYPHONIC ACTION INTO A THIRD - WHICH IS SEALED-CAUSING THE AIR TO BE FORCED OUT THRU THE WHISTLE --- Awakening the Sleeper

GETTING UP WITH A BANG
A 17th CENTURY PISTOL WITH A BUILT IN ALARM CLOCK!

Copr. 1949, King Features Syndicate, Inc., World rights reserved.

DURING THE REVOLUTION OF 1830 THE NATIONAL GUARD OF PARIS WAS ARMED WITH UMBRELLA GUNS TO PROTECT THEM AGAINST SUN AND RAIN

EDGAR SIMS of Sun City, Ariz. AT THE AGE OF 82 INVENTED A DEVICE TO IMPROVE HEARING --MOUSE-LIKE EARS

PASSAGE OF TIME WAS NOTED IN ANCIENT TIMES, AT NIGHT WHEN SUN-DIALS COULD NOT FUNCTION, BY BURNING LENGTHS OF ROPE KNOTTED AT REGULAR INTERVALS

PATENT #889,928 A PATENT FOR AN ALARM CLOCK THAT SPRAYS WATER ON THE FACE OF A SLEEPING PERSON WAS FILED AT THE U.S. PATENT OFFICE IN 1907!

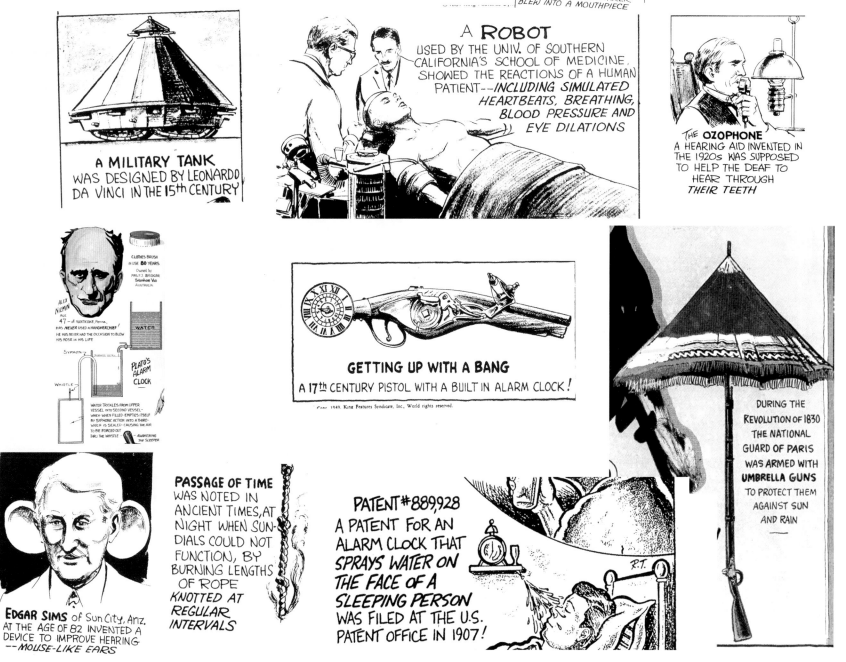

Rowland Emett's candy machine, as seen in the film "Chitty Chitty Bang Bang," dispenses treacle apples and candies that whistle. Circa early 1970s.

Rowland Emett and his Little Dragon Carpet Cleaner. Note that the Dragon wears high-magnification spectacles for optimum dirt-finding performance.

Rowland Emett with the Visi-Visi Television.

Rowland Emett's sketch for the Hush-a-bye hot air rocker, similar to the sketches drawn for Punch magazine that launched Emett's odd career.

ROWLAND EMETT'S WHIMSICAL GADGETS

Zany. Crazy. Potty. Loony. Nuts. These are the words often used to describe Rowland Emett, England's answer to America's Rube Goldberg. Emett quietly protested the moniker of "Zany Inventor" with which he was frequently labeled: "I'm not Zany. And I'm not an Inventor." he told Smithsonian magazine in July of 1973, "I make Things with a capital T."

When you examine a Rowland Emett creation, plenty of words come to mind—'sane' and 'ordinary' are never among them. Emett got his start in the 1940s, drawing whimsical cartoons for Punch magazine. In 1951, one of Emett's airy sketches was turned into a three-dimensional object, and the rest, as they say, is history.

Emett's devices drew adoring crowds wherever they were displayed. Henceforth, he earned his fame creating whimsical sculptures on commission for major corporations. Emett slyly mocked modern industry with his mechanical confections that did practically everything except the practical. He built everything from a bamboo elephant-shaped Forget-me-Not computer that didn't compute to a Vintage Car of the Future (complete with sausage barbecue) that didn't go anywhere.

Emett is probably best known for creating the wonderful gizmos in the 1968 film, *Chitty Chitty Bang Bang.*

Eight of Emett's fanciful creations were featured in the film, including the Humbug-Major Sweet Machine, which dispensed whistling candies and treacle apples. The Sweet Machine is one of five of Rowland Emett's devices that have found a happy home at Ripley's. It has joined its brethren, the Hush-a-Bye Hot Air Rocking Chair (complete with slippers and teddy bear) the Visi-Visi Television, the Clockwork Lullaby Machine and the Little Dragon Carpet Sweeper, all on display at various Ripley's Odditoriums around the world.

In 1990, Rowland Emett died at the age of 84, leaving behind a legacy of capricious drawings and whimsical inventions for future generations to enjoy. In his lifetime, Emett did more to (in the words of the late Shel Silverstein) "put somethin' silly in the world" than most of us could dream of.

Miniature MARVELS

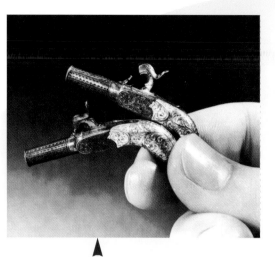

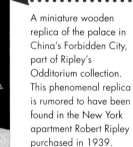

"Little Pumpkin", The world's smallest horse. This tiny stallion stood only 14" tall. He was raised by **J.C. Williams** of Inman, South Carolina, and appeared in a Believe It or Not! cartoon, in the Guiness Book of World Records, and on numerous television shows. (March 12, 1977.)

A MINIATURE CHANDELIER CREATED BY DON AND FRAN MEEHAN OF EAST WINDSOR, N.J., IS 4½" LONG, 3½" WIDE AND HAS 3,300 TINY PIECES OF AUSTRIAN CRYSTAL WITH 23 ELECTRIC BULBS THAT LIGHT UP!

These highly detailed miniature pistols were on display in Ripley's Niagara Falls Odditorium in the 1960s.

A miniature wooden replica of the palace in China's Forbidden City, part of Ripley's Odditorium collection. This phenomenal replica is rumored to have been found in the New York apartment Robert Ripley purchased in 1939.

Ripley poses with a miniature wooden replica of the Cathedral of Milan, carved by **Ed R. Turk** of Allenhurst, Georgia, who spent more than 5,000 hours over 5 years cutting, carving, and assembling hundreds of tiny parts—some so small that they required a microscope to be seen properly. The cathedral is currently on display in Ripley's Odditorium in Mexico City.

Miniature gold tea set inside a gold locket, from the **Jules Charbneau** collection. The document inside the locket's lid is Charbneau's miniature business card. This photograph was taken in 1968, when the Charbneau collection was purchased.

A working scale model carousel, with electric lights and moving horses. Created by **Frederick Turner** of Hounslow, England as therapy while he recovered from cataract surgery. Built from 1959 to 1967 and requiring 8,000 hours of labor, the carousel stands 6½ feet tall, weighs 450 pounds, and features 32 animals under 400 working lights.

A working box camera, built by **Harvey Libowitz**—and a print made from a negative taken by the camera, circa 1980.

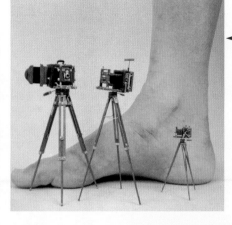

The world's smallest working miniature cameras, built by **Harvey Libowitz** of Brooklyn, New York, for the New Orleans Odditorium, circa 1980.

In addition to cameras, **Harvey Libowitz** built this functional miniature pool table, featured in a Believe It or Not cartoon on March 10, 1985.

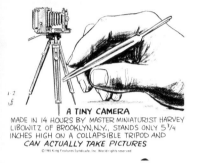

A TINY CAMERA
MADE IN 14 HOURS BY MASTER MINIATURIST HARVEY LIBOWITZ OF BROOKLYN, N.Y., STANDS ONLY 5³/₄ INCHES HIGH ON A COLLAPSIBLE TRIPOD AND *CAN ACTUALLY TAKE PICTURES*

This seemingly ordinary penny conceals a tiny slide-out drawer with a photograph of miniature collector **Jules Charbneau.** Circa 1930.

Miniature painting of the Crucifixion of Christ on a dime, by **Manuel Andrada** of Argentina. Part of the Charbneau collection. Circa 1930s.

Robert L. Ratte's mini-violin is only 5 1/2 inches long, yet it can produce musical tones. In the 1930s, Ratte gave a live concert on his mini-violin in Ripley's Radio Show.

OUR FATHER WHO ART IN HEAVEN HALLOWED BE THY NAME THY KINGDOM COME THY WILL BE DONE ON EARTH AS IT IS IN HEAVEN GIVE US THIS DAY OUR DAILY BREAD AND FORGIVE US OUR DEBTS AS WE FORGIVE OUR DEBTORS AND LEAD US NOT INTO TEMPTATION BUT DELIVER US FROM EVIL FOR THINE IS THE KINGDOM AND THE POWER AND THE GLORY FOR EVER AMEN

THE LORD'S PRAYER ON THE HEAD OF A PIN

Sing Sing Prison, the late 1800s: Two guards find convicted forger A. Schiller dead in his cell. On his body, they find seven pins, each with evidence of Schiller's amazing talent. Under magnification, it is revealed that he has engraved the Lord's Prayer, all 65 words and 254 letters, on every pin.

All of the pins were astonishing, but one gold pin, whose head measured 1.17 millimeters, or 47/1000ths of an inch in diameter, was absolutely flawless-every word and line perfectly spaced, every letter completely legible. When the pin head was magnified 500 times, the Lord's Prayer could easily be read. How could Schiller have accomplished this?

Schiller, an expert engraver, had been serving a sentence for forgery. He spent the last twenty-five years of his life creating this masterpiece, sacrificing his eyesight to complete it. Using a tool too tiny to be seen by the naked eye, Schiller made 1,863 separate cuts to the pin's head to form the letters of the prayer. The remarkable engraving was an exquisite testimony to craftsmanship.

The pin was put on display at a World's Fair exhibit in 1893, but was stolen from its display case and disappeared from the public eye for more than 40 years. Miniature collector Jacques Charbneau discovered it in an antique shop in the mid-1930s, and it re-entered the miniature market. Nearly twenty years later, Ripley's purchased the pin from Orville Elton of Seattle, Washington. Today Schiller's remarkable pin is on display at Ripley's St. Augustine, Florida Odditorium.

But Schiller's masterpiece is not the only pin of its type to merit a place in the Ripley legacy. A similar pin appeared in a Believe It or Not! cartoon on December 16, 1929. This pin, which allegedly took three years to complete, was credited to Charles Edward Baker of Spokane, Washington. Apparently, Mr. Baker went blind and insane from the effort!

Shortly after the cartoon was published, Ripley's received a letter from Alvin H. Hankins of Seattle, Washington, who claimed that Baker was a fraud. Hankins insisted that Charles Edward Baker didn't make the pin-the late Godfrey E. Lundberg did, before Hankins' eyes.

Hankins, a lens grinder, had been present during the entire time Lundberg worked on the pin. He told of the grueling conditions Lundberg imposed upon himself to complete the work: Lundberg worked from a barber's chair, strapping his hands to an iron bar to keep them from shaking. He also bound his wrists tightly with leather straps, because the rhythm of his pulse caused the engraving

tool to skip. Lundberg could only work on the pin in the evenings, when the rumbling trolley cars that passed by his shop had stopped running for the day. He destroyed more than two hundred pins in his attempt to create one perfect engraving.

How did Baker come to possess this controversial pin? Hankins claimed that after the masterpiece was completed, Lundberg made a tiny steel die, 110/1000ths of an inch in diameter, which was capable of stamping out copies of the original. Lundberg had sold his pin, as well as several copies, to Baker. The Lundberg pin, like the priceless Schiller pin in Ripley's Odditorium, had been engraved entirely by hand.

OPPOSITE PAGE: The Lord's Prayer on the head of a pin, greatly omagnified, engraved by **A. Schiller** in the late 1800s. The most legible of five, this pin is on display at the St. Augustine, Florida Odditorium.

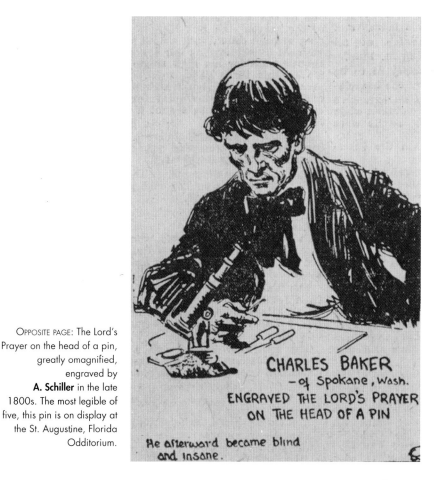

CHARLES BAKER
-of Spokane, Wash.
ENGRAVED THE LORD'S PRAYER
ON THE HEAD OF A PIN

He afterward became blind and insane.

Oversized
ODDITIES

The world's largest bass fiddle, built by **Arthur K. Ferris** of Ironia, New Jersey, stood 14 feet high, 6 feet wide, and 2 feet deep. Its sound-box alone stood a towering 7 feet. (December 15, 1934.)

Ripley stands before the world's largest sun dial in Manila, Philippines, during a 1932 visit.

6 million dollar shoe! **Elmer O. Chase** of Braintree, Massachusetts built this 10-foot long, 8-foot high shoe from $6 million in retired, shredded one dollar bills! (February 6, 1935.)

! *The famous "Maggie Murphy": **a potato weighing 96 pounds 10 ounces**, measuring 2 feet, 5 inches, was raised by **J. B. Swan**, Loveland, Colorado.*

Colossal Crustacean!

This enormous lobster was caught in the fall of 1934 off the Virginia Capes. It weighed 42 pounds 7 ounces, and was displayed in Boston's Museum of Science as the largest lobster ever recorded. The museum offered a reward to anyone who could bring in a larger lobster. The reward has never been collected.

The folks at the Chicago Furniture Mart constructed this giant chair which was at one time the world's largest. It stands 14 feet high and approximately 11 feet square, and is covered in brilliant rose-pink Naugahyde. (April 13, 1962.)

Wonder Weenie

The biggest hot dog of all time was stuffed by the German Butcher's Guild for their celebration in Koenigsberg in 1601. This hot dog was more than half a mile long (exactly 3,001 feet) and required the efforts of 103 butchers to carry it on parade. It weighed 885 pounds, and was later distributed among the members of the guild at a banquet table.

The world's biggest broom, 13 feet wide and 40 feet high, was created by the Deshler Broom Factory in Deshler, Nebraska, to celebrate its 50th anniversary. The huge broom was later taken apart and made into 1,440 ordinary-sized brooms. (November 14, 1940.)

This photo of **Mrs. Nelson Green** of Starke, Florida and her 22-pound turnip was submitted to Ripley's by E.L. Matthews, editor of the *Bradford County Telegraph*, with a note that read, "With 40,000 hungry soldiers to feed at Camp Blanding 8 miles away, Bradford County farmers are doing their bit"

The Pearl of Lao Tze, valued at several million dollars. This huge brainlike pearl was on display in the New York City Odditorium in 1940. Replicas of the pearl can be seen in Ripley's Odditoriums today.

"THE WORLD'S BIGGEST 'SCRABBLE' GAME" A GIANT 'SCRABBLE' GAME COVERED THE ENTIRE SOCCER FIELD at Wembley Stadium in London, AND HAD LETTER PIECES THAT REQUIRED TWO MEN EACH TO LIFT THEM! (Oct 1998)

The world's largest duck decoy. Circa 1950.

The BIGGEST SAILING SHIP IN THE WORLD VANISHED WITHOUT A TRACE! THE FIVE-MASTED BARK "KOBENHAVEN" DISAPPEARED INTO THE UNKNOWN! —ALTHOUGH SHE CARRIED RADIO EQUIPMENT and AUXILIARY ENGINES. 70 CADETS-MEMBERS of the MOST PROMINENT FAMILIES IN DENMARK-VANISHED WITH HER. HER FATE IS UNKNOWN

Francisco Calabaga of Tampa, Florida rolled this **7 foot, 8½ inch cigar** in honor of the 50th anniversary of the Tobacco Industry in Ybor City, Tampa, Florida's Cuban district. Calabaga's cigar weighed 22 pounds 2 ounces, took 96 hours to roll, and was valued at $350.00 in 1935. (February 21, 1935.)

THE OCTOBASSE A MUSICAL INSTRUMENT INVENTED IN THE 19th CENTURY RESEMBLES A VIOLIN IN LOOKS BUT IS 10 FEET HIGH

A SINGLE FINGERNAIL OF THE STATUE OF LIBERTY WEIGHS 100 POUNDS

I.R.S. MANUAL

Believe It or Not! THE OFFICIAL MANUAL for THE U.S. INTERNAL REVENUE SERVICE IS 38,000 PAGES LONG!

Send you 5728 Ma

VAN GOGH'S SELF-PORTRAIT IN POSTCARDS:

Ripley's Largest Exhibit

Over the years, Ripley's has struggled with some pretty awkward-sized objects. Figuring out ways to ship monstrous truck tires, giant animals made from car bumpers, and other bizarre objects of all shapes, sizes and weights has caused the folks at Ripley's more than a few headaches. But you'll be surprised to learn that the largest exhibit Ripley's has ever owned wasn't nearly as hard to haul as you might imagine.

Ripley's discovered Cornel Bierens' gigantic Van Gogh self-portrait in postcards in Chicago at a touring show of lesser-known Van Gogh works. In spite of its huge size—and perhaps partially because of it—the piece seemed to belong in a Ripley's Odditorium. Standing 25 feet tall and 20 feet wide, the reproduction of Van Gogh's famous self-portrait before an easel had been lovingly recreated from 3,000 postcards, each postcard itself a picture of a Van Gogh masterpiece. The artist, Cornel Bierens of the Netherlands, had carefully worked the nuances of shading and color from 113 different postcards. Bierens hadn't specifically intended to create such an enormous work, but the piece's size was simply a result of using postcards as his medium.

Cornel Bierens was born in the Netherlands in 1949. He embarked on a short career as a psychologist, then switched to art. "I didn't want to solve problems," he explained, "I wanted to create puzzles, artistic puzzles, as food for thought." Bierens studied for three years at the Academy of Gerrit Rietveld in Amsterdam, specializing in collages. The enormous Van Gogh collage came about in 1989, when Bierens was contacted by the Netherlands Bureau of Tourism who wanted to commission work from him for their 100th anniversary celebration of Van Gogh, which included an international tour. Ripley's met up with the artist in Toronto at the end of the tour, and purchased the collage just before it was to be sent back to the Netherlands.

Imagine you've just bought a piece of art 25 feet tall and 20 feet wide. You're in Toronto, Ontario. You've got to figure out a way to get the thing to Orlando, Florida. What do you do? Strap it to the belly of a 747? Duct-tape 250 skateboards together and pray for no rain? Fortunately, Bierens thought ahead, and designed his postcard masterpiece so that it could be disassembled into 12 relatively manageable pieces, all of which fit into an 8½' by 5' by 2' crate.

Thankfully, the 3,000 postcards were mounted on foam core board, so the whole thing is surprisingly light. The colossal collage arrived safely in Florida, and is currently on display in Ripley's Orlando Odditorium. When Ripley's last spoke with Bierens, he was considering doing a portrait of Russian novelist Anton Chekhov from the written words of his works.

Mother Nature's MISCHIEF

Naturally occurring wood snail. Photo 1991.

Bill Luyk of Marne, Michigan and **Christopher Powers** of Grand Rapids, Michigan found this naturally occurring pirate face peering at them from a tree root along Green Lake Trail in Michigan's Interlochen State Park. (February 18, 1976.)

Eerie skeleton of the **Devil Fish**. The Devil Fish skeleton and the Crucifix Fish skeleton were displayed together in the New York City Odditorium in 1940. Photo 1968.

Wilfred Larson of Roslyn, Washington discovered this natural **driftwood duck head** at Lake Kachess, Washington. (April 28, 1961.)

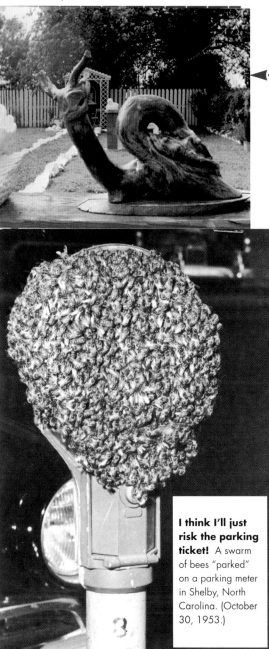

I think I'll just risk the parking ticket! A swarm of bees "parked" on a parking meter in Shelby, North Carolina. (October 30, 1953.)

When Biology Gets Creative

This rabbit, raised by **Mr. and Mrs. E. T. Humphrey** of Sanford, Florida, was entirely toothless except for two long tusks. One tusk snapped off when she attempted to get at some food in a gunny sack. The remaining tusk grew to 1 ½ inches. (September 24, 1949.)

A turtle with the face of a "Chinaman" was caught in 1933 by **Travis Robinson** of Texarkana, Texas.

The Jordan family of East Falls, Pennsylvania owned this black **dog with a perfect five-pointed white star on his chest.** Coincidentally, the dog's name was "Rip!" (August 30, 1947.)

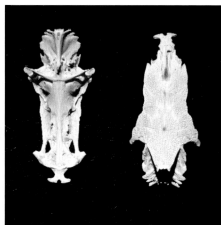

The skeleton of the **Crucifix Fish** so closely resembles a depiction of the crucified Christ that it is used by many West Indian peoples as a crucifix. Photo 1968.

Signs of the Times

Dreadlocked goat: how many combs would you go through to get the tangles out of this thing? (August 11, 1932.)

Sweetheart, owned by **Mrs. Weaver Blake** of Humboldt, Kansas. (May 7, 1939.)

Evil Omen: This calf was born with a naturally occurring swastika on its forehead on the farm of **Max Granzow** of Wrist-Holstein, Germany in 1933. (April 10, 1934.)

Just in case you weren't sure... this feline had **the word "CAT" spelled out in its fur!** Owned by **Larry Heaney** of Annapolis, Maryland. (November 18, 1972.)

Vickie, a black cat with a natural white "V" on her chest, born on V-Day! Owned by **Lily Gimlin** of Fort Lauderdale, Florida. (August 17, 1969.)

A rare **white alligator,** born in 1983 from the only brood of white gators ever found. This young gator and his brothers (alligators always bear same-sex broods) are not true albinos because their eyes are blue rather than pink. This gator and his kin now measure eight feet or more in length, and are displayed in zoos and aquariums around the world.

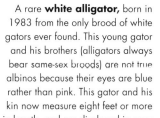

...Those Little Extras...

Mrs. Frank Allen of Bellview, Florida owns a Chihuahua with two full sets of teeth. (July 9, 1987.)

This calf was born on the farm of **Alex Harpe** of Buckley, Michigan with **a nearly complete "twin" growing out of its back.** The birth of this calf proved fatal to its mother. The calf was taxidermed and later sold as a curiosity to a passing stranger. Its whereabouts today are unknown. (November 2, 1954.)

This chicken with four drumsticks was owned by **John Worseley** of Lindsay, Ontario. (November 17, 1955.)

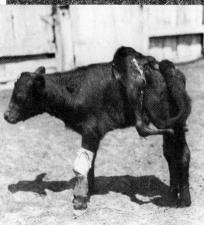

The "Bayswater Calf", a five-legged, two-tailed, hermaphrodite owned by **W. Taylor,** made the carnival sideshow circuit in West Australia in the 1970s. (November 17, 1975.)

THE DOUBLE-FOOTED HORSE
Owned by R. VAN WERT—
CINCINNATI, Ohio

Crab with a bonus claw, caught in Barnaget Bay, New Jersey. Submitted by William S. Yavorn. (December 5, 1982.)

Six-legged frog, owned by **Glen Lawrence** of Cross Plains, Texas, kept by schoolchildren as a classroom pet— the subject of many a science project! (February 17, 1954.)

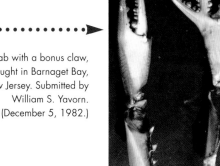

In his 22 years at Lederle Laboratories, **Dr. Reginal Hewitt** of Pearl River, New York bred and handled more than 25,000 mice per week, but had never before seen a **two-tailed mouse.** (December 11, 1952.)

Confucius Jones, Jr., one of a rare breed of **four-horned sheep** considered sacred by the Navajo. Confucius was born in Arizona and was later flown to Hawaii, where he lived out his days at Dairymen's Waialae Ranch, munching on his favorite snack: hula skirts! (June 9, 1948.)

H. O. Langley of St. Albans, New York photographed this **two-headed snake** found in Bronx Park in 1899. Although the snake only lived a few days, it was alive at the time of this photograph.

Two-nosed Llewellen setter, owned by **John E. Glenn** of Benton, Arkansas... does this mean he "smells" twice as much as other dogs? (August 20, 1946.)

Unlike the vast majority of two-headed animals, this **two-headed turtle,** owned by **Frank Cliffe** of Schenectady, New York remained alive after birth and was kept as a pet. Its heads operated independently of one another at the ends of a "Y" shaped spine, and could be fed separately. (March 22, 1992.)

Less is More

This **beakless chicken** was owned by **Barney Lederman** of Chicago, Illinois, and was displayed in a Chicago bar. (August 18, 1933.)

A cow bearing the silhouette of a prizefighter, owned by Laddie Tolley of Hamilton, Ohio. (January 19, 1954.)

A colt born with **no front legs** whatsoever, on **Jeff Drake's** farm in Sedalia, Montana. The colt could walk upright when held, and could take about a dozen steps alone. (August 2, 1940.)

NO HAM ON THIS PIG!
— BORN WITHOUT HIND LEGS
Owned by J. E. CHEWNING.

A. A. Rankin of Puyallup, Washington owned this collie/spaniel pup, who was **born without hips or hind legs.** At three months old, the pup was able to run around almost as fast as a normal dog. (September 6, 1932.)

Is Your Produce Trying to Tell You Something?

Potato plane, grown by **J. J. Brophy** and submitted by **Charles A. Shinn** of Hines, Oregon. The aerodynamic spud grew all in one piece, and weighed three pounds. Only the paper propeller was added. (May 2, 1935.)

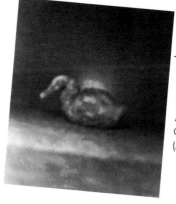

Sweet potato duck, submitted by Arthur Armstrong of Cincinnati, Ohio. (April 19, 1936.)

This kind won't make you fat: a tomato doughnut, 15 inches in circumference, grown by **E. C. Knott** of Summerland, British Columbia. (December 2, 1973.)

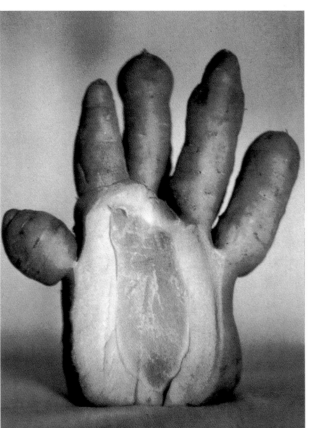

Ripley's archives are packed with photos of hand-shaped carrots, potatoes, and turnips. This particularly handlike carrot was found by Tommy Andrews at the Palace Cafe in Redlands, California. (May 11, 1935.)

Duck-shaped peanut, submitted by **Bea Johnson** of Huntsville, Alabama. (August 25, 1985.)

Spiro Agnew Eggplant: Johnny Brenner discovered this eggplant bearing the silhouette of former Vice President Spiro Agnew. (April 12, 1974.)

A PROPHESY FULFILLED

The Birth of the Sacred White Buffalo

August 20th, 1994, 6:00AM: Janesville, Wisconsin farmer David Heider headed out to see if his pregnant buffalo cow had given birth during the night. He was in for a shock: the little newborn calf Heider found standing beside her mother was not the usual red-brown, but a creamy white.

David Heider and his wife Valerie knew the calf was unusual, but being unfamiliar with Native American spirituality, they had no inkling that within the next few months, the tiny white buffalo calf would draw thousands of pilgrims, some from as far away as Ireland and China. The Heiders soon learned that the Native Americans spiritualists flocking to see the calf believed her to be the long-awaited harbinger of a new era of peace for all humankind. They named her "Miracle."

Geneticists disagree on the exact odds of producing a white buffalo; some place the odds at one in 10 million; others place them as high as one in 6 billion. Suffice it to say, white buffalo don't come along every day. But to Native Americans, particularly the Sioux and Cheyenne, Miracle was expected. She signals the long-awaited return of Wohpe, the White Buffalo Woman, one of the most sacred figures in Native American Plains religion.

One summer long ago (some reckon it as about 500 years ago) the people of the Plains were starving. Two men went out to hunt, and saw a woman in a shimmering white robe moving gracefully towards them. One of the men desired the woman, and tried to touch her, but was enveloped in a silvery cloud which reduced him to a pile of worm-eaten bones. The woman told the remaining man to return to his village and prepare for her coming.

When the woman appeared in the village a few days later, she brought with her a sacred pipe, which she gave to the people. She taught them to live virtuous lives, to value their women and children, and to respect and care for the buffalo that provided for their earthly needs.

She told the people she would return to them after another time of tribulation, at the dawn of a new era of peace. She then transformed into a white buffalo calf and rolled over four times, at each turn changing into one of the colors of the four races of humankind: yellow for Asians, black for Africans, white for Europeans, and red for Native Americans. Then she rose and galloped away. Since that day, the Lakota have kept tradition as she taught them.

To the Native American faithful, Miracle's birth signals the beginning of a new era of global spiritual unification, a healing time when all people will be of one heart and one mind. Floyd Hand, Chief Medicine Man of the Oglala Sioux, came to Miracle's birthplace to perform a ceremony of peace and unification. His grandfather told him he would live to see the birth of the anticipated white buffalo calf. His people have been praying for her for 500 years. The hopes that Miracle represents to Native American spiritual leaders are echoed in the tenets of many other faiths.

An ecumenical spiritual movement is currently taking place around the world, which speaks of an approaching time when all people will live together in peace.

Since Miracle's birth, tribal leaders have come to perform sacred ceremonial rites and to speak about righteous living, urging listeners to use their common sense to judge the difference between right and wrong, and to cherish and strengthen their families. Dr. Arvol Looking Horse came with the sacred White Buffalo Calf pipe, the very same pipe given to his people by Wohpe, the White Buffalo Woman.

Even when the little calf's color began to darken, the faithful were not deterred. Spiritual leaders explained that part of the prophesy indicated that the sacred white buffalo would manifest each of the four colors representing the four races: white, yellow, black, and red. Indeed, Miracle's coat went from a milky white to a yellow-gray, then to a dark charcoal. As she matured, it began to show tinges of coppery red.

The Heiders have truly witnessed a miracle on their farm: they have seen people from many diverse races, religions, and backgrounds come together joyfully over the hope that the little white calf represents. They have vowed to care for her, never to sell her, and to make sure that anyone who wants to see her will be welcome.

THE FIRST *PURE WHITE BUFFALO* BORN in the U.S. SINCE 1933 **WAS BORN in 1994** near Janesville, Wisconsin.

Nutty NAMES

And modesty is my most endearing quality...
Ripley's cartoon for Sunday, November 2, 1941 features a none-too-humble king with a wrist-cramping signature.

East meets West: **Mr. E. E. East** of West Virginia shakes hands with **Mr. E. E. West** of east Virginia. (February 5, 1937.)

Golden Ruel resided in Milwaukee, Wisconsin.

California Poppe lived in Inglewood, California. (July 8, 1933.)

Ms. Cali Fornia lived in San Pedro, California. (October 28, 1931.)

Mr. Ten Million lived in Seattle, Washington. (1929.)

Mr. Thrift of **Keepit**, Australia won the £30,000 first prize in a lottery.

Helen Fernal lived in Portland, Oregon. (May 21, 1930.)

Nina Clock lived in St. Paul, Minnesota (June 3, 1931.)

Nellie May Fly probably did—she was married to a pilot in Fresno, California. (February 4, 1936.)

Another Smith of New York City signed his letters "Just Another." (August 29, 1932.)

William Williams lived on Williams Street in Williamsburg, Kansas. (May 13, 1936.)

Annie Rainer Shine resided in Luverne, Alabama. (March 3, 1933.)

Merry Christmas Day was born in Bellingham, Washington on December 5th, 1903. (December 25, 1932.)

England's River Wye was once known as the **We,** for it was fed by three springs named I, **Thou,** and **He.**

Dina Might kept things bright in Flint Michigan (September 22, 1932.)

Iccolo Miccolo played the piccolo for the Los Angeles Philharmonic Orchestra. (July 26, 1935.)

A. Fish was a fish distributor in Oregon. (November 20, 1932.)

Dr. Besick was a doctor in Chicago, Illinois.

H. E. Passmore was a
Deputy Customs Inspector in
San Francisco, California.

Dr. H. A. Toothacre worked as a dentist for the
Burlington Iowa Independent School District.
(November 30, 1932.)

The Clipper Brothers worked as barbers in Bakersfield,
California. (November 9, 1951.)

George Kopman was a police officer in San Francisco, California.
(April 22, 1935.)

H. M. Balmer was a funeral director in Fort Collins, Colorado. (November
8, 1934.)

B. R. Parsons: a parson who lived in the parsonage on Parson Street in Sarnac
Michigan. (October 13, 1935.)

A. C. Current was an electrical contractor in Tontogany, Ohio. His son's name?
D. C. Current. (December 16, 1931.)

Jack Frost sold refrigerators in Washington D.C. (February 12, 1931.)

I. Teller worked as an information clerk at New York City's Hudson Terminal
Post Office. (March 9, 1935.)

Mr. Tuf owned the Tuf Steak Market in Lexington, Oklahoma.

Sam Heller was a ham seller in Richmond, Virginia. (March 30, 1931.)

Doctor Lawyer was a mayor in Ironwood, Michigan. (August 6, 1947.)

Iona Fiddle of St. Paul, Minnesota, never did... own a fiddle, that is.
(February 23, 1935.)

Mr. A. Ball Pitcher of Melrose Park, Illinois never pitched a
ball. (September 23, 1933.)

Deep C. Fisher hated fishing. He was a real estate
agent in San Francisco.

Austin Graham Dodge of Myrtle Point,
Oregon drove a Buick!

Question: where do
North, South, East,
and West come to-
gether? Answer: in
Eureka, California-
over a hand of
bridge! Buddies **Bill
North, Doug
South, Ivan East,**
and **Bill West** met
regularly to play
cards. (October 14,
1951.)

Alexander, Graham, and Bell:
telephone operators.
**Jeanette Alexander,
Loretta Graham,** and
Bonnie Bell worked for the
Newcastle, Indiana telephone
company. (May 10, 1954.)

Les Cool and **Les
Hot** worked together
at Rabeck Music
Company in Olympia,
Washington. (July 28,
1953.)

Did she love him for his name? In 1938 **Miss Birdie Snyder** married **C. Canary** and became **Birdie Canary** (January 6, 1938.)

A. WELCOME GUEST LIVES IN Eureka, Calif.

He was Welcome wherever he went! **A. Welcome Guest** lived in Eureka, California… and he was Welcome there, too! (March 5, 1961.)

A. SICKMAN IS A DOCTOR
—Lock No. 4, Pa.

CONNEC**T**ICUT
I**D**A**H**O
TENN**E**SS**FF**
KAN**S**AS
SOUTH DAKOTA
MARYL**A**ND
MISSOU**R**I
WI**S**CONSIN
GEORGI**A**
ARKA**N**SAS
RHO**D**E ISLAND
NEBRA**S**KA
WASHING**T**ON
VI**R**GINIA
I**O**WA
PENNSYLVANIA
MINN**E**SOTA
LOUI**S**IANA
OREGON
FLORIDA
NOR**T**H DAKOTA
O**H**IO
KENTUCKY
UTAH
MAINE
MICH**I**GAN
MON**T**ANA
NEW J**E**RSEY
DELAWARE
MAS**S**ACHUSETTS
TEXAS
ARIZONA
WEST **V**IRGINIA
N**E**W HAMPSHIRE
SOUTH CAROLINA
ILLINOI**S**
NOR**T**H CAROLINA
OKL**A**HOMA
N**E**VADA
I**N**DIANA
CALI**F**ORNIA
WY**O**MING
VER**M**ONT
MISSISSI**PP**I
NEW M**E**XICO
AL**A**BAMA
COLORADO
NEW YORK

Alphabet Girl

Liverpool Laundryman Arthur Pepper got ambitious when it came to naming his new baby daughter. Not wanting any letter of the alphabet to feel jealous at being left out, he used all of them, naming the child **Anna Bertha Cecilia Diana Emily Fanny Gertrude Hypatia Inez Jane Kate Louise Maude Nora Ophelia Prudence Quince Rebecca Sarah Teresa Ulysis Venus Winifred Xenophon Yetty Zeno Pepper.** They usually just called her Alphabet Pepper for short.

MELVIN M. STRAUBE, Paris, Mo.
HIS WHITE HAIR AND BEARD TURNED **BLACK** AT THE AGE OF 73

Harde and **Sharpe** were members of the New York Stock exchange.

Sweet and **Sauer** were business partners in Chico, California.

Love, Sunshine, and **Bliss** once owned a candy store in Johnstown, Pennsylvania.

Harry G. Faith and **Clide E. Sin** were roommates at the Colorado Sanitarium in Los Angeles, California. (July 13, 1954.)

Mrs. Harold E. Rich of Gary, Indiana was the daughter of **Mrs. Harley W. Poore.** (December 28, 1967.)

Once upon a time, the mayor of Gaastra, Michigan was **Looney.** The town clerk was **Battey.**

I. M. Wiser was married to **May B. Wise**r in Washington D.C. Their child was a little Wiser. (May 2, 1941.)

Ms. B. A. Gentleman lived in Kendall, Florida.

I. Etta Hamburger lived in Madison, Wisconsin.

A. Fortunat Mann lived in Indianapolis, Indiana.

AB C Defghi lived in Villa Park Illinois. (May 28, 1935.)

Monsieur Wzs lived in the French village of Ws.

Ed Ek of Brockton, Massachusetts, once held the record for the shortest name in the United States.

Z. Z. Zizz was an engineer on the Northern Pacific Railroad.

In Sweden, there is a city named **A.**

In the Netherlands, on the Zuyder Zee, there is a bay called **Y.**

The river **Aa** runs through Pas de Calais, France.

SIGNATURE OF
D. SHARP
RADIO TENOR,
Station KFBK,
Sacramento, Calif.

❗ *Between February 15 and April 15, 1931, Judge J. C. Davis of Dillon County, South Carolina married the following couples:*

Ransome Blue to **Elizabeth Redd**
Russian White to **Mary Ann Black**
Nathaniel Green to **Amanda Brown**
Solomon Gray to **Josephine Orange**
Navy Blue to **Aurelia Chocolate**
Josephus Drab to **Blanche Walnut**
Willie Lemon to **Juanita Tann**

Shakespeare Couldn't Spell His Own Name!

The immortal bard was no slouch when it came to drama, but he seemed to have a bit of trouble spelling his own name. In his will, he writes, "I, William Shackspeare." Yet in another instance, he calls himself, "Shakspeare." And even, "Wilm Shaxpr." Robert Ripley came to the conclusion that there were 4,000 different ways to spell the man's name, none of them authenticated. What follows is but a smidgen of the total:

SHAKESPEARE	SHAKSPARE	SHAXPERE
SHAXPUR	SAXPERE	SHAKESPER
SCHAKESPEIRE	SHACKSPEARE	CHACSPER
SHAGSPERE	SHACKSPIRE	SHAKEYSPEERE
SHAXESPUR	SHAXKESPEYR	CHACKESPEARE
SCHAXPEIRE	SHAXEPER	CHACSPEAR

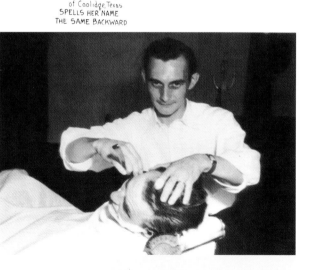

Drawn by Fred Williams

NILWON NOWLIN
of Coolidge, Texas
SPELLS HER NAME
THE SAME BACKWARD

• • • • • • • • • • • • • ▶
Would you trust a razor to someone named Cutlip?
Howard Cutlip worked as a barber in Dump's Barbershop, Spencerville, Ohio. (August 1,1949.)

❗ *How do you pronounce the name*
PHTHOLOGNYRRH?
It's "Turner."

Phth	*as in* phythsic	= T
olo	*as in* colonel	= ur
gn	*as in* gnat	= n
yrrh	*as in* myrrh	= er

Welcome to HOT COFFEE

BELIEVE IT OR NOT! IN MISSISSIPPI THERE IS A TOWN CALLED "HOT COFFEE" and in FLORIDA THERE IS A TOWN CALLED "TWO EGG"!

The 1792 Family

lives in Coulomiers, France. At the time Robert Ripley discovered them (in the 1920s) the family had three sons: January 1792, February 1792, and April 1792. A fourth son, March 1792, died in September 1904.

Mattie L. Coffin, who lived behind a **graveyard** in Beltsville, Maryland, claimed that her "neighbors" suited her because they were always peaceful and quiet. (June 23, 1936.)

Mr. Block & Mr. Cleaver owned a butcher shop in Toronto, Ontario. (July 29th, 1948.)

Meet Abraham Kaleialohakahohoholokuakiniokeanuenueonalanialiikoulana Imihia Kealohu.

His middle name means, "The Wreath of Love, Bearing the Colors of the Rainbow of the Heavens, Which a Swift Running Messenger is Carrying from the Great King." His third name means "Seeker of Mysterious Objects." His last name means "Beloved One." (September 11, 1949.)

A BABY BOY BORN IN TORO, Central Africa, TO A MOTHER WHOSE FIRST SON DIED IN INFANCY, WAS GIVEN THE NAME "BITAKARAMIRE", MEANING, "I EXPECT WE WILL LOSE THIS ONE TOO"—THE CHILD SURVIVED

Chargoggagoggmanchauga goggchaubunagungamaug is the local Native American name for a lake in Massachusetts. Its name translates as, "You fish on your side; I fish on my side; nobody fishes in the middle."

Death Becomes Him

J.R. Wilson of Salt Lake City, Utah worked the graveyard shift in the **Coffin Mine,** at the head of **Deadman's Gulch,** near **Tombstone Flat,** in the **Funeral Range,** 25 miles from **Poison Springs,** in **Death Valley.**

Ripley makes a stop in a Welsh town with the **second longest name in the world.** The longest name in the world belongs to a town in new Zealand. Photo circa 1933.

Graves and Toombs belong together! **Kim Ann Graves** married **Jackie Gerald Toombs, Jr.** on July 14th, 1979. (February 2, 1980.)

When little **Kananinoheaokuuhomeopu-ukaimanaalohilohinokeaweawealamakaokalani** was born in Honolulu in 1936, he held the record for the longest name. His name contains 63 letters, more than five times the number of the Hawaiian alphabet. The boy's sister, shown holding him, says that his name means, "The Beautiful Aroma of My Home at Sparkling Diamond Hill is Carried to the Eyes of Heaven." But they called him "Joe" for short. (November 22, 1936.)

Lawless lawman! **Greg Lawless** is a police officer with the Bellefontaine Police Department in Bellefontaine, Ohio. (December 13, 1973.)

Mrs. Triplett had Twins! Mrs. Wendell Triplett of Quincy, Illinois gave birth to twin sons on November 14th, 1950.

Sign for hungry travelers in Kent, England. Submitted by J. Carmichael of Toronto, Canada. (September 30, 1972.)

KUMARREKSITUTEESKENTELEENTUVAISEHKOLLAISMAISEKKUUDELLISENNESKENTELUTTELEMATTOMAMMUUKSISSANSAKAANKOPAHAN
IS A FINNISH WORD of **103** LETTERS — Meaning "TO BOW"

TO HELL WITH RIPLEY!

Highway to Hell: Ripley going completely to Hell, Norway, 1928.

Ripley went to all kinds of extremes in his relentless pursuit of the weird, but who'd have thought he'd go to Hell for it? Well, in 1927, he did. In his 1929 *Omnibus*, he wrote, "I admit that it had been so often suggested that I go there, that a year or so ago I did. And I liked it very much." Hell is a lovely little rural village in Norway, located on the Trondhjem Fjord near the city of Trondhjem. On his Scandinavian journey, Rip unashamedly let himself go completely to Hell, writing of this pastoral purgatory, "Beautiful wild flowers illuminate a velvety green carpet of grass that rolls down a 'gentle slope' to the fjord ('gentle slope' is the correct meaning of the word 'Hell' in Norwegian.)" Ripley even went so far as to slyly proclaim that Scandinavian maidens were the most beautiful in the world.

Ripley came away from his Hellish experience with a penchant for Akvavit with a beer chaser, and an understanding of the Scandinavian toast, "SKÅL", an acronym which means:

Skonhet = Beauty
Karlek = Love
Ålderdom = Long life
Lycka = Happiness

"Go to Hell!" Ripley urged, "I mean it!"

Ripley poses before the train station in Hell, Norway for a photo he sent back to his secretary, Cygna Conley, who first came to his attention as a "fast-talker" on his radio show before she began working for him.

To Cygna— With the WARMEST REGARDS from Rip IN HELL NORWAY -1928 BELIEVE IT OR NOT

Peculiar PLACES

THE GREAT LAKE OF SODA
EAST AFRICA

MYSTERIOUS LAKE 22 MILES LONG AND 10 MILES WIDE WITH A CRUST 8 FT. THICK OF PURE BAKING SODA - THE SAME AS USED BY HOUSEWIVES. — THE SODA IS REPLACED FASTER THAN MACHINERY CAN REMOVE IT!

SACRED SOURCE!
OF THE PLATANIA RIVER
THIS FAMOUS RIVER OF OLYMPIA, GREECE FLOWS OUT OF THE HEART OF A TREE!
INSIDE OF ITS TRUNK IS A CHAPEL LIGHTED BY A LANTERN WHICH HAS BEEN BURNING FOR THE PAST 2000 YEARS

Ripley's Believe It or Not! for New Year's Day, Sunday, January 1, 1939 depicts the lantern-lit tree housing the sacred spring that becomes Greece's Platania River.

HALEMAUMAU
The "HOUSE of EVERLASTING FIRE"
3000 FEET WIDE — 1000 FEET DEEP
THE FIRE PIT OF KILAUEA VOLCANO, HAWAII — ONE OF THE MOST STUPENDOUS SPECTACLES ON EARTH
ALTHOUGH KILAUEA IS THE LARGEST ACTIVE VOLCANO IN THE WORLD - ITS CRATER CONTAINS A HOTEL, U.S. MILITARY CAMP AND LANDING FIELD

! *A statue stands in Budapest, Hungary, in honor of a great 12th-century historian. We must assume he was great, at least, because no one remembers who he was!*

Ripley stands at the Center of the Universe in Beijing's Forbidden City during a visit to China in 1932.

PARAMECIUM
A SINGLE CELLED ANIMAL WAS NEVER BORN NOR DIES AND WILL NEVER DIE
IT MERELY DIVIDES INTO 2 SEPARATE ORGANISMS

The CENTER
OF THE WORLD — HUB OF THE UNIVERSE
"ALTAR OF THE MOST HIGH GOD"
THE CENTER STONE IN THE HIGHEST PLATFORM OF THIS REMARKABLE ALTAR IS CONSIDERED THE CENTER OF THE UNIVERSE BY THE CHINESE

The ONLY PLACE ON EARTH WHERE EVERYBODY WEARS A HALO!
Vethylensa Fjord, Iceland
A PERSON PEERING INTO THE FOG SEES HIS REFLECTION SURROUNDED BY A CONCENTRIC RAINBOW IN BRILLIANT COLORS!

WHO WAS THE FIRST NATION TO OFFER THE INFANT UNITED STATES ITS FRIENDSHIP?
Answer Next Sunday

IS THE ONLY OUTSIDER TO SIGN THE DECLARATION OF INDEPENDENCE!
HE WAS NOT A DELEGATE ON INDEPENDENCE DAY (1776) AND WAS PERMITTED TO SIGN AS A UNIQUE HONOR 4 MONTHS LATER

BLACK SANDS OF KALAPANA
ONE OF THE STRANGEST AND MOST BEAUTIFUL BEACHES IN THE WORLD IS THIS UNUSUAL JET-BLACK BEACH MADE OF DISINTEGRATED LAVA
- TRULY A LONG TO BE REMEMBERED SIGHT AS THE FOAMING TURQUOISE SEA CRASHES AND WITHDRAWS LEAVING THE SANDS GLISTENING

THE POWDER RIVER in Wyoming
DURING LIGHTNING STORMS
ACTUALLY EXPLODES LIKE GUNPOWDER-
THE INDIANS GAVE THE RIVER ITS NAME BECAUSE
THEY THOUGHT IT CONTAINED GUNPOWDER, BUT THE
EXPLOSIONS ARE CAUSED BY LIGHTNING TOUCHING
OFF BUBBLES OF NATURAL GAS IN THE WATER

THE PATH THAT IS ALWAYS GREEN !
THE GREEN WAY
between Winterbourne and Clarendon, England,
IS COVERED WITH THICK GREEN GRASS
EVEN IN WINTER - WHEN THE REST OF THE
COUNTRYSIDE IS BURIED UNDER SNOW

! *In 1927, the thermometer registered 158.8°F in the Oasis of the Tuaregs in Northern Africa.*

THE CASTLE OF CELLE-LES-BORDES
in the forest of Rambouillet, France,
HAS THOUSANDS OF ANTLERS AND
OTHER TROPHIES OF THE CHASE
COVERING THE WALLS, CEILINGS AND
EVEN LINING THE STAIRWAYS
-OF EVERY ROOM AND HALLWAY

NATURE'S
BEAUTY
PARLOR
THE WATERS OF SOAP LAKE,
Washington, TINT BATHERS'
HAIR STRAWBERRY BLONDE

THE SACRED BRIDGE AT NIKKO,
- RESERVED FOR THE GODS ALONE !
WAS DYED RED WITH HUMAN BLOOD

THE 5 CHAPELS
of the Capucine Church,
in Rome, Italy,
ARE LINED WITH HUMAN
SKELETONS AND BONES
-SOME OF THE SKELETONS
ATTIRED AS MONKS

The Lake Above the Clouds

Ripley wrote in 1929 of his visit to Lake Titicaca, the "Wash Basin of the Gods." He called it the strangest body of water on earth. Titicaca is nearly as large as Lake Erie, yet its elevation is higher than two Mount Washingtons stacked one atop the other. Rip wrote of the lake that the Incas held sacred: "Here it is possible to utterly lose sight of land, although on top of the Andes Mountains and in the center of a continent. Its waters are mysterious... iron will not rust in it, eggs will not boil in it, and only one kind of fish will live in it." Rip sailed Titicaca in the ship Goya, which had been built in England, sailed to Peru, taken apart, carted piece by piece over a mountain pass 17,000 feet high, and reassembled on Titicaca's shores.

THE STANDLEY CHASM IN THE
MacDonnell Mountains of Australia,
20 FEET WIDE AND 500 FEET DEEP,
IS A CLEFT SO DARK THAT A MAN
STANDING AT THE BOTTOM OF IT
CAN SEE STARS IN THE DAYTIME

CITY OF **THE DEAD**

MESHED — IRAN

A PERSIAN CITY PAVED WITH TOMBSTONES

THE SPACE AROUND THE SHRINE IS ONE VAST GRAVEYARD PEOPLE PAY FROM $50 TO $500 FOR THE PRIVILEGE OF INTERMENT WITHIN ITS SACRED PRECINCTS

THE PERILOUS PAGODA OF MOUNT BA DEN
Indo-China
IT WAS CARVED OUT OF SOLID STONE BENEATH A HUGE BOULDER SO DELICATELY BALANCED THAT *IT TEETERS TO AND FRO AT THE TOUCH OF A FINGER*

THE **PULPIT** OF THE CHURCH OF TRAUNKIRCHEN, Austria
— A FISHING PARISH —
IS SHAPED LIKE A BASKET OF FISH, FROM WHICH WATER APPEARS TO BE CASCADING

THE **TREE** OF **FEAR** near Palma, Spain
WHICH FOR **400** YEARS HAS BORNE FRUIT ONLY WHEN *"FRIGHTENED" IN THE SPRING BY DRUMS AND RATTLES*

Residents of Palma on the Spanish Island of Mallorca gather around this olive tree every spring with drums and rattles to "frighten" it into blossoming with a horrendous racket. They have done this every spring for 400 years, claiming that without this noisy jump-start, the tree would not bear fruit.

! **Forecast: Rain — For the Next Million Years:** There's a small stretch of land near the Parana River in Paraguay where rain has been falling ceaselessly for millions of years.

! *Le Cimetiere des Noyes (The Graveyard of the Drowned Ones) in the Archipelago of Glenans in the Department of Finistere, France, is the final resting place for victims of the sea. The graveyard is located on the bottom of Forest Bay, which is completely submerged every time the tide comes in.*

THE **MONTECITO GRAPEVINE**

LARGEST IN THE WORLD ~ COVERING 10,000 SQ. FT.

GROWN FROM A RIDING WHIP, FASHIONED FROM A GRAPEVINE AND GIVEN TO THE BEAUTIFUL SEÑORITA MARCELINA FELIZ BY HER LOVER. SHE PLANTED THE WHIP AS A MEMENTO OF THEIR PLIGHTED FAITH!

A **BIRD REFUGE** near Stonewall, Manitoba, HAS A 400-YARD POND *IN THE SHAPE OF A DUCK* Submitted by PAM DE WEESE, Long Beach, New York

Duck-shaped pond inside a bird sanctuary east of Stonewall, Manitoba. Photographer Robert R. Taylor took this aerial photo just as the sun lit up the duck pond's surface. (March 31, 1974.)

! *Old Granny Kempoch, a stone in Gourock, Scotland, was regarded with such fear in the 17th century that nine persons suspected of plotting to throw it into the sea were burned at the stake.*

The PALACE OF A THOUSAND GATES
TOMB OF AKBAR
EACH GATE INDICATES A NOBLE VIRTUE OF THE GREAT RULER
996 GATES ARE FALSE · 4 ARE TRUE GATES
The CATAFALQUE of AKBAR STANDS IN SOLITARY GLORY
ON THE TOP TERRACE OPEN TO THE SKY. AT ONE TIME
THE FAMOUS KOH-I-NOOR DIAMOND WAS INCRUSTED ON TOP

THE HALL FIREPLACE
IN RABY CASTLE,
near Durham, England,
HAS HAD A BLAZE IN IT
CONSTANTLY FOR 700 YEARS

The CITY OF NO CHILDREN! (1816)
WHEN THE SOVEREIGN CITY OF RAGUSA, Dalmatia, WAS CONQUERED
BY THE AUSTRIANS — IT DECIDED *NOT* TO BEAR THE ALIEN YOKE.
SO SECRETLY THEY VOWED NOT TO HAVE CHILDREN —
WITH THE RESULT THAT THEY DIED OUT COMPLETELY IN 2 GENERATIONS

THE CELEBRATED **LATIN PUN** of **DEAN SWIFT**
Latin	English
MOLLIS ABUTI	MOLL IS A BEAUTY
HAS AN ACUTI	HAS AN ACUTE EYE

Believe It or Not!
IN Cornwall, England,
THERE IS A
PET CEMETERY
WITH A SECTION
DEVOTED ENTIRELY
TO ELECTRONIC
"TAMAGOTCHI" PETS!

IT'S COOL, MAN!
FULLY DRESSED DINERS
on the Greek island of Mykonos
OFTEN EAT IN SEASIDE
RESTAURANTS AT TABLES
*THAT ARE PARTIALLY
UNDER WATER*

NAN MADOL,
A 700-YEAR-OLD CITY IN
THE ISLANDS OF MICRONESIA, IS A
POPULAR TOURIST CENTER WITH
8,000 VISITORS A YEAR, YET
THERE ARE NO HOTELS AND
TOURISTS NEVER STAY
OVERNIGHT BECAUSE OF
AN ANCIENT
CURSE!
WARNING
VISITORS
MUST
LEAVE BY
SUNDOWN

THE MOST HAZARDOUS BRIDGE IN THE WORLD!
The ADUNG RIVER BRIDGE on the border between Burma and Tibet
CONSISTS ONLY OF A ROPE 150 FEET IN LENGTH
STRUNG 40 FEET ABOVE THE WATER
WOMEN CROSS THE BRIDGE WITH BABIES STRAPPED TO
THEIR BACKS BY HAULING THEMSELVES ACROSS THE SPAN WHILE
HANGING UPSIDE DOWN IN A CANE RING BENEATH THE ROPE!

THE SKY BATHERS
A HOTEL ON HONSHU, JAPAN'S WAKAYAMA PENINSULA,
OFFERS HOT-SPRING BATHS IN A CABLE CAR
AS IT TRAVERSES A DEEP GORGE

The BLOOD SPRING - Glastonbury, Eng.
IT IS BELIEVED THAT ST. JOSEPH OF ARIMATHEA
BROUGHT THE **HOLY GRAIL** TO ENGLAND **1900** YEARS AGO AND BURIED IT HERE
RED WATER ISSUES FORTH CONTINUOUSLY
FROM THIS SPRING - ALTHOUGH
THE CUP IS NOT VISIBLE TO ANY
BUT THE PURE AND HOLY
Luke 23:50

BIG BIRTHA!

The **HOLY CANNON** of BATAVIA, Java
—TO WHICH JAVANESE WOMEN PRAY FOR BABIES
They come from all parts of the Island to worship - Bringing gifts of Incense and Flowers

RESTAURANT DINERS in Zahle a resort town in Lebanon, SIT AT TABLES THAT STRADDLE BRANCHES OF THE BARDUNI RIVER

Believe It or Not! YOU COULD GO TO JAIL JUST for BEING A TOURIST! TOURISTS VISITING London's Bixtum Priory CAN STAY OVERNIGHT IN A CELL AND HAVE A TYPICAL PRISONER'S BREAKFAST BEFORE THEY'RE RELEASED THE NEXT MORNING.

A monument to a bed stands in Columbia, South Carolina. Submitted to Ripley's in 1939 by **Charles B. Walker.**

TO A BED — ON WHICH MOST OF US ARE — BORN — DIE — AND SPEND SOME OF OUR SUBLIMEST MOMENTS.

Ripley's cartoon for November 18, 1945 features the beautiful torii gateways that grace Japan.

OUR SOLDIERS OF OCCUPATION WILL SEE THE FAMOUS "BIRD ROOST" MIYAJIMA - INLAND SEA OF JAPAN -
TORIIS - MEANING BIRD RESTS -ARE PLACED BEFORE ALL SHINTO SHRINES AND SACRED SPOTS.
THE TORII WAS ORIGINALLY A PERCH FOR SACRED FOWL THAT HERALDED THE RISING SUN

TOMB OF SANTA CLAUS
SANTA CLAUS REALLY LIVED — HE WAS THE BISHOP OF MYRA - IN ASIA MINOR.
HE DIED DEC. 6, 342 A.D. AND IS BURIED IN THE CHURCH OF ST. NICHOLAS, BARI, ITALY.
ST. NICHOLAS WAS NOT ONLY THE PATRON SAINT OF CHILDREN -BUT OF THIEVES AND PAWNBROKERS

DRAWN IN BARI, ITALY CHURCH OF "SAN NICOLA" 1937

Copr. 1942, King Features Syndicate, Inc., World rights reserved

THE STATUE of EMPEROR MARCUS AURELIUS IN ROME, ITALY, WAS USED IN THE MIDDLE AGES AS A GALLOWS-- CRIMINALS WERE HANGED BY A ROPE LOOPED AROUND THE HORSE'S HEAD

A VACATION DOWN BELOW

JULES' UNDERSEA LODGE (named after "Twenty Thousand Leagues Under the Sea" author Jules Verne) IS LOCATED IN A FORMER MARINE RESEARCH CENTER OFF FLORIDA'S KEY LARGO. FOR $295 A NIGHT, GUESTS CAN ENJOY ALL THE COMFORTS OF HOME -- WHILE GAZING AT LIFE UNDERSEAS, 30 FEET DOWN

THE BLACK HOLE OF CALCUTTA

"CALCUTTA, India, February 8, 1923: This city should be called "Calcootie." The hotel at which we stopped—and it ranks high—is without a rival, a bath, or a bedspring. It is not uncommon for a wealthy native to hire a servant to go to bed first and allow the bugs to bite their fill, so that when he retires later he may obtain a little rest. An army would be required at this hotel. I got up early this morning to get some rest! Recalling vaguely the story of the famous "Black Hole" of Calcutta, I hailed a ghari and was determined to see the historic place for myself and compare it with my hotel."

Upon arriving at the Black Hole of Calcutta, Ripley's visit to the teeming city went from merely itchy to decidedly somber. Ripley found himself gazing at a stout marble slab surrounded by a spiked iron fence. Directly below the slab there once had lain a dank underground prison cell in which 123 people had died an excruciating death—in one night.

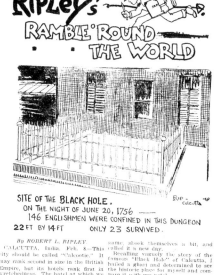

When the British East India Company founded the city of Calcutta in 1690, a number of native leaders harbored resentment against foreign domination. On June 20, 1756, the Nawab of Bengal, Siraj Ud Daua, captured Calcutta and imprisoned most of its British garrison. His means of dispatching his prisoners is one of the cruelest in history. He forced 146 soldiers into an guardroom 14-feet-long by 16-feet-wide, with only two small windows. After a night of excruciating confinement in intense heat, of the 146 who had gone into the "Black Hole", only 23 remained alive.

In 1901 Lord Gurzon, Viceroy and Governor-general of India had the prison sealed with a marble slab and marked with a plaque, a grim monument to those whose lives were taken by one of the cruelest means of torture ever devised, "the memory of which," Ripley wrote, "still makes an Englishman shudder."

Personal PROJECTS

Herman Melheim of Ray, Minnesota carved this grandfather clock from a single tree trunk using only an ordinary pocket knife. (April 8, 1947.)

Extraordinary Works from Ordinary Objects

Ripley displays yards of continuous wooden chain whittled by **H. T. Stewart** of Chicago, Illinois, from a single 20' by 1' plank. 1934.

How'd he do that? A wooden arrow pierces a glass bottle without shattering the glass. **Joseph Shagena** of Sebring, Florida created these seemingly impossible artifacts. He offered his works to Ripley's, including pierced light bulbs and perfume bottles, provided that the secret to their creation was sealed inside a vault. The secret remains locked away to this day. Circa 1986.

93 strands of thread through an ordinary sewing needle, by **Harold Blahnik** of Kewannee, Wisconsin. Circa 1960s.

The Mona Lisa on Toast: Tadhiko Okawa recreated Da Vinci's Mona Lisa and other famous works of art from pieces of burnt toast. Okawa creates these edible works by etching the picture on aluminum foil, wrapping each piece of toast in a section of foil, cutting out the design, then toasting it in a horizontal toaster.

Batfence: Old bats got a new lease on life when **J. Milton Beam** of Battle Creek, Michigan recycled them as a fence. (January 29, 1952.)

One of A Kind

"In the Beginning, there was the Word...": a portrait of Jesus made from the words of the Gospel, written in miniature, created by a Korean artist (name unknown) in the 1950s.

Symphony in Glass: **Billy Glass** of New York City built an entire orchestra out of plexiglass. (March 20, 1947.)

Bottle o' Bones: **Clarence W. Pearson** of Mt. Vernon, Illinois whittled the bones of this skeleton out of maple wood, then assembled them inside the bottle using tweezers, clamps, and wire. The project, which took 600 hours to complete, was displayed in Ripley's Odditorium at the New York World's Fair in 1939.

! **Vincent Hart** of *Clayton, Georgia lost both his arms decades ago. Yet he built his own two-story house. He even wall-papered it, wired it, and installed the plumbing.*

Do-It-Yourself Surgery: When **"Chief" Couzzingo** of Oxford, Ohio broke a rib, he calmly fastened it back to his breastbone using an ice pick, a screwdriver, and two 1" screws. He used no anesthesia whatsoever. The surgery was successful. While the rib healed, he took the screws out daily to sterilize them. He was 70 years old at the time of his self-surgery. (October 10, 1942.)

"A+" For Effort!

6,300 matches balanced on a beer bottle, without any artificial support, by **Jean Phipps, Carrie Welling, Dick Lightcap,** and **Dorothy Taylor** of Pittsburgh, Pennsylvania. (September 2, 1935.)

Stamp ball created with 4,655,000 ordinary-sized postage stamps. 32" in diameter and weighing 600 pounds, the ball is solid stamps throughout. Owned by the Father Flanagan Boys' Home in Boys' Town, Nebraska. (July 17, 1955.)

Drunkard's Calling Card

Impoverished artist William Gould got in the habit of exchanging his artwork for liquid refreshment at local public houses around Port Arthur, Australia. So great was his thirst, that eventually, every pub in Port Arthur boasted at least one Gould original!

A KNIFE WITH **384** BLADES
EACH BLADE IS DIFFERENT
Made by John Hayes, Limerick, Ireland

Francis Johnson of Darwin, Minnesota collected this enormous ball of twine singlehandedly. The ball required a railroad jack to lift, and sat chained to a tree in Johnson's yard for more than 40 years. It is now sheltered by the top of Johnson's own silo, and sits across the street from the Stringball Cafe, where visitors can purchase their very own Stringball T-shirt. (June 17, 1971 and March 18, 1979.)

T. **Rassmuson** of Victoria, British Columbia claimed that this chair he made from the antlers of moose he shot in Saskatchewan was quite comfortable. (January 19, 1950.)

Match Schtick

Matchstick "Peterbuilt" truck made by **Ken Applegate** of Florida, 1974

Countess Roza Branicka of Poland was diagnosed with terminal breast cancer at the age of 63. Doctors urged immediate surgery. Not wanting to alarm her family, the countess made several shopping trips to surgical supply stores in Switzerland and France over the following year. She purchased a scalpel, a lancet, and other surgical necessities, but only bought one item at a time, secretly, so as not to arouse suspicion. When she had accumulated all the necessary supplies, she locked herself in a Paris hotel suite and performed surgery on herself, successfully removing the cancerous tumor from her breast. She lived in excellent health for 19 years afterwards.

Close-up of the Reg Pollard matchstick Rolls Royce, showing the detail of the cockpit.

Fritz Meng of Bad Homburg, Germany built this violin using 8,000 matchsticks. He claimed that the violin's tone was perfect. (September 1, 1954.)

A phenomenal replica of a 1907 model Rolls Royce Silver Ghost, built in 1983 by **Reg Pollard,** out of more than one million matchsticks. The Rolls Royce can be seen at Ripley's Orlando, Florida Odditorium.

Faith and Luck: **Hildegard Horn** of Bethlehem, Pennsylvania placed a four-leaf clover on every page of her 1,046-page King James Bible. (January 17, 1971.)

London Tower Bridge, constructed from approximately 350,000 matchsticks, currently on display at Ripley's St. Augustine, Florida Odditorium. Built in 1980 by **Reg Pollard** of Manchester, England.

MASAKICHI
Lifelike Legacy

"Love and death are a strange combination," wrote Robert Ripley of Hananuma Masakichi, an ailing Japanese sculptor who, facing death, created a unique parting gift for the woman he loved. When the wood-carver discovered that he was dying of tuberculosis, he sought a way to keep the image of himself before his loved one, even after he could no longer be with her in the flesh. The image he offered her was so precise a replica of himself, that artists and anatomists alike cannot resist using words like "alive" and "human" to describe it.

Ensconced in his Yoko-hama studio before a set of adjustable mirrors, Masakichi assembled each part of his body separately from strips of dark wood. The figure is largely hollow inside. Some texts say that he used more than 2,000 individual strips of wood, others claim more than 5,000. But all marvel at the fact that when Masakichi assembled the parts together, using only dovetail joints, wooden pegs, and glue—not one metal nail—he joined them so expertly that no seam can be seen, even with a magnifying glass.

Masakichi handcrafted glass eyes to provide windows for his creation's soul. They are so precisely like his own that they baffle members of the optical profession. He painted and lacquered the statue's exterior to match the hue and texture of his own skin. He captured every nuance of muscle, sinew, bone and crease.

But it is what Masakichi did next that seems to cause the most astonishment among his admirers. The sculptor bored one minute hole for every pore on his body, plucked the corresponding hair from his own flesh, and inserted it in its exact position on the statue. He covered his creation with all of his own hair, from his

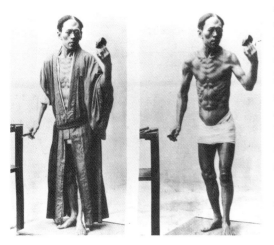

The famous double-image photograph depicting the wooden statue's remarkable likeness to its live creator. Hananuma Masakichi himself is on the left; the statue is on the right.

head, beard, body, even from the backs of his hands—millions of individual hairs in all. He added his own eyebrows and eyelashes. Then excruciatingly, painstakingly, he pulled out his own fingernails, toenails, and teeth, and carefully affixed them on his likeness.

The figure appears somewhat emaciated, as Masakichi, at 53, was already beginning to waste away from his consumptive disease. Yet the eyes are fiery and full of concentration. Masakichi sculpted himself in the act of sculpting: in its left hand the figure holds up a tiny mask, and appears to inspect its handiwork. In its right hand, the figure holds a sculpting tool. Masakichi placed his own spectacles on the statue's face, and wrapped his own loincloth around its waist.

In 1885, the figure was complete. Hananuma Masakichi held a private exhibition of his work. He stood beside his model to the utter confusion of the audience, who were unable to distinguish the artist from the statue. Ten years later he died in poverty, leaving behind a unique legacy, and willing all his worldly goods to the wooden image of himself.

Robert Ripley fell in love with the story of the Masakichi statue, and in 1934, he purchased it from an Asian curio shop. He displayed it in his Chicago Odditorium.

After Ripley's death in 1949, the Masakichi statue made the rounds to various Odditoriums, until it encountered the misfortune of being on display in Los Angeles in 1994, during the devastating Northridge earthquake. The statue fell from its pedestal and sustained considerable damage. Today, it rests in a quiet corner of Ripley's secret warehouse, gazing out upon row after row of oddities, awaiting a day when a sculptor whose hands match the skill of Hananuma Masakichi can restore it to lifelike perfection.

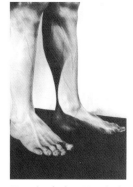

"Detail of the Masakichi statue showing veins, pores, and the artist's own toenails.

Queer CUSTOMS

The DANCING CORPSES
A WEALTHY NATIVE OF THE **KAPSIKI** TRIBE—AFRICA IS PREPARED AFTER DEATH FOR THE GAY LIFE A PERSON OF STANDING IS EXPECTED TO LEAD IN THE NEXT WORLD BY HOISTING THE CORPSE ON THE SHOULDERS OF THE VILLAGE BLACKSMITH —AND GIVING IT A DANCING LESSON THAT LASTS FOR HOURS!

The Tlingit Tribe of Alaska cremated all their dead except shamans, whom they believed would not burn. Shamans were embalmed and placed in primitive shelters, along with a slave sacrificed to serve them in the afterlife. (Submitted by Emery F. Tobin of Vancouver, Washington.)

A South Sea Islands cannibal skull. Cannibals rarely ate the heads of their victims, but skulls were considered powerful talismans and prized trophies.

Ripley's owns an impressive collection of silver, brass and jewel-trimmed Tibetan skull bowls. Ripley's president, **Bob Masterson**, keeps his business cards in one.

A Peruvian Moche Indian head with skin still intact. The man's testicles hang from a string fed through a hole bored in his skull. Circa. 1000 A.D.

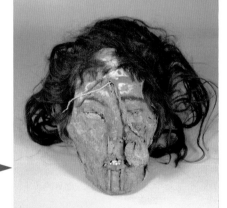

A Peruvian Moche Indian skull with parrot feathers inserted in the cranium, copper eyes and ponytail, on display in Ripley's Dallas museum. One of the oldest anthropological exhibits in Ripley's collection. Circa 800 A.D.

WIDOWS' WEEDS IN THE TIRIO TRIBE OF NEW GUINEA, COMPRISE AN ACTUAL COVERING OF WEEDS **FROM HEAD TO TOE**

A feather-decorated cannibal skull from the South Sea Islands.

Robert Ripley once owned this Tibetan skull drum. Made by monks, the drum is covered in lizard skin and studded with silver and turquoise. Purchased in 1937.

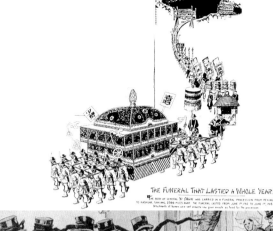

THE FUNERAL THAT *LASTED A WHOLE YEAR!*
THE BODY OF GENERAL *SU CHUN* WAS CARRIED IN A FUNERAL PROCESSION FROM PEKING TO KASHGAR, SINKIANG, 2300 MILES AWAY. THE FUNERAL LASTED FROM JUNE 1ST, 1912 TO JUNE 1ST, 1913. Detachments of farmers were sent ahead to sow grain and vegetables along the route for the procession.

Present, but Not Voting

In 1929, Ripley wrote, in his first book, of an unusual custom that took place at the board of trustees meetings of University College Hospital in London. Jeremy Bentham, who founded the hospital in 1827, willed that he be allowed to attend every board meeting, in perpetuity. So, even though he died in 1832, every meeting of the board has found him sitting at the table: "His gaunt form is erect," Ripley wrote, "his sightless eyes stare outright, and his broad-brimmed beaver hat is never removed from the long locks that dangle down his shoulders." Jeremy was consulted on every pressing matter that came before the board, and when no answer came from his grinning teeth, he was recorded as "Present, but not voting."

A MUMMIFIED HAND CUT FROM THE BODY OF A HANGED MAN WAS USED BY BURGLARS IN ANCIENT ENGLAND IN THE BELIEF *IT COULD OPEN LOCKED DOORS*

MASKED MEN MEMBERS OF A RELIGIOUS FRATERNITY, COLLECT ALMS ON THE STREETS OF MALTA FOR 3 DAYS BEFORE THE EXECUTION OF EVERY CRIMINAL—TO PAY FOR THE CONDEMNED MAN'S FUNERAL

...RD of Asia, HE TIP OF ITS ...S 7 FEET

3-21

FUNERAL ON SKATES
IN THE LAND OF THE WENDS, ON THE RIVER SPREE IN GERMANY, A NETWORK OF LAKES AND STREAMS TAKES THE PLACE OF ROADS — MOURNERS IN FUNERAL PROCESSIONS *WEAR ICE SKATES IN WINTER — USE BOATS IN SUMMER*

Grave Robers

The natives of Imerina Province on the island of Madagascar don't believe in letting their dead lie in peace. Instead, every September they hold an annual ceremony of Famadiana, in which the bodies of the departed are dug up, provided with a new change of clothing, then either reinterred in the same spot or moved to a newer, showier spot, depending on the family's financial health. The ceremony is repeated annually until either the bereaved themselves die or there is nothing left to reclothe and rebury.

Tibetan ram's skull, jeweled and silver-plated. When the use of human skulls was outlawed in 1949, ram and monkey skulls were substituted.

SKULLS MADE OF CANDY AND SOLD ON A FIESTA DAY IN MEXICO, ARE GIVEN BY YOUTHS TO GIRLFRIENDS AS A SIGN OF THEIR HIGH REGARD

YOUTHS in Lapland, PRACTICE LASSOING REINDEER ON FRIENDS WHO DASH ABOUT HOLDING ANTLERS TO THEIR HEAD

New Guinea clay-covered ancestor skull.

THE MOST HAZARDOUS SAFE CONDUCT PASS IN HISTORY

ANY TURKISH SUBJECT WITH A GRIEVANCE AGAINST THE GRAND VIZIER COULD WIN AN IMMEDIATE AUDIENCE WITH THE RULER BY BALANCING UPON HIS HEAD *A BLAZING FIRE POT*

BUT IT WAS ONLY A ONE-WAY PASS -- AND IF HE FAILED TO PROVE HIS COMPLAINT *HE WAS IMMEDIATELY BEHEADED*

THE 6-HORSE SLEIGH used by the mother of Czar Peter the Great, of Russia, WAS ALWAYS ACCOMPANIED BY 12 GROOMS-ONE FOR EACH HORSE-AND 6 OTHERS WHO PUSHED THE SLEIGH TO INCREASE ITS SPEED -ALL THE GROOMS HAD TO RUN STEADILY FOR MILES

In the Komti caste of Bellalpur, India, a girl is purchased in the marriage market at the rate of 100 rupees ($21) for each year of her age, up to the age of ten. Once she passes the age of ten, she is considered worthless and must be content to marry anyone who desires her.

! The Human Pincushion

The rural population of Wottawa, Bohemia holds an annual pin-sticking contest to determine who will hold each years title of Human Pincushion. Bagro, king of the local gypsy tribe, carried off the honors in 1928 by embedding 3,200 needles in his arm for 31 hours. This heroic feat has not been equaled either before or since.

! *Among the Thais of Vietnam, a baby boy must decide his future vocation on his first birthday. Symbols of various occupations are put in front of him and the object he first grasps will determine his life's work.*

Library Propriety

Lady Gough, distinguished blue-nose of England, wrote a book on etiquette in 1863, on page 80 of which appears this passage:

The perfect hostess will see to it that the works of male and female authors are properly separated on her bookshelves. Their proximity unless they happen to be married should not be tolerated.

TEENAGERS in the Sudan, Africa, MUST WEAR A HEADDRESS FROM WHICH 3 SHELLS DANGLE IN FRONT OF THEIR FACE THEY HAVE TO WALK IN A DIGNIFIED MANNER OR THE SHELLS WILL BOUNCE AGAINST THEIR NOSE

TWINS in the Yoruba Tribe of Africa ARE CONSIDERED WITH SUCH RESPECT THAT A MOTHER CARRYING HER TWINS MUST BE GIVEN A GIFT BY EVERY PASSERBY SHE GREETS

WOMEN OF THE BALANTA Tribe, in Binar, Portuguese Guinea, ANNUALLY PERFORM A DANCE IN WHICH THEY BALANCE ON THEIR HEADS A HUGE BASKET CONTAINING THEIR HUSBAND OR SWEETHEART

! *Rumanian peasants believe that a man suffering from rheumatism can recover his full health by having a trained bear walk back and forth on his back for half an hour!*

ENGLISH SCHOOLBOYS WERE FORCED IN THE 1800s TO WRITE HOLIDAY GREETINGS TO THEIR PARENTS TO DEMONSTRATE THEIR WRITING ABILITY--AND THESE WERE ACTUALLY THE FIRST ENGLISH CHRISTMAS CARDS

© 1979 King Features Syndicate, Inc. World rights reserved.

MARRIED MEN in the Akela Tribe, Africa ALWAYS CUT THEIR MEAT INTO SMALL CHUNKS WITH A KNIFE HELD BETWEEN THEIR TOES -BECAUSE BEFORE THEIR WEDDING THEY WERE REQUIRED TO KNOCK OUT ALL THEIR OWN TEETH!

116

A **TREE** CUT DOWN IN SWEDEN, BY LAW, MUST BE REPLACED BY A NEW PLANTING

TINGUIANS of the Philippines PLAY THE FLUTE WITH THEIR NOSES

On request, sent with stamped, addressed envelope, Mr. Ripley will furnish proof of anything depicted by him
Copyright, 1935, King Features Syndicate, Inc., Great Britain Rights Reserved.

Sinkies of the World, Unite!

Believe It or Not, there is an "International Association of Sinkies"—people who like to eat over the sink—based in Santa Rosa, California! (April 23, 1996.)

It was customary in ancient Egypt for a man to carry a skeleton around the table at the end of a meal.

! *Since 1837, there has been an annual world Black Pudding Championship held in Ramsbottom, England, which challenges contestants to hurl black pudding onto the roof of a pub! (October 26, 1996.)*

A **PLACE** IS SET AT THE TABLE IN POLAND ON CHRISTMAS EVE TO ACCOMMODATE ANY STRANGER WHO MIGHT DROP IN

5 CLAMS FOUND IN ONE SHELL by Joseph D. Salo Santa Rosa

SIAMESE CUCUMBER Grown at Pearl Harbor Lake Washington Washington

THE **HEJNAL** OR "BROKEN NOTE" FAMOUS HISTORIC SIGNAL OF POLAND

SIGNATURE FRANK J. LOGUE NEW YORK CITY

THE OFFICIAL TOWN DRUNK
AN ELECTED OFFICIAL in ancient Sparta WAS REQUIRED TO GET INTOXICATED EVERY DAY AND REEL THROUGH THE STREETS *AS AN OBJECT LESSON FOR THE YOUNG CITIZENRY*

THE DINNER THAT MUST BE EATEN UNDERWATER
Hatta, India

A **SACRED POOL** IN WHICH ONCE EACH YEAR 5,000 PILGRIMS EAT A FULL MEAL *WHILE SWIMMING BENEATH ITS SURFACE*

LONG HAIR INDICATED NOBLE RANK AMONG THE ANCIENT GAULS, AND WHEN JULIUS CAESAR CONQUERED THEM *HE ORDERED THEIR HAIR CUT AS A SIGN OF SUBMISSION*

A **SADDLED HORSE** TO ENABLE EACH CALIPH OF BAGHDAD TO ESCAPE IN THE EVENT OF REVOLT WAS KEPT IN CONSTANT READINESS FROM 760 TO 1258 —A PERIOD OF 498 YEARS!

Count On It!

Instead of counting by tens as Westerners do, the people of the Min tribe, in western Papua-New Guinea, count by 27s. Where do they get the number 27? By counting not only on their fingers, but on various other body parts. They begin counting on the little finger of their left hand, then when they run out of fingers, they count the left wrist, forearm, elbow, bicep, shoulder, side of the neck, ear and eye—that's 13. The bridge of the nose makes 14. Then the right eye, ear, side of the neck, shoulder, bicep, elbow forearm, wrist and five fingers make a total of 27!

Ice sitting contest, held at White City Casino, Chicago, Illinois on July 31, 1933. The Winner, **Gus Simmons** (second from the right), was disqualified, even though he remained on his block of ice for 26 hours, because the judges discovered he was running a fever of 102.5°! This photo was featured on a Ripley's Believe It or Not! postcard in the early 1990s. (October 17, 1933.)

April 14, 1946: seven cheerful lads promote National Laugh Week. The second man from the right is **David Caidin** of New York City, World Champion Laugher. Caidin's laugh, which he could produce on demand, could be heard for three miles. Today, Ripley's holds an annual laughing contest.

WAS WORTH EXACTLY THE COST OF A HAM

THE FIRST PRESIDENTIAL POLLS
INFORMAL POLLS DETERMINING THE POPULARITY OF PRESIDENTIAL CANDIDATES WERE CONDUCTED BETWEEN 1880 AND THE 1900s BY PUTTING THEIR PICTURES ON CIGAR BOXES--AND THEN NOTING WHICH SOLD THE BEST.

THE MOST BURGLAR-PROOF "BANK VAULT" IN HISTORY!
MASUD I, KING of GHAZNA AND RULER of INDIA, ALWAYS CARRIED THE ENTIRE STATE TREASURY –AS MUCH AS $150,000,000– ON THE BACKS OF 3,000 PERSONALLY-TRAINED CAMELS!
EACH CAMEL OBEYED A DIFFERENT PASSWORD KNOWN ONLY TO THE KING, WHO WOULD GIVE A CREDITOR THE PROPER PASSWORD FOR A CAMEL CARRYING EXACTLY THE SUM HE WAS TO COLLECT— ONLY WHEN THE PROPER CODE WORD WAS UTTERED WOULD A CAMEL PERMIT ITSELF TO BE LED AWAY AND UNLOADED OF ITS PRECIOUS CARGO
(1030 - 1040)

GOOD LUCK CHARMS WERE WRITTEN BY TAOIST PRIESTS IN CHINA, AS A MEANS OF CURING ALL DISEASES-- *THEN THE FORMULA WAS BURNED BY THE PATIENT AND SWALLOWED*

Two Bad!

In the United States, the $2 bill is considered bad luck. The notion may have started with gamblers, who called the $2 bill a deuce, a slang term for the Devil. To rid themselves of the $2 bill's bad luck, gamblers would tear off a corner of the bill to form a triangle, which brought good luck. Each person receiving the bill must tear off a corner, or the bad luck stays with them. If you're the unlucky person who receives a bill with no corners left, you're supposed to tear it all up. Cashiers today still ask customers if they mind taking a $2 bill; some will even kiss it before handing it over.

JIVARO HEAD SHRINKING
An Ancient Secret is Exposed

Ripley holds a shrunken head with long hair. Ripley acquired the head in the 1920s, but it dates back to the 1800s. New York City Odditorium. Circa 1939.

Robert Ripley took delight in all kinds of strange customs, but he seemed to have a particular inclination towards the grislier rituals human beings inflicted upon one another. Ripley frequently wrote of the Jivaro Indians of the Amazon and their practice of head shrinking, a closely guarded tribal secret. Ripley recounted the legend of a red-bearded German scientist who disappeared into the Amazonian jungles, determined to learn the Jivaro's secret. The scientist was never seen alive again, so the story goes, but months later a trader arrived from Jivaro country offering for sale the red-bearded shrunken head of a white man!

The secret which that unfortunate German scientist (fictional or not) lost his life attempting to discover, you are now about to learn. A Jivaro headhunter began the head shrinking ritual by hacking off the head of his victim as close to the body as possible. He then slit the scalp from the crown of the head to the nape of the neck and carefully teased the skull out through this opening. He stretched the skin over a knob of wood and submerged it in boiling water, which made the skin begin to contract. Next, the Jivaro sewed a ring made of vine into the base of the neck to keep it open during the shrinking process. Then, hot stones and sand were dropped inside the head, which the Jivaro kept in constant motion so that the head was heated uniformly. Whenever the sand began to cool, it was emptied out, reheated and poured back into the head. As the head dried and grew smaller, the Jivaro kneaded and pinched

The Jivaros of South America believed that an individual's spiritual powers resided in the head. To decapitate an enemy and possess his head was to keep for one's self all the powers of its original owner. The mouths and other orifices of shrunken heads were often sewn shut to keep the soul from escaping. This shrunken head has been on display at the Niagara Falls Odditorium since 1963.

the facial features constantly to help them retain their lifelike appearance. Finally, if the head was that of a man, its lips were sewn shut with sinew to keep his soul from escaping. If it was that of a woman (female shrunken heads are far rarer) the mouth remained unsewn, because it was believed that women had no soul. The finished product was small enough that it would fit into your hand like a baseball.

The whole head shrinking process was interspersed with magical rites and ceremonies. The Jivaros believed that when they decapitated an enemy and possessed his head, they inherited all of his supernatural powers. It was a way of humiliating an enemy and of robbing him of a normal rebirth in the next world. It was also a grisly means of bookkeeping: the number of heads a warrior owned served as a record of his bravery. The Jivaros were by no means the world's only headhunters. The practice flourished throughout South America, as well in Northern India, Malaya, Indonesia, Melanesia, the Philippines, Formosa and the Northwest coast of America.

Ripley kept three fine examples of shrunken heads in his personal collection. He swore that the hair on the heads grew by several inches while they were in his possession—proof that hair growth continues after death!

A very rare shrunken female torso, on display in Ripley's Blackpool, England Odditorium. Since traditionally the Jivaro did not shrink female heads (shrunken heads are war trophies, and women traditionally didn't go to war), this torso was probably prepared in the early 20th century, deliberately to sell to white tourists.

Remarkable ROYALTY

Wax figure of **Chin Shin Huang Ti,** First Emperor of China, builder of the Great Wall and the man who gave China its name, was formerly on display at Ripley's Niagara Falls Odditorium.

CONDEMNED TO PRISON BECAUSE HIS TROUSERS SPLIT!
EMPRESS ANNE of RUSSIA FORCED WAR MINISTER VON LOEWENBURG (WHO WAS 6 FEET 11½ INCHES TALL) TO BOW SO LOW TO KISS HER HAND THAT HIS PANTS RIPPED—AND THE KISS WAS A FAILURE
AS A PUNISHMENT HE WAS CONFINED FOR 20 YEARS IN A CELL 4½ FEET LONG—4½ FEET WIDE AND 4½ FEET HIGH

THE JACKAL THAT BECAME A KING!
The RAJAH OF PARTABGARH in India, AS A GESTURE OF CONTEMPT FOR A DEFEATED MONARCH CROWNED A JACKAL AS RULER OF GARWARA "AND THE ANIMAL REIGNED FOR 12 YEARS!

Ripley pays a visit to the Tomb of Queen Min's Finger in Seoul, South Korea, 1932.

ACCENT ON YOUTH!
ISABEL of FRANCE – QUEEN of ENGLAND
ENGAGED AT THE AGE OF 2
MARRIED TO KING RICHARD II, of England, AT THE AGE OF 7
BECAME A WIDOW AT THE AGE OF 11
MARRIED CHARLES of ANGOULEME AT THE AGE OF 16
DIED IN CHILDBIRTH AT THE AGE OF 20
SHE WAS THE RICHEST AND BEST-DRESSED WOMAN IN EUROPE AT THE AGE OF 7
F.E. MALE IS A MALE DRUGGIST Union Sq. San Francisco

OUR SOLDIERS OF OCCUPATION WILL SEE THE TOMB OF THE QUEEN'S LITTLE FINGER – SEOUL, KOREA
WHEN QUEEN MIN, of KOREA, WAS MURDERED AND HER BODY BURNED BY THE JAPANESE IN 1895.
THE KOREANS SEARCHED THE RUINS AND ALL THEY COULD FIND WAS A BONE OF HER LITTLE FINGER,
SO AN ENTIRE CITY WAS DESTROYED TO MAKE A BEAUTIFUL BURIAL GROUND FOR HER FINGER
Copr. 1945, King Features Syndicate, Inc., World rights reserved.

Abdallah Es-Zaghal (The Valiant), Moorish king of Granada (1485–1491) who sold his kingdom for five million golden maravedi ($17 million today) enjoyed his wealth for only a short time. When he crossed over to Africa on his way to a life of luxury and ease, he was arrested by King Benimerin of Fez, who confiscated the former king's wealth, blinded him and turned him out into the streets. For the next 12 years, Es-Zaghal was reduced to begging, going about the streets with a bit of ragged parchment on his back, reading, "This is the unfortunate king of Andalusia."

QUEEN VICTORIA
(1819-1901) ENGLAND'S LONGEST-REIGNING MONARCH, WAS THE GRANDMOTHER OF THE TWO MAJOR ANTAGONISTS OF WORLD WAR I
KING GEORGE V AND KAISER WILHELM II

Hindu King Kusinaba was the father of 100 daughters, all of them hunchbacks. To commemorate his great family tragedy, the king founded a city and named it Kanyakubja, "The City of the Deformed Maidens." The city remains today, although its name has been shortened to Kanauj.

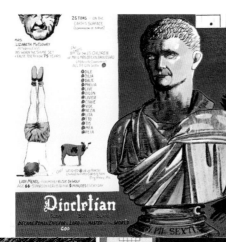

25 TONS — ON THE EARTH'S SURFACE
(COMMON TO ALL MEN)

MRS. LIZABETH McCLOVARY
HAS WORN THE SAME SET OF FALSE TEETH FOR 75 YEARS

THE MOTHER OF 25 CHILDREN OF MR. & MRS. DION PAOUSSAU
—ALL LIVING WITH NAMES ALL BEGIN WITH "D"

DOLE · OLIA · OPHELIA · OLIVE · DILON · OLIVIER · OCTAVE · DIDIER · MEZIA · OLITA · OTTO · OTIS · OMEA · DELIA

LADY MENDL — FORMERLY ELSIE DeWOLF
AGE 66 — STANDS ON HER HEAD FOR 5 MINUTES EVERY DAY

Diocletian
SLAVE · SON · SLAVE
BECAME ROMAN EMPEROR LORD and MASTER of the WORLD
GOD

PR. SEXTI

In 1800, Russia's Czar Paul I ORDERED A HORSE FORMALLY COURT-MARTIALED and BEATEN FOR HAVING REARED BENEATH HIM IN A PARADE!

THE MAN WHOSE DANCING HELPED MAKE HIM A KING
KING STANISLAW II (1732–1798)
the last Polish monarch
BEGAN HIS POLITICAL CAREER
BY DANCING WITH ONE GIRL CONTINUOUSLY
FOR 12 HOURS TO WIN HER FATHER'S VOTE
STANISLAW WAS ELECTED TO THE POLISH
PARLIAMENT IN 1754 – AND 10 YEARS LATER
BECAME KING OF POLAND

PRINCESS RADZIWILL of Poland AT A MEETING OF THE SKATING CLUB IN ROME, ITALY, IN 1910 DROVE A ROMAN CHARIOT DRAWN BY A LEOPARD AND A LION

TO TRACE THIS AND TURN AN ANGLE AT EVERY POINT
TAKE THE OUTERMOST LINES IN TWO CIRCLES.

Roman Emperor VITELLIUS GREATEST GLUTTON IN ALL HISTORY
SPENT MORE THAN $375,000 A DAY ON FOOD ALONE!
$90,000,000 IN 8 MONTHS
HE ATE 1,000 OYSTERS A DAY — AND INDULGED IN SUCH DISHES AS NIGHTINGALE TONGUES, PEACOCK BRAINS, LIVERS OF PARROT FISH, LAMPREY MILK, ETC.
YET – HE STARVED HIS OWN MOTHER TO DEATH!
(TO FULFILL A PROPHECY THAT HE WOULD RULE LONG – IF HIS MOTHER DIED FIRST.)

The entire court of Louis XIV and XV had to be present during the delivery of a baby to verify that the offspring was indeed royal and not a commoner smuggled in from a village mother.

KING LOUIS XIV (1638-1715) of France WAS SO VAIN THAT HE COULD OFTEN BE HEARD SINGING AND HUMMING SONGS WRITTEN IN PRAISE OF HIS RULE

Believe It or Not!

THE MEN WHO THREW THEMSELVES UNDER A CARRIAGE TO CUSHION ITS WHEELS!
ALI PASHA (1741-1822) Ruler of Janina, Albania TO PREVENT HIS CARRIAGE FROM BOUNCING ALWAYS HAD A DOZEN MEN RUN AHEAD OF HIS HORSES AND THROW THEMSELVES INTO ANY DEEP HOLES IN THE ROAD!
FOR ALLOWING THE COACH AND HORSES TO PASS OVER HIM, EACH MAN WAS PAID 3½ LBS. OF BREAD EACH DAY

BEST KNOWN FACE IN HISTORY
Elizabeth of York
QUEEN of HENRY VII of ENGLAND
HER PORTRAIT HAS APPEARED 8 TIMES
IN EVERY DECK of PLAYING CARDS for 400 YEARS

Mother of Monarchs

Marie-Laetitia Ramolino, born on the island of Corsica in 1750, was the mother of four kings, two queens, a duchess and a prince. Of her thirteen children, the most famous was her second child, Napoleon, who became Emperor of France. Joseph, her eldest son, became the King of Spain. Jerome was crowned King of Westphalia; Louis was the King of Holland. Her daughters Maria Annunciata and Caroline Elisa became Queen of Naples and Queen of Toscana. Of her other famous children, Lucien became the Prince of Canino and Marie Pauline was the Duchess of Guastalla. She outlived them all by more than twenty years and died in 1836.

Punishment by Proxy

In Germany during the nineteenth century all princes of blood had a prugelknaben: a boy who was brought up with the young prince and who was spanked every time the prince misbehaved.

THE $75,000.00 TOAST!
SIR THOMAS GRESHAM DRANK TO THE HEALTH OF *Queen Elizabeth* WITH A GLASS OF WINE CONTAINING A LARGE PEARL CRUSHED TO DUST AND WORTH $75000.00

CATHERINE -THE GREAT of RUSSIA HAD 32 LOVERS!
SHE SPENT 99,820,000 RUBLES ON THEM (ABOUT A BILLION DOLLARS IN PURCHASING POWER TODAY) IN ADDITION SHE GAVE THEM 107,800 HUMAN BEINGS AS SLAVES. SHE WAS THE FIRST TO CALL A MAN A "WOLF" (IN LETTERS TO POTUMKIN)

THOMAS KEN (1637-1711) BRAVED THE WRATH OF KING CHARLES II BY SCOLDING HIM FOR HIS DISSOLUTE HABITS –*AND* AS A REWARD YEARS LATER, THE MONARCH NAMED HIM BISHOP OF BATH AND WELLS

! England's Queen Victoria had her chef chew a clove of garlic, then breathe over her food before serving it to her.

A LANTERN IN THE TOMB OF THE BUDDHIST PRIEST KOBO DAISHI in the Monastery of Koya San HAS BEEN BURNING CONTINUOUSLY FOR 1,126 YEARS Nara, Japan

Ripley's— **Believe It or Not!**

THE STRANGEST TREASURE MAP IN HISTORY A CIRCLE OF STONES near Dongarra, Australia, HAS HELD THE CLUE TO A BURIED TREASURE OF $30,400 IN DUTCH GUILDERS FOR 300 YEARS. THE MONEY WAS SALVAGED FROM THE DUTCH SHIP "GILT DRAGON" BY SURVIVORS OF ITS CREW, BUT THEY DIED WITHOUT RECLAIMING IT OR REVEALING THE SECRET OF THE STONE TREASURE MAP

A FOSSIL LEAF IMBEDDED IN A ROCK NEAR Camberwell, England, FOR 2,000,000 YEARS

HENRY BERNHARD KOSTER 1662-1749 A PENNSYLVANIA PASTOR, PRAYED EACH DAY IN 4 LANGUAGES: GREEK, CZECH AND HEBREW HE WROTE HYMNS IN LATIN, HEBREW, GREEK, GERMAN, FRENCH, CZECH, ENGLISH, DUTCH, ARABIC, PERSIAN, SWEDISH AND DANISH

THE GREAT STONE PYRAMID near Ichang, China, 482 FEET HIGH AND ON A BASE 750 IS ALMOST AN EXACT REPLICA OF THE PYRAMID OF CHEOPS YET IT WAS FASHIONED BY...

THE MONARCH WHO HID BEHIND A WOMAN'S SKIRTS! KING CHARLES II of England PURSUED BY CROMWELL'S SOLDIERS AFTER THE BATTLE OF WORCESTER TOOK REFUGE IN COAXDON HALL AND WAS SAVED BY MRS. ELIZABETH COGAN WHO HID HIM BENEATH HER VOLUMINOUS HOOPSKIRTS! Sept. 24, 1651

Ripley's

THE PINK LADY EMPRESS ELIZABETH of Russia (Daughter of Peter the Great) WHOSE FAVORITE COLOR WAS *PINK*, ISSUED A DECREE THAT NO WOMAN MIGHT WEAR THAT COLOR-EITHER VISIBLY OR CONCEALED, UNDER PAIN OF DEATH!

A LOBSTER CHANGES 8 TIMES THE... 5 TIMES THE... 3 TIMES THE... AND THEREA... MALE CHANGES... AND THE FEM...

The QUEEN of HEARTS QUEEN MARGUERITE de VALOIS (1552-1615) of Navarre HAD POCKETS IN THE LINING OF HER VOLUMINOUS HOOPSKIRT SO SHE COULD CARRY WITH HER ALWAYS THE HEARTS OF HER 34 SUCCESSIVE SWEETHEARTS – EACH EMBALMED AND SEALED IN A SEPARATE BOX !

A Hot Bath Changed His Mind

After Emperor Constans II of the Eastern Roman Empire was assassinated in his bath in Syracuse, Sicily, it took a little convincing to get his successor, General Misizi, to ascend the throne. To help him make up his mind, the army commanders scooped up the general, fully clothed and armored, and dumped him into the same bath in which the former emperor had died. The commanders informed the soggy general that he would have to stay there until he changed his mind. It didn't take long; the water was hot and July in Sicily is uncomfortably warm—not a nice combination when you're fully armored. Misizi accepted the crown. He died after ruling for one year.

THE MONARCH WHOSE AILMENT STARTED A FASHION!
KING CHRISTIAN IV (1588-1648) of Denmark WORE HIS HAIR LONG AND IN A PIGTAIL TIED WITH RIBBONS BECAUSE HE SUFFERED FROM A SCALP CONDITION *THAT MADE IT IMPOSSIBLE FOR HIM TO GET A HAIRCUT* HIS COURTIERS ALL ADOPTED THE KING'S HAIR STYLE

"SIR QUACK"
SIR WILLIAM REED, AN ITINERANT TAILOR WHO COULD HARDLY READ OR WRITE, SO CONVINCED QUEEN ANNE OF ENGLAND OF HIS SKILL AS AN OCULIST THAT SHE BECAME HIS PATIENT AND KNIGHTED HIM

❗ *At the court of England's Queen Victoria, who reigned from 1837 to 1901, when the monarch put down her knife and fork, the plates of everyone else at the table had to be removed!*

NELL GWYN the British actress WON A TITLE FOR HER 6-YEAR-OLD SON BY HOLDING THE CHILD OUTSIDE A WINDOW IN THE PRESENCE OF KING CHARLES II - AND THREATENING TO DROP THE BOY TO THE STREET
"THE ALARMED MONARCH CRIED "SAVE THE EARL OF BURFORD"

KING HENRI III of France
SENT EACH CRITIC OF HIS ACTIONS A GIFT OF $100 *WITH THE SUGGESTION THAT HE PURCHASE HONEY* **TO SWEETEN HIS MOOD**

The KNIGHT IN ARMOUR FOR 7 YEARS

TO FORM A MAGIC CIRCLE ADDING UP TO 69 - USING ONLY DIGITS FROM 1 to 9 PLACE #8 IN THE CENTER

5

Enguerrand de Saint-Cloud OF FRANCE VOWED *NEVER TO REMOVE HIS ARMOUR* OR THAT OF HIS HORSE UNTIL THE HONOR OF HIS GODFATHER - (who was wrongly executed) **BE RESTORED BY KING LOUIS X**

HE WORE HIS ARMOUR *Day and Night* for 7 yrs.

A stunning wax replica of **Catharine of Aragon,** wife of Henry VIII, graces Ripley's Louis Tussaud's museum in Niagara Falls.

The Fetus King

Sapor II, King of 4th-century Persia, was crowned before his birth. When Shah Hormouz died without an heir, his loyal subjects feared a civil war as the princes of the house of Sassan greedily eyed the empty throne. Hormouz's magi determined that his widowed queen had conceived before the king's death and that the child would be a boy. Upon his word, an unusual coronation ceremony took place: the queen was laid upon a royal bed and the crown of the Sassanids was placed on her belly, while the subjects of their presumed king-to-be knelt in homage. The magi proved to be right. Months later, the queen gave birth to a son, who lived to enjoy a lengthy reign.

Sultan Malik Al-Salih Najm Al-Din Ayyub, who ruled Egypt from 1240 to 1249, died from squatting down on a poisoned floor mat. He was accustomed to squatting barefoot on the mat each evening to play his usual game of chess. His wife, Queen Shajar Al-Durr, saturated the mat with a highly corrosive substance. The Sultan contracted a gangrenous sore on his bare ankle and died 48 hours later.

THE MONARCH WHO WAS REARED IN AN IRON CAGE
SULTAN ABDUL HAMID I (1725-1789) of Turkey
IMPRISONED IN A SMALL CAGE AT THE AGE OF 6
DID NOT LEAVE IT UNTIL HE WAS ENTHRONED
AS RULER OF ONE OF THE MIGHTIEST EMPIRES ON EARTH
—43 YEARS LATER!

The LOST TREASURE OF THE CZAR!
$ 330,000,000 IN GOLD
DUMPED FROM CARTS BY ADMIRAL KOLCHAK IN HIS FLIGHT FROM THE BOLSHEVIKI!
LAY ABANDONED BESIDE A SIBERIAN ROAD FOR WEEKS!
THE TREASURE FINALLY DISAPPEARED AND NO TRACE OF IT HAS EVER BEEN FOUND

KING ALARIC
OF THE VISIGOTHS
WAS BURIED IN 410 IN THE BED
OF THE BUSENTO RIVER, IN
COSENZA, ITALY, MOUNTED ON HIS
FAVORITE CHARGER
—THE RIVER BEING DIVERTED
DURING THE INTERMENT
THE SLAVES WHO HELPED SHIFT
THE RIVER WERE SLAIN TO KEEP
HIS FINAL RESTING PLACE
A SECRET FOREVER

Wax figure of **Richard the Lion Hearted,** King of England. On display at Ripley's Louis Tussaud's wax museum in Niagara Falls, Canada.

ELEANOR OF AQUITAINE
WAS QUEEN OF FRANCE FOR 15 YEARS
AND THEN
QUEEN OF ENGLAND FOR 23 YEARS
AND THEN
A STATE PRISONER FOR 12 YEARS

SHE DIVORCED KING LOUIS VII OF FRANCE
AND MARRIED HENRY II OF ENGLAND
SHE WAS IMPRISONED FOR TREASON

❗ *King Charles I of England, a lifelong stammerer, uttered only one sentence without stuttering: his farewell message on January 30, 1649, just before he was beheaded.*

KILLING A SWAN IS PUNISHABLE BY DEATH IN ENGLAND A MEDIEVAL STATUTE WAS NEVER BEEN REPEALED

THE RIVER OF FAMINE
Beaudricourt, France
IT FLOWS ONLY IN YEARS OF WANT— AND BECOMES STAGNANT DURING PERIODS OF PROSPERITY!

CHARLEMAGNE
—Emperor of the Holy Roman Empire
SAT ON HIS THRONE FOR 397 YEARS!
HE WAS INTERRED ON HIS MARBLE THRONE IN 814 AFTER A REIGN OF 46 YEARS—AND HIS CORPSE WAS STILL SEATED ON IT WHEN THE TOMB WAS OPENED IN 1165!

THE MONARCH WHO WAS FRIGHTENED TO DEATH BY A LETTER
KING GEORGE I
(1660-1727) of England
KEPT HIS WIFE, SOPHIA DOROTHEA, IMPRISONED FOR 32 YEARS —UNTIL SHE DIED IN 1726 ON JAN. 10, 1727, A NOTE FROM HER WAS TOSSED INTO HIS COACH, SUMMONING HIM TO DIVINE JUDGMENT A YEAR AFTER HER DEATH — AND THE KING DIED ON THE SPOT!

Portrait of **King Bhumibol Adulyades** of Thailand made of laundry lint, commissioned for Ripley's Thailand Odditorium in 1994. Artist **Slater Baron** of Long Beach, California patterned her creation after a formal court portrait.

Ripley visits with the Crown Prince of Italy, a fellow passenger aboard a ship bound for Egypt. Circa 1933.

THE HIGHEST PAID JUGGLER IN ALL HISTORY!
ALPTEGIN A SLAVE OWNED BY AHMED, PRINCE OF SAMANI, BECAUSE HE COULD JUGGLE WHILE RIDING A HORSE AT FULL GALLOP, WAS GRANTED HIS FREEDOM—BECAME COMMANDER OF THE PRINCE'S ARMY AND GOVERNOR OF A PROVINCE—AND IN 960 BECAME KING OF AFGHANISTAN!
THE FORMER SLAVE FOUNDED A DYNASTY WHICH RULED AFGHANISTAN AND A LARGE PART OF INDIA FOR MORE THAN 200 YEARS

THE CASKET OF QUEEN ELIZABETH I
WHILE ON VIEW IN Whitehall Palace, London, ON THE EVE OF HER INTERMENT MYSTERIOUSLY EXPLODED!
THE COFFIN WAS SHATTERED AND HAD TO BE REPLACED - YET THE QUEEN'S BODY WAS UNHARMED (Mar. 24, 1603)

THE MONARCH WHO WAS FRIGHTENED TO DEATH BY AN ECLIPSE!
LOUIS le DEBONNAIRE
778 - 840
KING OF FRANCE AND EMPEROR OF GERMANY DIED OF FRIGHT WHEN THE SUN SUDDENLY DARKENED AND STARS APPEARED IN THE DAYTIME

CLOCKWISE FROM TOP RIGHT:

King Edward IV of England, at the Niagara Falls Tussaud's.

King Hussein of Jordan and Palestine Liberation Organization leader Yasir Arafat, side by side at Tussaud's Copenhagen.

King Christian II of Denmark, on display at Tussaud's Copenhagen.

King Henry VIII of England, Tussaud's, Copenhagen.

Comtesse du Barry of French Revolution fame, on display at Tussaud's, Niagara Falls.

Queen Elizabeth I of England, at Tussaud's, Niagara Falls.

England's beloved Queen Victoria, who reigned from 1837–1901.

WAX MAJESTY

Royalty on Display

Wax figures have a timeless appeal. Their striking realism gives museum visitors the illusion that they are in the presence of the famous, the infamous and the larger than life. Folks in the wax museum trade have come to rely on a "holy trinity" of wax replicas that attract visitors' attention: political figures, entertainers and especially, royalty. Unlike political figures and entertainers, many of whom are still alive (or were alive recently enough in most visitors' memories) royal figures give visitors a unique opportunity to come face to face with history. The lifelike qualities of Ripley's Henry VIII or Queen Victoria, for example, bring history to life in a way that no textbook can.

The "holy trinity" of popular wax figures: royalty, political figures and entertainers. Shown here are King Henry VIII of England, English Prime Minister Margaret Thatcher and American entertainer George Burns, on display at Ripley's Niagara Falls Tussaud's.

maintains one full-service wax works studio in Orlando, Florida, plus one small "urgent care" facility in Niagara Falls for repairing damaged figures. The figures in Ripley's two Tussaud's wax museums and in various Odditoriums around the world keep both shops busy.

But bringing the past to life is no easy task. Ripley's boasts two talented full-time professional wax artists among its ranks: Irv Wurst and Barry Anderson. Pieces are also occasionally bought from other artists, especially Jose Ballester of Valencia, Spain.
Theirs is an unusual, highly developed skill, involving numerous steps.

Ripley's Wax artists begin the creation of a new wax sculpture (which, start to finish, can take several months) by hitting the books. They carefully research the person they will be recreating, to assure that the figure will be as accurate as possible. Then they set to work sculpting the figure's head and hands of clay. Only the head and hands are sculpted; the rest of the body is cast. Occasionally, the artists will hire a model of similar body type to be used to make the body cast.

All exposed areas of the figure's skin are made in wax; the rest is molded from plastic. Each wax shop has its own favorite blend of wax, generally a mix of bee's wax, paraffin and other waxes. The figure's teeth are cast in porcelain; the eyes are glass. Wax artists insert real human hair into their figures, carefully placing one strand at a time, using a tiny forked needle. Then the figure is painted, using oil paints as makeup to give it realistic variations in pigmentation. Its hair is cut and styled and eyelashes are added. Finally, costumers move in to dress the figures in carefully researched garments, reproduced in exact detail.
Ripley's

A wax studio looks something like a cross between a potter's shop and a mechanic's bay. Shelves full of heads, hands and molds for various body parts line every available wall space. Extras of Ripley's most popular figures crowd every corner, at the ready in case a display figure is damaged. The more you look, the more you'll recognize familiar faces: Robert Wadlow, the world's tallest man, Liu Chung, the man with two pupils in each eye, Wang, the human unicorn and the Lighthouse man, complete with an electric "candle" in his skull. The center of Orlando's waxworks is dominated by an enormous yellow grid of steel that would look at home in a sci-fi movie. Body molds are clamped into this device, which spins like a gyroscope. The machine's motion causes the wax or plastic molding agent to be pressed into the molds by centrifugal force, leaving the inside hollow, thus making a lighter, less expensive figure.

Orlando's waxworks keeps a small corner of its wax shop curtained off as a "retirement home" for damaged and aging wax figures. As the wax ages, it darkens. Anyone entering this curtained area is greeted by the heads and hands of the four Beatles and row upon row of other famous figures, looking as though they had been out in the sun far too long.

Through a small door, you'll come across a room that looks for all the world like a backstage dressing room: mirrors, lights, makeup palettes. This is where the assembled figures receive their finishing touches. Waxy complexions gain a blush across the cheeks, hair is coiffed, lavish clothing and sparkling jewels are added. Finally, the figures are draped in protective plastic and crated, awaiting their chance to take their place on display among Ripley's "beautiful people."

Talented TOTS

Stanwurt von Schilling could play the sousaphone at the age of three. (May 10, 1936.)

C. W. Moeller, child contortionist from Spirit Lake, Iowa. At age five, she was the youngest child able to attain this challenging position. (January 8, 1937.)

Ripley poses with sensational 1930s and 1940s child star, **Shirley Temple.**

BELIEVE IT OR NOT—By Ripley

The son of Harvard professor Dr. Boris Sidis could recite the alphabet at the age of six months. At two, he could read and write. At the age of eleven he matriculated in Harvard and astonished his professors by discussing the fourth dimension.

Jean-Louis Cardiac (1719–1726) of Cardiac Castle, France knew the alphabet at three months, could read and write Latin when he was three years of age, knew English, German and Hebrew at the age of four, was versed in mathematics, geography and history at age six—and died at the age of seven!

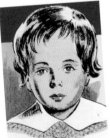

! *Elie Gourbeyre of Nouara, France, could lure any bird to her shoulder merely by crooking her finger! Her strange powers lasted only 6 years until she was 12 years of age.*

Boy Marvel Truman Henry Safford of Royalton, Vermont (1836–1901) was able to multiply two four-digit numbers and extract the square and cubic roots of ten-digit figures in his head—at the age of six! By the time he was nine, he had plotted the elliptical orbit of a comet and when the comet arrived on course, passing Earth three years later, Safford was proven correct. Before he was eleven, he had published two almanacs based solely on his own calculations. At the age of ten, he extracted the square root of 365,365,365,365,365,365 in less than one minute. Professor Benjamin Pierce declared that the boy's powers of abstraction and concentration were of an incredibly high order. Safford grew up to become Professor of Astronomy at the University of Chicago and Williams College, fulfilling the promise of his early boyhood.

At the age of five, **Johnny Charles Reed** of Brawley, California took a malfunctioning #5 Underwood typewriter completely apart. When his dad threatened to spank him if he didn't put it back together, he did—and had it in good running condition in less than two hours! (April 24, 1947.)

By the time he was two and a half months old, **Ralph Roland Dowell** of Grand Junction, Colorado could do a perfect "wrestler's bridge" (January 9, 1932.)

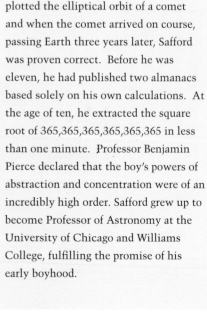

Judith Elaine Entine of Philadelphia, Pennsylvania could balance on one foot on the palm of her daddy's hand at the age of eleven months. (September 17, 1947.)

Lynwood Ganza of Los Angeles, California could perform a "flag" at the age of three and a half years. (August 31, 1947.)

Tiny Renee Marie LeFebvre of Fullerton, California could hang from a bar at the age of three months, nineteen days. Her father submitted this photograph in response to a Believe It or Not! cartoon of a four month old boy who could perform this feat. Little Renee was ahead of the boy by several days! (September 1, 1940.)

Roylene Smith, age two-and-a-half, the world's youngest trick rider, performing a "fender drag" on her pony, "Small Fry." Roylene performed across the West with Roy Knapp's Rough Riders, a troupe of trick-riding youths age 2 1/2 to 14. (October 16, 1939.)

Miracle Baby!

Two year old Christopher Falcon, son of David Falcon and Beatriz Templa of Cebu, Philippines, was pronounced dead on the morning of Good Friday, March 26, 1948. He had "died" of whooping cough. Friends and neighbors gathered to hold vigil over his tiny white coffin. Six hours had passed, when, to the amazement of those gathered around him, Christopher suddenly revived! The incident created a wide-spread sensation and young Christopher went on to live a normal, healthy life.

! *Sandra Sheffield of Wainwright, Alberta, Canada balanced upright on her father's hand at the age of five weeks!*

KIM UNG-YOUNG
Child Genius

What does the world look like to a super-genius? How do you have a conversation with your peers when their IQs are hardly more than half yours? When other kids your age are studying addition and subtraction and you're finishing up a PhD in mathematics, where do you find common ground? What would you think of yourself if all the world seemed to look upon you as an oddity?

These are the questions that surely must have plagued the parents of little Kim Ung-young, who, at the age of four, was found to have the highest I.Q. ever recorded. They wanted their son to have a chance to develop his special abilities, yet they didn't want him to miss out on a normal childhood. And above all, they wanted to protect him from the harsh light of public curiosity.

Kim's parents knew there was something unusual about their son when they discovered that he could read at the age of nine months. Kim had finished reading his first book before he could walk. At the age of ten months, Kim was speaking fluent English in addition to his native Korean. His parents knew they had a special little boy on their hands.

At the age of three, Kim had a better grasp of arithmetic, chemistry, literature and philosophy than most professors. At six, Kim designed a solar-powered space ship. In 1969, when Kim was four, his parents allowed him to take a battery of intelligence tests to measure his I.Q. The average human I.Q. falls between 90 and 130; 130 to 140 is bordering on genius and only 1% of human beings are known to have an IQ over 140. IQs bordering on 200 are almost unheard of. Kim's measured 210.

How do you parent a child like Kim? Kim's mother and father agonized over this question for years as they watched their brilliant child leave his peers further and further behind. His parents realized that giving their son the stimulus and training he needed to develop his astonishing ability was far beyond their capacities. In 1973, when Kim graduated with his doctorate from Seoul's Konguk University at the age of eight, his parents decided to send him to America to be raised by an aunt who was a professor at a Colorado University.

Kim traveled to America with his younger brother, Chang-young and two younger sisters, Ye-young and Myong-young, all of whose I.Q.s were almost as high as Kim's.

The children's parents insisted that they be sheltered from public scrutiny and that they be brought up in the Korean way. Ripley's file on Kim Ung-young and his family ends abruptly in 1973. Ripley's researchers attempted to find the young genius in various American Universities, to no avail. Perhaps Kim's family changed their name to avoid unwanted attention. Perhaps Kim quietly disappeared into some exclusive government think tank. Suffice it to say, when your IQ is 210, you probably have no trouble thinking up plenty of ways to disappear. If he is still alive, Kim would only be 34 today.

The YOUNG GENIUS UNG-YONG KIM of Seoul, South Korea, COULD SOLVE MATHEMATICAL PROBLEMS BASED ON EINSTEIN'S THEORY OF RELATIVITY — LIKE THIS ONE TO DETERMINE THE INDEFINITE INTEGRAL— AT THE AGE OF 4

$$\int \frac{x}{\sqrt{x^n + 4}} \, dx$$

Witnessed by Professor Kentaro Yano, Department of Applied Mathematics, University of Waterloo, Ontario

Terrific TRANSPORTATION

"THE TURTLE" FIRST AMERICAN SUBMARINE USED BY GEORGE WASHINGTON IN THE REVOLUTIONARY WAR Invented by DAVID BUSHNELL

AUTOMOBILES IN ENGLAND, UNTIL 1896, COULD NOT BE DRIVEN FASTER THAN FOUR MILES AN HOUR PRECEDED BY A MAN CARRYING A RED FLAG

◀ • • • • • • • • •

The Hondime, a 1973 Honda covered in American dimes. (January 4, 1992.)

Dust Schooners

An annual regatta is held in Alice Springs, Australia on the Todd River. However, the river is dry for most of the year, including the day of the regatta. So competitors build special bottomless sail boats and "sail" the regatta on foot!

"ONLY" BRIDGE IN THE WORLD THAT STEAMSHIPS PASS OVER! Håverud, Sweden IT CARRIES THE DALSLAND CANAL OVER A WATERFALL AND UNDER ANOTHER BRIDGE!

◀ • • • • • • • • • • • • • • • •

Chinese imperial rickshaw made from over a ton of jade, standing approximately ten feet high and sixteen feet long. Jade, which retains its own temperature, was once used as a primitive air conditioning system. This rickshaw is fully functional, but its enormous weight makes its use impractical. Ripley's purchased the rickshaw in Ghoungzhou, China in 1996.

Tortoise Boat INVENTED BY LI SOON SIN—1591 THE FIRST IRONCLAD WARSHIP EVER BUILT! IT ENABLED KOREA TO INFLICT A MOST DISASTROUS DEFEAT UPON THE JAPANESE IT COULD MOVE BACKWARDS, FORWARDS AND SIDEWAYS, and SUBMERGED LIKE A SUBMARINE - ALMOST UNAIDED IT DEFEATED THE JAPANESE NAVY

THE SHIP THAT CLIMBED A HILL! A SMALL STEAMER ON THE LAKE OF LOEN, NORWAY, WAS STRUCK BY A GIGANTIC WAVE - Caused by a landslide - AND HURLED OVER A PERPENDICULAR CLIFF 300 FEET HIGH 1906

MOTOR-DRIVEN ROLLER SKATES INVENTED BY ALPHONSE CONSTANTINI IN 1906 COULD TRAVEL 40 MILES AN HOUR

THE CANADIAN NATIONAL RAILROAD IS 3 MILES LONGER IN SUMMER THAN IN WINTER

THE "COOSA" A RIVER STEAMBOAT, WAS BUILT IN CINCINNATI, OHIO, IN 1845, THEN SAILED DOWN THE OHIO RIVER TO CAIRO, ILL., AND ON THE MISSISSIPPI AND MOBILE RIVERS TO WETUMPKA, ALA. - BUT IN ORDER TO TRANSPORT IT TO THE COOSA RIVER IN ALABAMA IT HAD TO BE DISMANTLED COMPLETELY AND CARRIED 100 MILES OVERLAND ON WAGONS DRAWN BY TEAMS OF OXEN

Charles Miller of Portland, Oregon stretches out on the roomy back porch of his charming clap-board house truck and admires his spacious green lawn. Miller lived in his 3'9" wide, 6' long vehicle for more than two years and toured the country in it nine times. The chassis had more than 200,000 miles on it when he purchased it; Miller added 200,000 more. (October 7, 1933.)

E. G. Hartley of Casper, Wyoming covered his car with 37,700 stamps from 60 different countries. (December 18, 1936.)

MOUNTED POLICEMEN in Australia, USING CAMELS, OFTEN PATROL AN AREA OF 168,000 SQUARE MILES

John Martin of Sarasota, Florida had his head so severely mangled in an elevator accident that it was necessary to remove both his eyes. Yet he went on to build this astonishing house-car (note that the flowers in the window boxes are real!) in which he and his wife toured the country. (April 27, 1941.)

The one-of-a-kind Longhorn V12, built by hand by **Oliver Albert** of Gonzalez, Texas. Albert claims he used the "best parts" from 14 different makes of car: Cadillac, Chevrolet, Chrysler, Dodge, Ford, Jeep, Lincoln, Mercedes, Mercury, Nash, Plymouth, Pontiac, Renault and Terraplane. (March 17, 1985.)

THE FIRST HORSELESS CARRIAGE A CARRIAGE BUILT BY HANS HAUTSCH of Nürnberg, Germany, IN 1649 COULD BE PEDALED AT A SPEED OF ONE MILE PER HOUR—AND AT THE SAME TIME SPRAY PERFUME ON PASSERSBY THROUGH AN ATOMIZER IN THE DRAGON'S HEAD, WHICH ALSO SERVED AS ITS TILLER

The Whole Town Rides The Rails

The town of Lakewood, Australia, a community in the heart of a lumber and gold mining region, has its homes, shops, post office and police station mounted on railroad cars.

Joseph Steinlauf, builder of whimsical bicycles, appeared in Ripley's cartoons seven times between 1931 and 1951. This brass bed bicycle, weighing 75 pounds, was one of many Steinlauf creations, along with a spike-wheeled bicycle for riding on ice, a bicycle built for five inspired by the Dionne quintuplets and a two-person gangstercycle with 15 antique guns. A classic Believe It or Not! figure, Joseph Steinlauf died in 1982.

Henry Langer, better known as Cloudbuster Hen Langer, went up in an airplane 479 times, but never landed in one. He parachuted to earth during his first plane ride in 1932 and did so during every plane ride afterwards. (May 5, 1957.)

EGG TURNED ITSELF IN THE PAN! H. R. HOLT Southern Pines, N.C.

DOG TRICYCLE INVENTED BY GUITU, A FRENCHMAN THE WHEELS WERE REVOLVED BY 2 RUNNING DOGS - SPEED 6 MILES AN HOUR

ONE MAN'S JUNK IS
ANOTHER MAN'S TREASURE

Ripley's *Mon Lei*

Imagine you're sitting quietly on the banks of the Hudson River, taking in the sights, when suddenly, a vision of the exotic Far East flies up before your eyes: a brightly painted Chinese junk, all reds and golds and blues, barreling past at a blazing 15 knots, her sails flapping backwards, a boisterous party of Mandarin-clothed passengers waving their cocktails at you and the only Western-dressed figure aboard, a man clad in American sailing duds and a buck-toothed grin.

The Mon Lei under sail, one of only two known watercolor paintings by Robert Ripley, both dated 1948. The other painting, similar in design and color, depicts a majestic Spanish galleon. The galleon painting was set into the center of a giant compass on the floor at BION Island.

If the time period were the late 1940s, you would have just seen Ripley's *Mon Lei,* a common, if startling, sight to all who frequented the riverbanks. Ripley purchased the exotic vessel in 1946 and for a time used it as his daily means of commuting from BION Island to his New York studio. He maintained a flashy Mandarin wardrobe aboard for his guests, although he himself always dressed in a traditional American yachting outfit. While aboard the Mon Lei, he insisted on being called "Commodore Rip Lee."

The *Mon Lei* was built, one source tells, as early as the 1780s. Like all junks of her construction, a design virtually unchanged for a thousand years, she was made to haul fish and cargo along the Foochow River. Her blunt nose and shallow draw helped her navigate muddy bottoms and treacherous shoals. In 1939 she was refurbished to serve as a pleasure yacht for a distinguished Chinese military man, but in 1941, the officer and his boat were seized by the Japanese. Rumor has it that the military man was "dispatched," and

Ripley wears his perennial captain's hat. The woman in the Chinese outfit is Ripley's close friend, author Li Ling Ai.

the *Mon Lei* lay at anchor for several years with a prize crew while the war played itself out.

But one night during the war, the story goes, a group of Europeans and one American surprised and murdered the prize crew, stole the *Mon Lei* and sailed her on a harrowing 86 day voyage across the Pacific, through the Panama Canal and to the Florida coast. The exotic boat became mired in customs battles and lay anchored dejectedly in the mud, until one Robert Ripley discovered her and greased the wheels of bureaucracy by buying her outright.

Ripley had the junk repainted in the original colors of all Foochow fishing boats; each Chinese seaport and river has its own color scheme. He installed a powerful 165 horsepower Gray marine engine, which he painted with eyes, claws and whiskers, to honor the ancient Chinese belief that boats were fast because a dragon lived inside them. He cleverly hid the engine behind a gilded altar to the Chinese god of joy, Ho Tei. The little boat was no slouch under sail, cruising at a brisk 7 knots, but now with sails up and engine full bore, she could blaze along at 15 knots. Under engine power alone, her sails would be blown aft, hence the illusion that the little craft was sailing backwards.

Ripley decorated her with art from his own private collection. Below decks, she was all sumptuous carvings, silks and tapestries, including a blue pillow embroidered with the "Forbidden Stitch", a

The Mon Lei's 165 horsepower diesel engine was hidden behind an altar to Ho Tei, Chinese god of joy. Ripley painted dragonlike features on the powerful engine.

Costumed guests aboard the Mon Lei take in the sights off Long Island Sound.

Ripley decorated the Mon Lei's interior with sumptuous imported Chinese carvings and textiles. Most of the Mon Lei's decor below decks has since been destroyed by fire.

design so intricate that Chinese embroiderers lost their eyesight creating it, until the Empress forbade it.

The name *Mon Lei* means Ten Thousand, or Infinity, the Chinese equivalent for Bon Voyage ("Ten Thousand Voyages".) The Great Wall is also called Mon Lei because of its association with infinity. Ripley painted every available space with traditional Chinese sailing proverbs. The characters forward of the wheelhouse translated as: "May she sail like a flying dragon and move like a leaping elephant;" those behind the wheelhouse read "Peace be with you on your trip." On her port side: "Fast time long voyage." On starboard: "One way peace." And aft: "straight wind, straight water." Her wheelhouse was filled with Chinese gods, her bow bore a butterfly of good luck and a pair of bright eyes so that she could see where she was going. In her teak and camphor woodwork, black, red and gold lacquered dragons scampered all about.

Not surprisingly, Ripley saw his new acquisition as yet another excuse to have a party. But something about the *Mon Lei* seemed to bring out the "Believe It or Not" in her passengers. In 1947 the *Mon Lei* got herself into an entanglement that resulted in headaches for her owner.

Several of Ripley's closest friends received an invitation in the mail to board the *Mon Lei* for a luncheon cruise to salute the *U.S.S. Missouri* as it returned home from the war. The battleship's return was to be a grand event with all manner of festivities and a speech from the President. But what Ripley forgot to mention to his guests was that the navy had not invited Ripley.

As crowds gathered on every bank, bridge and pier to welcome the great warship, their attention was drawn instead to a colorful little Chinese junk skipping over the waves, gaily flying the Chinese flag, her decks swarming with passengers in flamboyant Mandarin costumes. The *Mon Lei* literally stole the thunder from the Missouri's triumphant parade.

Not knowing whether the "foreign looking" boat was friend or foe, the navy quickly grew suspicious. The *Mon Lei* picked up a navy patrol escort. It didn't help their case that just as the navy boat pulled along behind, guests were sitting down to their Chinese luncheon when a strong wind blew their fried rice overboard. The navy following behind found themselves pelted by a steady stream of Chinese food.

A navy patrolman hoisted a megaphone and asked for their names. Bugs Baer yelled back, "We can't tell you! We're smuggling in dope from the Orient!" The President was due to appear at any moment. The navy patrol had ceased to find the situation amusing and told the captain of the *Mon Lei* to either drop anchor or pull over to the Jersey shore, at which Ripley's friend Walter Shirley pointed to the Chinese flag and hollered, "We're here to call for the laundry, but it's all right with us if you want a dirty navy."

At this, the navy patrol boat began bumping the *Mon Lei* into the nearest berth, which just happened to be at Pier 90, where the Queen Mary customarily dropped anchor. Ripley tried his best to disappear amidst the fans pressing him for his autograph. But alas, Ripley was never known for his ability to blend in. His guests quietly changed out of their Mandarin costumes and slipped away, leaving a bewildered Ripley alone in the clutches of the authorities, sheepishly paying fines and calling upon the spirits of all the *Mon Lei's* gods and dragons to save him.

Ripley's shikara boat awaits at the dock on BION island, circa 1939. Ripley had special mirrored costumes made for guests to wear on moonlight rides.

The Mon Lei was only the largest and most impressive craft in Ripley's "navy", which included a round guffa boat like the one Moses used, a Kashmir shikara gondola and an Indian dugout, all of which were routinely made available to Ripley's part guests.

Whimsical WONDERS

Jeff de Boer's cat armor— never worn! On display in Ripley's Myrtle Beach Odditorium.

How much is an Easter egg worth? Well, if it was made by Faberge, court jeweler to the czar of Russia, it can be worth millions. Faberge presented a royal egg to the court each Easter. He decorated the shells with rubies, pearls and diamonds. Inside the eggs were miniature crowns, rings, picture frames, carriages and platinum swans. One egg held a miniature train, perfect in every detail. Of the 57 eggs Faberge made, 53 are still in existence, worth an estimated $5 million apiece.

A **TOWER**, EXHIBITED IN OSAKA, JAPAN, *CREATED OUT OF 5,000,000 POSTCARDS*— THEY WERE PART OF 93,000,000 CARDS MAILED IN A CONTEST TO SELECT THE 8 MOST BEAUTIFUL SIGHTS IN JAPAN

Antler Christmas tree, made of approximately 700 elk antlers and decorated with lights, submitted to Ripley's by Ed Matukonis of Forty Fort, Pennsylvania. (December 25, 1988.)

A HUGE SILVER FOUNTAIN BUILT FOR MONGOL PRINCE MANGU KHAN IN THE 13TH CENTURY HAD 4 SPOUTS—*EACH DISPENSING A DIFFERENT ALCOHOLIC DRINK*

"NOT A CHIP OFF THE OLD BLOCK"

"ZIPPY CHIPPY" THE GRANDSON of THE GREAT RACEHORSE "NORTHERN DANCER" HAS LOST 85 RACES IN A ROW!

AN EYEGLASS CASE OWNED BY "DIAMOND JIM" BRADY WAS ADORNED WITH A MINIATURE LOCOMOTIVE MADE WITH 210 DIAMONDS
© King Features Syndicate, Inc., 1969. World rights reserved.

Jim Garry's scrap metal allosaurus holds a dragonfly in its mouth.

Whimsical dinosaur skeleton assembled from scrap car parts by Jim Garry of Farmingdale, New Jersey. Garry appeared on Ripley's 1980s-era television show. (December 9, 1990.)

A MONUMENT TO A LIAR A FOUNTAIN IN BODENWERDER, W. GERMANY, DEPICTS BARON KARL von MUNCHAUSEN RIDING HALF A HORSE—A MEMORIAL TO HIS TALL TALE THAT DURING THE TURKISH WARS HE RODE HALF A HORSE TO VICTORY... Submitted by Jules Marr, Albuquerque, N.M.

! A mysterious skull of pure quartz was discovered in Lubantuum, British Honduras by Anna Leguillon in 1927. Authorities disagree on whether its origin is European or Central American, but they claim that it must have taken approximately 150 years of polishing with the primitive technology that existed in the region to achieve the skull's perfectly smooth surface. When lit from below, the skull's eyes glow.

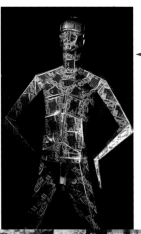

Coca-cola Man made of flattened soda cans, on display in Ripley's San Francisco Odditorium, created by **Theresa Tozer** of Osprey, Florida, circa 1982.

Detail of Coca-cola Man's face. **Theresa Tozer** also created a Coca-cola Woman, made of crushed rather than flattened cans, also on display at Ripley's San Francisco Odditorium.

BICYCLE BUILT FOR 10
THE **DECEMTUPLE**, BUILT IN 1896, *CARRIED 10 RIDERS*

Detail of an intricate camel-bone carving by the Ghuongzhou Zonghua Jingyi sculpture factory of Guangzhou, China, circa 1990. A shortage of ivory has turned the company to other materials, notably, cow and camel bone. This huge, intricate sculpture, titled "Fairy Cave" and featuring blooming flowers, pines, dancing cranes and more than 200 gods, was created by master sculptors **Jin Zhao Guang, Xie Mai Hua** and **Xie Zhong Din,** as proof that fine results can be gained with alternate materials.

Larry Fuente's bespangled, full-sized horse.

Anton Schiavone of Bangor, Pennsylvania created this life-sized replica of **Da Vinci's** Last Supper from brown paper grocery bags his neighbors helped him collect from the local A&P. Circa 1985. On display recently at Ripley's Copenhagen Odditorium.

Desert Bookmobile

Abul Kassem Ismael "Saheb" (938–995) the scholarly Grand Vizier of Persia had a library of 117,000 books that went with him wherever he traveled. As the great warrior-statesman traveled, his library followed him on the backs of 400 camels. The beasts that carried this huge portable collection were specially trained to travel in alphabetical order and were attended by a host of camel-driver librarians, who could locate any book their master desired in a short span of time.

THE
**CHAIN
TREE**
A BOX ELDER
Grown by
A.N. ERLANDSON
Santa Cruz,
Calif.
5-26

The remarkable Erlandson trees, grown by **A. N. Erlandson** of Santa Cruz, California. Erlandson's wonderful trees were featured in numerous Ripley cartoons in the 1950s. Most of the trees died soon after Erlandson's death. Ripley's attempted to buy the entire Erlandson forest, then later tried to purchase sections of the trees, unsuccessfully.

A SCULPTURE OF A GIANT BLOCK OF CONCRETE WITH CARS EMBEDDED IN ITS SURFACE IS USED AS A ROAD MARKER NEAR THE CITY OF JIDDAH, SAUDI ARABIA!

5-17

A limited edition 5-inch by 19-and-½-inch blown-glass replica of the carriage that carried **Princess Diana** and **Prince Charles** on their wedding day. One of only fifty made by Litchfield Glass Sculptors. July, 1981.)

This Japanese sushi made from laundry lint by **Slater Barron** of Long Beach, California, looks delicious, but requires more than the usual amount of saki to wash down! Circa 1985.

Turrtle shell fiddle and armadillo-armor charanga, originally owned by Robert Ripley.

Hubcap guitar and **crutch bass,** two of several unusual instruments built by Ken Butler of upstate New York. All are playable and were featured on a music album. The instruments were purchased for the Ripley collection in 1991.

SCAVENGED SCULPTURE

Leo Sewell's Trash Art

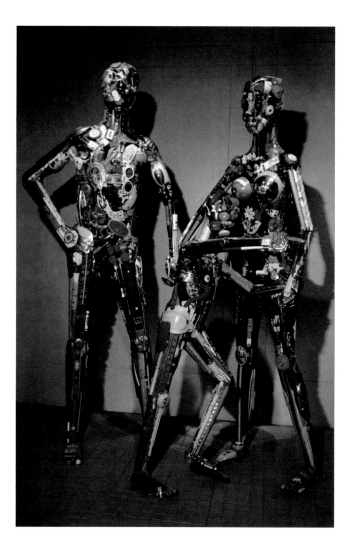

A stroll down the sidewalks of Philadelphia might be a pretty mundane exercise for most of us. But for artist Leo Sewell, it's a treasure hunt. A self-styled dumpster diver, trash-picker and junk lover, Sewell turned a childhood fascination with everyday objects into an art form. His sculptures, every piece of which is an object somebody else threw away, now sell for $1,500 a square foot.

Sewell maintains a sculpture studio in Philadelphia jam-packed (albeit tidily) with more than 100,000 found objects, everything from thermometers to yo-yos, waiting to find a home on one of his sculptures. Most of Sewell's creations are animals and people, although he has been known to make furniture and musical instruments, as well as a statue of Christ on the cross made with collection plates and rosaries and a reproduction of sorts of a classic work of art, which Sewell dubbed Venus de Junko. He even made Rocky and Rambo figures for film actor Sylvester Stallone. Most fans, however, are probably more familiar with his ducks, bears, armadillos, dinosaurs and elephants. It's the familiarity of the objects, in combination with the way they're portrayed, that seem to elicit smiles.

Recently, Sewell and his work have become involved in Philadelphia's recycling campaign. Sewell created a three-foot-long football out of recycled aluminum cans for display at football stadiums across the state. Fans were encouraged to guess the number of cans used in the sculpture in exchange for prizes. Admittedly, Leo Sewell's form of recycling is a bit unusual, but it gets people's attention.

Leo Sewell's works are featured in nearly all of Ripley's Odditoriums, where they receive a great deal of attention from visitors. Sewell's colorful creations are always whimsical, often laughable and sometimes meaningful. He admits that the money he gets for his creations is an added perk. And he says it's nice to know that the work he does is making people think. But if you ask him the real reason behind his creations, he'll tell you, "I just want to make you smile."

ABOVE: Junk art people, created by Leo Sewell of Philadelphia, Pennsylvania from found materials. Sewell's art appears in almost every Ripley's museum. This colorful trio is on display at Ripley's Niagara falls.

RIGHT: Leo Sewell created this colorful duck from plastic and metal garbage he found on the streets of Philadelphia. 1980.

Wonderful WEDDINGS

THE MOST DAZZLING PROCESSION IN HISTORY!
India
THE WEDDING PARTY at the marriage of the daughter of King Deva Raya I of Vijayanagar to Sultan Firoz Shah of Kulbarga WALKED FROM THE CITY GATE TO THE ROYAL PALACE - A DISTANCE OF 6 MILES - ON A CARPET OF GOLD CLOTH (1406)

Mrs. Theresa Vaughn, age 24, was arraigned in the Police Court of Sheffield, England on December 19, 1922 on a charge of bigamy. In the course of the hearing Mrs. Vaughn confessed to 61 bigamous marriages which she contracted without obtaining a divorce from her first husband. Her husbands were scattered all over the British Isles, Germany and South Africa, and all her marriages took place within the span of five years.

RIPLEY'S

The BRIDE WHO MARRIED A SEVERED HEAD
PRINCE RONALD of Multan, India, ORDERED TO GO TO WAR ON HIS WEDDING DAY, KILLED HIMSELF AFTER DIRECTING THAT HIS HEAD BE CUT OFF AND SENT TO HIS FIANCEE - THE MARRIAGE WAS PERFORMED ON SCHEDULE!

THE MAN WHO MATCHED HIS WIVES TO HIS INITIALS!
JETHRO ALEXANDER CUMMINGS (1855-1924) of London, England, WAS MARRIED 3 TIMES -- THE MAIDEN NAMES OF HIS WIVES WERE:
JANE JETHRO ...
ALICE ALEXANDER ...
CLARA CUMMINGS

The MAN WHO MARRIED HIS OWN WIFE - AND DIDN'T KNOW IT!
HUMPHREY KYNASTON (1466-1534) AN ENGLISH OUTLAW, DIVORCED A NOBLEWOMAN NAMED ISABEL OF ASTON AFTER 10 YEARS OF MARRIAGE AND 15 YEARS LATER MARRIED A WOMAN NAMED MARION OF OSWESTRY
NOT UNTIL HE WAS ON HIS DEATHBED 13 YEARS LATER DID HE LEARN THAT BOTH ISABEL AND MARION WERE THE SAME WOMAN!

THE BELL HARRY TOWER of Canterbury, England MODEL FOR THE TOWER OF LONDON'S HOUSES OF PARLIAMENT HAS A BELL THAT HAS NEVER BEEN HEARD DURING THE DAYLIGHT HOURS -- EXCEPT TO TOLL A KNELL FOR A DEAD SOVEREIGN OR ARCHBISHOP OF CANTERBURY -- IN 463 YEARS!

MARRIAGES THAT LASTED BEYOND THE GRAVE!
THE DIVORCE LAWS of the Byzantine Empire MADE IT EASY TO GET RID OF A LIVING SPOUSE -- BUT THERE WAS NO LEGAL WAY OF ENDING A MARRIAGE TO A DEAD WIFE OR HUSBAND

When Venetia Anastasia Hanley married English author/adventurer Sir Kenelm Digby in 1625, she brought 300 pairs of false eyebrows into the marriage. Each pair was different in size, shape and color. Public gossip had it that she never wore the same pair of eyebrows two days in a row. When she died, the inventory set up for the benefit of the Surrogate's court still listed among her "movable" assets 300 pairs of slightly used eyebrows, assorted.

Ripley giving away his sister Louise at her wedding in New York's "Little Church Around the Corner," famous for celebrity weddings.

SUSAN LANE OF TOLUCA LAKE, CALIF., CREATED A WEDDING DRESS AND BOUQUET OUT OF RECYCLED TRASH INCLUDING PLASTIC BAGS, EGG CARTONS AND COTTON BALLS!
8-3

Kehna, Algerian Queen of the Berbers, had a harem of 400 husbands!

The Marriage Racket

Widows of Africa's Kavati tribe have a "sound" way of acquiring a new husband. Custom requires a widow to remain near her departed husband's grave, screaming at the top of her lungs and drumming ceaselessly on the walls of the grave with a cudgel. She keeps up this noisy display until some eligible male offers to marry her, thereby restoring peace and quiet.

Cakhi Nebat jilted a king! Translated, her name means, "a piece of sugar,"—a clue to her loveliness. She was so enchanting that she inflamed the hearts of two of the most prominent men of her age. One was Shuja, king of the Persian province of Fars. The other was a local boy of her native Shiraz whose name was Hafiz. Hafiz was one of Persia's immortal poets, a master of lyricism and glowing imagery. Having the choice of these two suitors, Chakhi Nebat jilted the king and married the poet. But she did not live happily ever after. The poet was a brute, who mistreated her and caused her early death. Yet even after she was gone, Hafiz's poetry lives on, extolling his wife's beauty in glowing verse.

The Man Who Married the Bible

Shebbatai Zebi, the most famous of the self-styled "messiahs," was a 17th-century charlatan and a mystic who deluded his Jewish brethren by claiming to have come to "fulfill their Messianic hopes." His greatest piece of effrontery was the celebration of his marriage to the Bible. The sacred scrolls of the Law were arrayed in bridal vestments and the swindler proceeded to wed the Bible with great pomp and solemnity. The community of Salonika, Greece turned out to witness the wedding. Shebbatai, whose purpose was to bolster up his pretended mission, eventually embraced Islam to escape punishment at the hands of the Sultan of Turkey.

THE **BRIDE** WHO DIDN'T HAVE A **STITCH** TO WEAR MRS. **HANNAH WARD** A WIDOW, AT HER MARRIAGE TO MAJOR MOSES JOY in Newfane, Vt. WORE AS A BRIDAL GOWN A **WOODEN BOX!** IN EARLY NEW ENGLAND A WIDOW'S SECOND HUSBAND BECAME LEGALLY RESPONSIBLE FOR ALL THE FIRST HUSBAND'S DEBTS IF THE BRIDE BROUGHT ANY OF HER PREVIOUS POSSESSIONS TO THE WEDDING— EVEN CLOTHING! Feb. 22. 1789

EASTER EGG 101 YEARS OLD owned by MRS. R.M.CATES Tuscarawas, Ohio

THE GREATEST WEDDING IN HISTORY KING SIVAJI of Tanjore, India, MARRIED 17 WOMEN IN ONE CEREMONY!

A BRIDE IN OLD ENGLAND, TO BE ASSURED OF GOOD FORTUNE, HAD TO BE KISSED AT HER WEDDING BY A CHIMNEY SWEEP

Dorothy Ford of South Pool, England is probably the only English woman to have married a corpse. A few days before her wedding on June 11, 1666, Dorothy was heartbroken to learn that her fiance, Reverend William Streat, had died. But oddly enough, Dorothy's friends began having disturbing dreams of her dead fiance. In these dreams, the reverend insisted that he could not rest until his pledge to marry was redeemed. At her friend's urging, Dorothy agreed to have her fiance's body disinterred. Finally, on November 27, 1667, Dorothy Ford stood beside her fiance's coffin before the altar and took the vows. From that moment on, Dorothy's dead husband stopped tormenting her friends in their dreams.

The Lahlas of Africa have the most "picturesque" wedding ceremony on earth. The marriage rites consist of painting the bride's portrait on a framed canvas the groom wears on his nuptial headdress. The divorce proceedings are even simpler. The husband erases his wife's features from the wedding frame and presently she passes out of his life.

Their relationship is always up in the air... yet they get along fine! Commercial airline pilots **Tom** and **Jackee Gerber** are husband and wife and work for the same airline. They manage to get assigned to the same flight, as co-pilots, about 80% of the time (April 18, 1982.)

The women of the Acholi tribe in the Upper Nile Valley, Africa, must marry the same man three times before the marriage is considered legal. The three successive ceremonies, separated by intervals, are designed to protect men from hasty entanglements. The groom may change his mind any time prior to the final ceremony.

JIMMY **BURNTHET** of Ennerdale, England INCENSED WHEN THE GIRL HE HAD COURTED FOR **40** YEARS BROKE THEIR ENGAGEMENT AND MARRIED HIS NEPHEW, RETALIATED BY, MARRYING HIS EX-FIANCÉE'S NIECE!

! *A Banda girl is not ready for marriage until she has eaten a whole chicken raw.*

MARRIAGE
AMONG THE ANCIENT AZTECS WAS SYMBOLIZED BY ACTUALLY TYING TOGETHER THE CLOAKS OF THE BRIDE AND GROOM

David Lamont (1733–1837) Minister of Kirkpatrick-Durham, Scotland for 63 years, married the girl who was the first infant he ever baptized. She was 21 when they were married and they lived together happily for 38 years.

HUNGARIAN BRIDES TRADITIONALLY WORE HEADDRESSES ADORNED WITH *FLOWERS, FRUIT AND COINS*

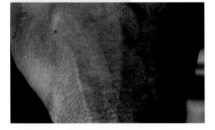

He knew she was the one...
Eugene H. Sloane of Annapolis, Maryland has the initials "M.R." spelled out in the veins on the back of his right hand—a fact that surely pleased his bride, Margaret Riley! (January 29, 1971.)

! *Among the Lodhi caste of Oshangabad, India, a bachelor is allowed to marry a widow—but only after he first undergoes a bizarre ritual. He must rid himself of his unmarried status by marrying a pair of earrings. The man must wear his "wife" for a full year before he is allowed to divorce the earrings and marry the widow.*

"ESPOSA" IN SPANISH MEANS BOTH "WIFE" AND "HANDCUFFS" Submitted by Dino Copetas, Pittsburgh, Pa.

A WOMAN IN FRANCE, WHO HAS BORNE CHILDREN TO A MAN, CAN BE LEGALLY MARRIED TO HIM *AFTER HIS DEATH*

HERE COMES THE BRIDE TA DUM TEE DUM

4 NATIVE DOGS in the Olemba Tribe, Africa IS THE STANDARD PRICE OF A WIFE

HOT CHOCOLATE
THE ISLAND WHERE EVERY MARRIAGE PROPOSAL WAS AN INVITATION TO DEATH!
A YOUNG MAN ON St. Kilda, in the Hebrides, Scotland WAS NOT PERMITTED TO MARRY UNTIL HE HAD PROVED HIS COURAGE BY STANDING ON THE TIP OF LOVER'S ROCK ON ONE LEG --*AND LEANING OFF BALANCE 850 FEET ABOVE THE SEA!*

THE STRANGEST COURTSHIP IN THE WORLD! A GIRL of the Mututsi Tribe Africa CARRIES HER FUTURE HUSBAND AROUND IN A SLING ON HER BACK! A WIFE IS USUALLY *10* YEARS OLDER THAN HER HUSBAND, AND THEY BECOME ENGAGED WHILE HE IS STILL AN INFANT

In Paris during the summer of 1862, two lovers made a vow to elope to England to be married. Sidney Nicholson of Melbourne, Australia and Angelique Desprats secretly planned to rendezvous under the Champs Elysees. But before they could carry out their plan, Angelique's parents spirited her away. Brokenhearted, Sidney traveled to Paris annually for the next twenty years, searching for some trace of his lost love.

In 1882, he decided that this year's trip to Paris would be his last. As Sidney toured an Art Exhibition at the Palais de L'Industrie, his eyes suddenly fell upon a small canvas entitled "Au bon Soleil" ("Sunshine".) To his astonishment, the pretty girl standing in a meadow that the painting depicted had the very same blue eyes and lovely face as his long lost Angelique—she even wore the same straw sun hat he remembered. He obtained the address of the painter, and hurriedly paid him a visit. The painter told Sidney that the young woman's name was Angelique, and offered an address in Rue Rousselet where she lived. A young woman answered his knock—a woman almost perfectly resembling the Angelique he once knew. When he explained himself to the young woman, she invited him in at once.

The young woman told him that the story of her mother's love affair with a dashing Australian man was well known to her, her favorite story when she was a child. She explained that her mother was very unhappy after the loss of her love and died young. After her father, Rouseche, died too, young Angelique was raised by her grandparents, never tiring of hearing the romantic tale of the dashing young man who won her mother's heart. Angelique even explained that it was indeed her mother's hat that she had worn for the painting. Angelique Rouseche and Sidney Nicholson were married in Paris that year. And they lived happily ever after.

In 1927, Zaro Agha of Constantinople, Turkey celebrated his 153rd year of life by getting married- for the 11th time. During his long and eventful life, Agha had buried 10 previous wives and 27 of his children.

147 YEARS OF WEDDED BLISS

The record for a long and happy wedded life belongs to Janos Roven and his good wife Sara. They lived together as husband and wife for 147 years—and almost saw their third golden jubilee.

Janos and Sara were born in the little village of Stradova, Hungary and both died there, Janos at age 172 years and Sara at 164.

The aged couple attracted considerable attention during the latter years of their marriage. The Dutch envoy in Vienna visited them and had their pictures painted. This painting was turned over to William Bosvilee, the trustee of the Earl of Northumberland, along with the original documents of their marriage.

Janos and Sara died within days of each other in 1825. Their son, age 116 years and his two great-great-grandsons, were at their bedside.

Ouch!

Theodore Kaufman of Astoria, Long Island was able to **lick a hot soldering iron.** (June 26, 1953.)

August L. Schmolt smacked himself on the bicep with a 4 pound hammer every day for 40 years, yet even severe blows would not bruise his skin. (August 15, 1944.)

Leona Young of Norwich, New York (who was also known as the Devil's Daughter) was able to withstand **the heat of a plumber's torch on her tongue.** (March 3, 1938.)

Rasmus Nielsen of Angel's Camp, California could **lift a 200 pound anvil** with a metal bar that pierced his nipples. (July 16, 1938.)

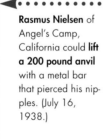

Phineas Gage's Skull Was Pierced With a Crowbar— Yet he Lived to Tell About It!

On September 13, 1847, Phineas P. Gage, a foreman of the Rutland and Burlington Railroad, was charging a hole with powder in preparation for blasting. When the powder exploded prematurely, a 3' 7" tamping iron, weighing 13.25 pounds, was driven completely through his skull. The iron entered Gage's face just under the zygomatic arch of his left eye, pierced his brain and protruded from the top of his head.

Despite his injury, Gage did not even lose consciousness. He was taken to a hotel a mile from the blast sight, where he dismounted the carriage and walked to his hotel room. An operation was performed to remove the crowbar. Throughout the day, Gage remained perfectly rational.

Gage's convalescence was rapid and uneventful and the only permanent damage he suffered was the loss of sight in his left eye. Later in life, however, Gage suffered a complete change of personality, becoming inexplicably violent and hostile.

H. H. Getty of Edmonton, Alberta discovered that **a match held to his skin caused neither pain nor blistering.** Getty visited several prominent physicians in an attempt to discover an explanation for his "asbestos skin." None was found. (May 20, 1940.)

In the summer of 1923 **Delbert C. Hughes** of Clarinda, Iowa **had his hat pinned to his head with a pitchfork** that fell from a hayloft! His father pulled the pitchfork from his skull by hand. Hughes recovered fully with no ill effects. (May 22, 1976.)

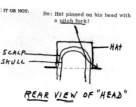

Gardner **A. Taylor** of Winner, South Dakota lifted a 155 pound anvil with his ears. (March 10, 1944.)

Amedeo Vacca the Human Volcano, of Long Island, New York. **Vacca swallowed lit cigarettes for a living,** yet never smoked them. (1935)

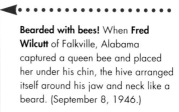

Bearded with bees! When **Fred Wilcutt** of Falkville, Alabama captured a queen bee and placed her under his chin, the hive arranged itself around his jaw and neck like a beard. (September 8, 1946.)

"Professor" Leo Kongee, who could hammer nails into his nose and could painlessly pierce parts of his body with sharp objects was featured at Ripley's Chicago Odditorium in the 1930s and appeared in Ripley's cartoons several times. Circa 1934.

Chicago Odditorium performer **Harry McGregor** could tow a wagon carrying his wife, Lillian-with his eyelids! 1933.

During the 1930s and 1940s, Odditorium performers endured pins, nails, hammer blows, blowtorches and innumerable other kinds of torture to astonish Odditorium visitors.

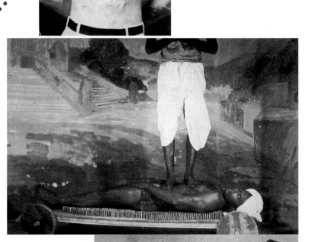

Odditorium performer in formalwear, aiming blowtorch into mouth, postcard was made of him.

Habu the Iron-Tongued Fakir performed at Ripley's Odditorium in the 1930s.

"Professor" Leo Kongee sews a button onto his tongue. Circa 1934.

Singlee the Fireproof Man performed in Ripley's Odditorium in the 1930s and was featured in a Believe it or Not! cartoon. Circa 1934.

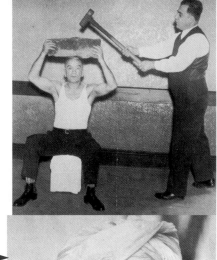

This fakir appeared at Ripley's Odditorium in 1933. He had taken a lifelong vow of silence and had placed a skewer through his tongue to prevent himself from talking.

THE IRON MAIDEN
OF NUREMBURG

During a visit to Germany in 1928, Ripley became quite fascinated with a particular maiden. He was so smitten with the maiden that he vowed he had to have her and immediately made arrangements to bring her home with him. Yet, enthralled as Ripley was with her, this was one maiden whose embraces no man would seek. Ripley had just purchased the infamous, dreaded medieval torture device, the Iron Maiden of Nuremburg.

The Iron Maiden of Nuremburg has been called the most famous instrument of torture and death in the world. A coffin-like iron chamber standing nearly eight feet tall, the maiden contained a lid studded with 13 sharp iron spikes to penetrate her victims through the skull, eyes, chest and heart. Those who died in the maiden's embrace were so horribly mutilated that no one could bear to see them. The maiden was equipped with a trap door through which the victims' bodies could be dropped into a moat or river.

At home on BION Island, Ripley placed his Maiden in a special suite decorated with scold's bridles, chastity belts and numerous other implements of torture. This room was generally kept locked when Ripley was entertaining, lest the faint of heart accidentally discover it.

The Maiden was on display at the New York City Odditorium from 1940 to 1972, at the St. Augustine Odditorium from 1972 to 1978 and at the Odditorium in Myrtle Beach, South Carolina from 1978 to 1988. Since 1988, Ripley's wicked Maiden has been horrifying visitors at the Buena Park, California Odditorium. She is such a popular exhibit that replicas have been built for nearly every Ripley's Odditorium across the globe.

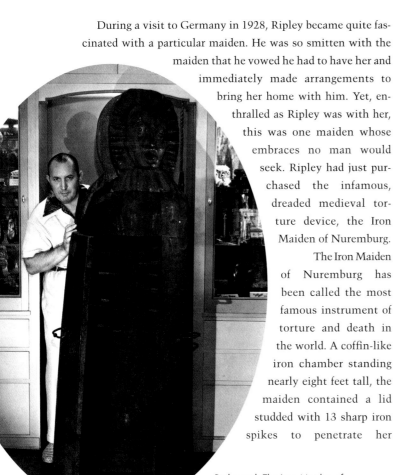

Ripley with The Iron Maiden of Nuremburg at his home on BION island. Circa 1934.

Numerous Odditoriums feature a replica of the Iron Maiden, like this one on display at the Myrtle Beach, South Carolina Odditorium. The authentic Maiden can be seen in Ripley's Buena Park museum.

"GENUINE TORTURE IMPLEMENTS!"

Huh?

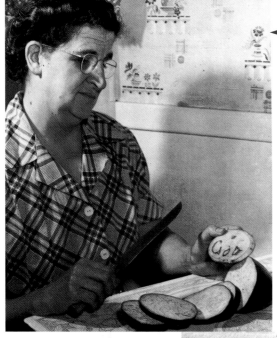

She found "God" in her eggplant! On Sunday, August 15, 1948, **Mrs. Henry G. Hesslink** of Amsterdam, New York was preparing dinner for her family when she discovered that the eggplant she was slicing had been "signed" by its creator! (September 25, 1948.)

Hitler in a Japanese suit appeared in the streaked wood of a turpentine tree belonging to **Mr. and Mrs. Louis F. Wagenblast** of Pinellas Park, Florida. The Wagenblasts claimed they only touched up with white paint the naturally occurring lines of the Führer's portrait. (May 17, 1947.)

Mr. M. C. Barker of Moundsville, West Virginia holds one of the exact shoes he sold in 1916 for $3.00 then bought back again, still in their original box and still in good condition, in 1948—32 years later! The price he paid to buy his shoes back? $3.00.

Bananagram: the arrival of this properly addressed, stamped and delivered banana to St. Raphael's Hospital surely must have brightened **Mrs. Rachel Collonna's** day! The banana, sent by her niece, bore two stamps and the words "I love you" in Italian. And yes—it was eaten and enjoyed. (July 19, 1988.)

"That carrot is wearing my ring!" While tilling her garden in the spring of 1923, **Mrs. Carolina Scufaca** of Canyon City, Colorado lost the wedding ring she had worn for 25 years. Not to worry—months later, she got her ring back when she harvested a carrot that had grown through it! (June 9, 1939.)

Dust rag dictator: Frank Olson of Garden city, Michigan looked down to the spot where he'd casually tossed his dust rag... only to find the profile of **Fidel Castro** staring back at him! (July 21, 1961.)

It never snows there—you've gotta get creative! Tarzana, California poultry farmer **Erling O. Wigg** constructed a ski ramp from the side of his barn, which he slicked with chicken feathers in lieu of snow! In 1979, after years of experimenting with numerous other materials, Erling invented Nordik Snow, a snow substitute derived of salt granules for use by off-season skiers. (May 28, 1949.)

TING CHENG
Holy man of Macao, Portuguese coast.
PLANTED 2 PALM BRANCHES
IN HOLES BORED IN HIS SKULL!
NOURISHMENT FROM CHENG'S BODY KEPT THEM GREEN FOR 10 YEARS
(1851-1860)

Heavyweight Fighter **Eddie Simms** of Cleveland, Ohio **never scored a knockout until he took up playing the accordion!** He claimed that his accordion skill was responsible for the perfect left hook he developed, which enabled him to score 18 consecutive knockouts! (September 5, 1933.)

He had a toothache in his ear! Veterinarian **J. A. Hodgson** of Niagara Falls, Ontario pulled a tooth from this horse's ear! He remembered that his father, also a veterinarian, had performed a similar operation on a horse 50 years before. Dr. Hodgson remarked that it could be another 100 years or so before this happens again! (March 2, 1973.)

FUR BEARING TROUT
Very Rare
CAUGHT WHILE TROLLING IN LAKE SUPERIOR OFF GROS CAP,
NEAR SAULT STE. MARIE, DISTRICT OF ALGOMA
It is believed that the great depth and the extreme penetrating coldness of the water in which these fish live, has caused them to grow their dense coat of (usually) white fur.

Mounted by ROSS C. JOBE, Taxidermist of Sault Ste. Marie, Ontario.

Naughty, naughty! These "fur-bearing trout" (which actually bear glued-on white bunny fur) were made and sold by **Ross Jobe** of Sault Saint Marie, Ontario, as rare trophies. Jobe was undoubtedly from the same school of taxidermy that stuck white-tail antlers on jackrabbits!

You can't get rid of the durned things! Soldier **Leroy Gibson** was followed home by a fruitcake! The cake was mailed from his home town of Monongahela, Pennsylvania in 1943 while he was away at war and followed him, always a stop or two behind, as he was transferred to various locales across the Pacific. It finally caught up with him back home in Pennsylvania, 12 years later!

NAVEL NOVELTY
One Man's Startling Adventure Inside His Own Belly Button!

In 1993, Choith Ramchandani of Kowloon, China contacted Ripley's about his unusual belly button lint and even included several choice samples of the lint carefully preserved in a baggie.

In 1993, Choith Ramchandani of Kowloon, China wrote to Ripley's headquarters with news of an astonishing discovery he had made inside his own navel: the lint in his belly button was white! Not merely pale, but snowy white. And furthermore, this astonishing phenomenon was not a one time aberration of nature. Ramchandani, at age 58, had extracted a clump of the eerily white belly button lint from his navel every day since the age of 23!

Of course, common knowledge tells us that navel lint generally confines itself to a spectrum somewhere between bluish-gray and brownish-beige. Yet inexplicably, Ramchandani's lint was white as new-fallen snow. And to back up this astonishing claim, Ramchandani furnished the proof: along with his letter, Ramchandani included a baggie containing 12 of his finest lint clumps. The lint remains carefully cataloged and preserved in Ripley's collection, awaiting the day when medical science may uncover an explanation for this bizarre phenomenon. To date, Ramchandani's astonishing snowy-white navel fluff has yet to make its debut in a Believe It or Not! cartoon or Odditorium exhibit. The world may never be ready.

Colonel J. Hunter Reinburg of Wabasso, Florida claimed that **he cured his own failing eyesight with primitive do-it-yourself acupuncture!** He was originally rejected as a midshipman because of his poor eyesight, but went on to a distinguished flying career after he pierced his ears and nose with paper clips! (May 7, 1982.)

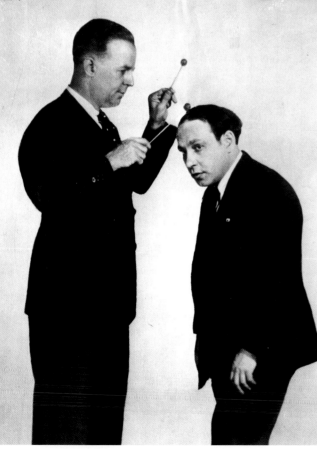

The man with the xylophone head! Professor Charles Cheer, being played here by **Elmer Cleve,** performed (or should we say, was performed upon?) at Ripley's Cleveland Odditorium and on Ripley's radio show. (December 16, 1936.)

MRS. MARY ENOS of Confluence, Pa. MARCHES REGULARLY IN PARADES AS A DRUM MAJORETTE *AT THE AGE OF 73*

A R

Sexy Sweet Potato Scandal!

If Ripley's had credited this lascivious "sweet patootie" cartoon
to Missouri's would-be governor,
it would surely have ruined his political career!

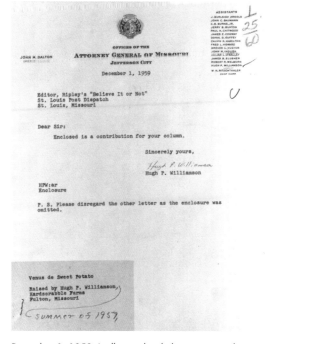

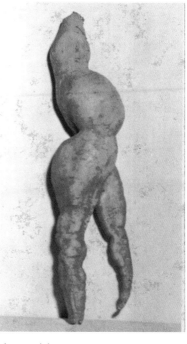

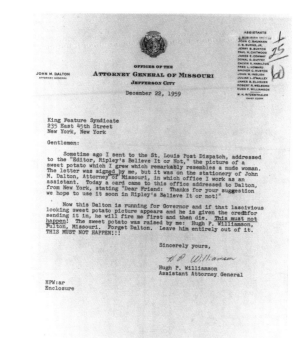

December 1, 1959: It all started with this innocent submission letter from assistant attorney general **Hugh P. Williamson** of Fulton, Missouri, offering his **ribald sweet potato** as a potential Ripley contribution. His one mistake: **he used his boss's letterhead!**

The scandalous sweet potato in question, grown by **Mr. Williamson**. Note the voluptuous curves—**positively shocking!**"

"THIS MUST NOT HAPPEN!" A horrified Williamson learns that Ripley's has responded not to him, but to the name on the letterhead: his boss, a future gubernatorial candidate!

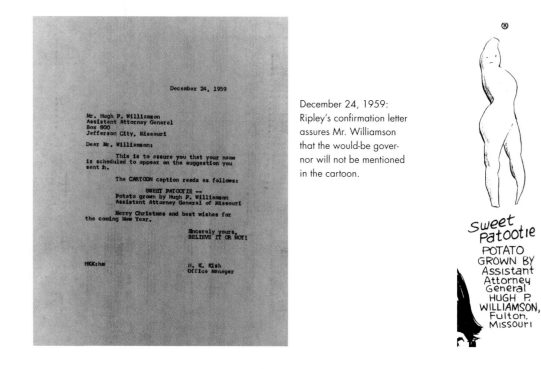

December 24, 1959: Ripley's confirmation letter assures Mr. Williamson that the would-be governor will not be mentioned in the cartoon.

The sweet potato cartoon as it appeared on January 25, 1960: a lucky near-miss for attorney general Dalton's political career!

About Ripley ENTERTAINMENT

1939 Odditorium Poster. Ripley's got out of the live performance business shortly after Robert Ripley's death in 1949. Most states outlawed "freak shows" in 1972 and the custom has slowly died out since then. Shows like those at Ripley's Odditoriums in the 1930s and 1940s are a bygone phenomenon.

Believe It or Not! Odditoriums

Wax figure of **Vlad the Impaler** on display at Ripley's Gatlinburg, Tennessee Odditorium.

Ripley's Orlando, Florida Odditorium appears to be slipping into one of Central Florida's infamous sinkholes.

Ripley's Odditorium in Gatlinburg, Tennessee

Visitors to Ripley's Orlando, Florida Odditorium are greeted by the ghost of Robert Ripley.

Ripley's Odditorium, Grand Prairie, Texas.

! Robert Ripley opened the first permanent Odditorium in New York City in 1939. Ripley's unusual museum was such a tremendous success that within a few years, Ripley was opening Odditoriums in several other major cities. Today there are 27 Odditoriums in operation, each one unique.

Ripley's Odditorium in San Antonio, Texas.

Ripley's Odditorium in Branson, Missouri.

Visitors to Ripley's Odditoriums are encouraged to try their skill at tongue-rolling and girning.

United States Odditoriums

Buena Park, California
Hollywood, California
San Francisco, California
Key West, Florida
Orlando, Florida
St. Augustine, Florida
Branson, Missouri
Atlantic City, New Jersey
Newport, Oregon
Gatlinburg, Tennessee
Grand Prairie, Texas
San Antonio, Texas
Myrtle Beach, South Carolina
Wisconsin Dells, Wisconsin
Jackson Hole, Wyoming

International Odditoriums

Surfer's Paradise, Australia
Copenhagen, Denmark
Blackpool, England
The Peak, Hong Kong
Kyonggi-do, Korea
Guadalajara, Mexico
Mexico City, Mexico
Niagara Falls, Ontario
Manila, Philippines
Cavendish, Prince Edward Island
Pattaya, Thailand

Ripley's Believe It or Not! Odditorium in Wisconsin Dells, Wisconsin.

Visitors stumble, wobble and reel through the rotating tunnel illusion, a popular display featured in almost every Ripley's Odditorium. Shown here in the (now closed) Odditorium in Jakarta, Indonesia.

Ripley's Odditorium in Pattaya, Thailand.

Ripley's Odditorium in Atlantic City, New Jersey.

This wax gypsy figure is displayed inside an authentic gypsy caravan in Ripley's Atlantic City Odditorium.

The lobby of Ripley's Branson, Missouri Odditorium.

Louis Tussaud's Wax Museums

Ripley's owns two Louis Tussaud's Wax Museums, featuring astonishingly realistic wax figures of famous celebrities, royalty, political figures, accident victims and mythical characters. One Tussaud's is located in Niagara Falls, Ontario; the other is in Copenhagen, Denmark.

Ripley's Louis Tussaud's museum in Copenhagen, Denmark.

Ripley's Odditorium in Surfer's Paradise, Queensland, Australia, features the Culligan Water Faucet illusion that appears, in different incarnations, in several Ripley's Odditoriums.

Ripley's Aquarium

The newest addition to Ripley's family of entertainment, the first Ripley's Aquarium, is now open in Myrtle Beach, South Carolina. Ripley's Aquarium is a dazzling 74,000-square-foot facility with a 16-foot-tall waterfall out front and a massive shark tank inside. Visitors can ride a moving walkway through a curving 310-foot acrylic tube inside the tank! The aquarium also features live animal displays: stingrays, horseshoe crabs, piranhas, sea dragons and giant octopus, plus a multimedia playground and an educational resource center. Ripley's plans to open several more aquariums across the country.

Ripley's new aquarium in Myrtle Beach, South Carolina features the world's first curved underwater shark tank tunnel, where visitors ride a moving walkway past amazing sea life.

Guinness World of Records Museums

Ripley's owns and operates six museums devoted to Guinness's World Records. Guinness's Museums feature three-dimensional displays of the world's fastest, smallest, tallest, loudest, longest, fattest....

- Hollywood, California
- Copenhagen, Denmark.
- Las Vegas, Nevada
- Niagara Falls, Ontario
- Gatlinburg, Tennessee
- Taiwan

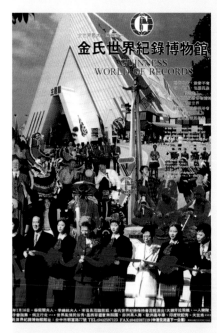

The opening ceremony, with guest of honor **Margaret Thatcher,** at Ripley's newest Guinness World of Records museum in Taiwan

Ripley's Motion Theaters

Ripley's has recently opened three thrilling Motion Simulator Moving Theaters, located in Myrtle Beach, South Carolina, Gatlinburg, Tennessee and Niagara Falls, Ontario.

81 Years of Believe-It Or Nots

RIPLEY ARTISTS	RIPLEY RESEARCHERS	RIPLEY EDITORS
Robert Ripley 1918–1949	Norbert Pearlroth 1923–1976	Robert Ripley 1918–1949
Paul Frehm 1949–1978	Charles Grant 1976–1989	Lester Byck 1949–1989
Walter Frehm 1978–1989	Karen Kemlo 1989–present	Edward Meyer 1989–1998
Don Wimmer 1990–present		Christina Favalo 1998–present

Behind the Scenes

RIPLEY'S OWNERS	RIPLEY'S LEADERSHIP
Robert Ripley 1918–1949	Bob Masterson: President
Doug Ripley 1949–1951	Norm Deska: Executive Vice President/Attractions
John Arthur 1951–1963	Jim Pattison, Jr.: Executive Vice President/Aquariums
Doug Storer 1950–1959	Edward Meyer: Vice President/Publisher
Alec Rigby 1963–1984	John Corcoran: Vice President/Franchise Operations
Jim Pattison 1985–present	Joe Choromanski: Vice President/Husbandry, Ripley's Aquariums
	Jeff Leaker: Vice President/Architecture, Engineering & Design
	Neva Richardson: Chief Financial Officer

WE'RE 'OUT THERE' TOO!

Ripley's Entertainment Meets the *X-Files*.

Ripley's Vice President of Publishing Edward Meyer knew things were about to get weird when he came home one evening to a message left on his answering machine, spoken in an eerie voice: "Edwaaard... this is the *X-Files* calling... we need youuu... help usss..." Meyer recalls, "My wife Giliane didn't erase the message for weeks until all our friends had heard it."

Ripley's "original" Fiji mermaid is currently on display in the Newport, Oregon Odditorium.

At the time, the *X-Files* folks were working on a story that would have the show's two main characters, FBI agents Mulder and Scully, investigating a murder in a bizarre Florida town populated by circus performers. The episode would feature assorted "freaks" and oddities, as well as the story's chief murder suspect, the Fiji mermaid.

Although the "detachable" twin character in the *X Files* episode "Humbug" was pure fiction, he was inspired by reality in the form of **Jean and Jacques Libbera** of Rome, Italy, conjoined twins.

The *X-Files* research team knew exactly where to look for the weird facts they needed to develop the episode. Not only does Ripley's own some of the finest Fiji mermaids, it is also home to the "Freak File", a collection of hundreds of photos of circus performers and human oddities. At first, *X-Files* researchers focused on the Fiji mermaid, but out of the show's contact with Ripley's came inspiration for other unforgettable characters. "They didn't know we had photos of an undeveloped twin until I told them," recalls Meyer, "and I supplied some general information on Jo Jo the Dog-faced Boy." Meyer also passed along several xeroxes of his "favorite freaks."

The episode, entitled "Humbug," refers to the term coined by P.T. Barnum, who used it to mean an object, either real or fake, offered to the public by means of persuasion. Barnum once called the Fiji mermaid "the genuine fake" because it didn't fool anyone.

In "Humbug," the Fiji mermaid becomes the focus of the investigation for a time, as Fox Mulder speculates that there may be more truth than fiction to the legendary hoax. He suspects that a real Fiji mermaid may be lurking about, feeding on unsuspecting circus freaks. The hirsute circus performer Jo Jo the Dog-faced Boy was the inspiration behind the relatively normal-seeming Sheriff Hamilton, who says of the town's unusual inhabitants, "On the inside, they're as normal as anybody..." Later in the episode, we discover that before he shaved, Hamilton made his living as "Jim Jim the Dog-faced Boy." Leonard, the vicious detachable conjoined twin who is actually responsible for the murders, is a greatly fictionalized take-off on the non-detachable Jean and Jacques Libbera of Rome, Italy, born in 1884.

Jo Jo the Dog-faced boy, who also went by **Lionel** the Lion-faced boy, was a popular freak show performer in the 1920s and 1930s.

"Humbug," written by Darin Morgan, aired on March 31, 1995, during the show's second season. It became an instant hit with fans and is now considered a classic episode. What did Ripley's Edward Meyer think of the finished product? "I'm a big fan of the show, so I loved it. Scully eating the bug was great, but the best scene was the motel clerk guessing that Mulder was an FBI agent based on what he was wearing. I howled!" When the weirdest TV show on the airwaves and the weirdest entertainment company in the world put their heads together, what else would you expect?

Ripley's New MILLENNIUM

You'll be seeing a lot of Ripley's in the new millennium. Ripley's is planning a number of major events for release within the next few years, most notably the first authorized biography of founder Robert Ripley, written by celebrity biographer George Mair, a "Barnum"-esque Broadway musical, and a major motion picture about Robert Ripley's life that is being co-produced with AEI/GP and George Clooney's Maysville Pictures.

Check your TV listings for the new "Ripley's Believe It or Not!" animated adventure series, produced by Cinar, as well as an all-new primetime "Ripley's Believe It or Not!" series from Columbia/Tristar airing on TBS beginning in January, 2000. You may be seeing a lot more of Ripley's at your local bookstore, too: Ripley's has a new line of amazing paperback books in the works, with a brand new look. And while you're surfing the net, stop by and see us at **Ripleys.com**, to check out the latest Ripley's news, museum events, contests, activities and cool stuff. In the new millennium, Ripley's will be the place to go for bizarre and amazing facts— Believe It!

Do You Have a Believe It or Not! for Ripley's?

Do you have an astonishing fact, weird talent, or strange phenomena that you think would make a great Believe It or Not? Ripley's wants to hear from you! Contact us at:

Ripley Entertainment
5728 Major Boulevard
Suite 700
Orlando, Florida 32819

www.Ripleys.com

BELIEVE IT OR NOT!

Terrific Teaching Tool!

Elementary school teacher Steve Freeman of Centralia, Washington has discovered what may be Ripley's finest application yet: Believe It or Nots as teaching tools! Inspired by a classic 1952 Ripley's cartoon featuring a gun that had grown through an oak tree, Steve and his students went on a quest to locate "The Gun Tree." During the research project, Steve made a startling discovery: the kids were having too much fun to realize how much they were learning!

Steve put together a 70-page workbook of Ripley-based research projects, and turned them over to his students. Through their work on the Ripley projects, Steve's students gained a vast array of new research skills. Their reading abilities skyrocketed, even among remedial readers. The more they got involved, the more their interest and enthusiasm grew. "It just exploded," Steve said, "they didn't realize how hard they were working."

Steve and his students also opened their own "Odditorium in the Auditorium" at their school: a display of class projects, as well as local oddities collected by the students and the community. The enthusiasm their homegrown museum of oddities generated is truly astonishing.

Freeman went on to launch the Ripley Research Projects Program, designed to bring his class's phenomenal success to a nationwide level. This Ripley-based educational series is designed to appeal to readers of all levels. The projects are intended to hone students' higher order thinking skills, as well as their skills in reading comprehension, communication and research. Steve was approached by Success for All, his school's new reading program, about writing a textbook to show other teachers how it's done. Soon students across the United States may be using Ripley's Believe it or Nots in their school projects.

And by the way, Steve's students did eventually find what was left of the "Gun Tree" in a Port Townsend antique shop. But before they could authenticate the item, an unknown tourist purchased the gun for cash and left no record. Who knows? Maybe a future classroom of Ripley fans will someday track it down!

INDEX

W

X

Z